Being Better Than You've Ever Been

13 UNCOMMON PEOPLE TELL YOU HOW TO SOLVE 13 OF LIFE'S MOST COMMON PROBLEMS

DR. FRANK FLEMING

Prentice-Hall, Inc.
Englewood Cliffs, N.J. 07632

Library of Congress Cataloging in Publication Data

Fleming, Frank.
  Being better than you've ever been.

  Includes index.
  1. Conduct of life.   I. Title.
BJ1581.2.F56 1983   158′.1   83-9766
ISBN 0-13-071795-9
ISBN 0-13-071787-8 (pbk.)

Epigram quote: S.I. Hayakawa, *Symbol, Status, and Personality*.
(New York: Harcourt Brace Jovanovich, 1953), p. 52.

ISBN 0-13-071795-9

ISBN 0-13-071787-8 {PBK.}

Editorial/production supervision: Marlys Lehmann
Cover design © 1983 by Jeannette Jacobs
Manufacturing buyer: Pat Mahoney

This book is available at a special discount when ordered in
bulk quantities. Contact Prentice-Hall, Inc., General
Publishing Division, Special Sales, Englewood Cliffs, N.J. 07632.

Prentice-Hall International, Inc., *London*
Prentice-Hall of Australia Pty. Limited, *Sydney*
Prentice-Hall Canada Inc., *Toronto*
Prentice-Hall of India Private Limited, *New Delhi*
Prentice-Hall of Japan, Inc., *Tokyo*
Prentice-Hall of Southeast Asia Pte. Ltd., *Singapore*
Whitehall Books Limited, *Wellington, New Zealand*
Editora Prentice-Hall do Brasil Ltda., *Rio de Janeiro*

FOR LECH WALESA

"They tear me to pieces," you said, feeling frustrated with the mounting demands on your time. Yet there was delight in your voice, too. Over the phone from your home in Gdansk you warmly accepted my invitation to participate in *Being Better Than You've Ever Been*.

The Polish Consulate in Washington assured me there would be no problem obtaining a visa. "Why should there be? Our government does not deny visas." None was issued.

In the middle of the night, twenty-two days after we talked, a knock on the door of the same Gdansk apartment signaled your arrest.

Your presence in this book is missed.

CONTENTS

What sort of a person would a genuinely sane individual be? What would he be like to have around, to talk with as a friend, to work with as a colleague? . . . There is plenty of literature on neurotics and psychotics, telling us how we got to be the messes we are. . . . We have thousands of descriptions of emotional disturbance and its causes, but we have too few descriptions of emotional health. And so, as I say, what does a sane person look like?

S.I. HAYAKAWA
Symbols, Status, and Personalities

PREFACE

Emotionally healthy people enjoy a reasonable degree of functioning in each of the basic coping skills. While all people vary in their levels of these skills day by day and from one situation to another, well-adjusted people, while not problem free, function sufficiently well to deal successfully with life's challenges.

Although they may maintain the highest standards and goals for themselves and the world around them, they accept that neither they nor their world is perfect. They look upon life's problems with good humor and an eye toward solutions. They are comfortable with themselves in terms of appearance and competence. The healthy pleasure at being themselves enables them to allow others into close physical and emotional contact without shying away or putting up defenses.

These individuals make decisions on the basis of their own best judgment, which is uncompromised by the need to win approval from others. They are bold in the face of potential failure because they recognize failure as an essential part of the human learning process. They enjoy their successes and learn from their failures without attempting to place credit or blame elsewhere.

Emotionally well-adjusted people are sufficiently assertive to voice opinions whenever appropriate. They express thoughts and feelings, including anger, in a constructive, self-enhancing manner with a genuine regard for the needs and feelings of others. Living in a manner that reflects their own beliefs, and dealing openly with those around them, they know that they are doing their best, and they are, therefore, free from guilt.

When speaking to others, and to themselves in the form of their own thoughts, they accurately represent reality rather than be Pollyannish at the one extreme or exaggerating negatively at the other. The resulting emotions ring true and without excess in either direction.

Finally, healthy copers incorporate these qualities into being the individuals they choose to be, and they play their roles consistently. They refuse to exaggerate certain qualities or diminish others in order to manipulate their environment.

If there are facets of your personality that you would like to modify in the direction of better coping, *Being Better Than You've Ever Been* offers the concrete information you need.

ACKNOWLEDGMENTS

Writing a book that is based on spending time with people who are among the world's most sought after would not have been possible without a tremendous amount of patience, good will, and a genuine belief in this project on the parts of the thirteen featured celebrities. They are the soul of *Being Better Than You've Ever Been*.

I would also like to thank by name just a few of those whose assistance, support, and camaraderie, in the complicated logistics of interviewing the celebrities, frequently exceeded anything I could have expected. Janice Barbieri, Drew Bundini Brown, Jr., Richard L. Buckle, Eric Cohn, Richard Gerstein, Steve Gersztoff, Abdel Kader, Halina Kanopaka, Virginia Kouyoumdjian, Mabel K. Nuttle, Ken-Ichiro Ohe, George and Eleanor Pavloff, Mrs. Ruth Peale, Wayne Poston, Layon F. Robinson, Felix Schlesinger, Wayne Smith, Tony Zonca, and the officials, the Indian inmates, and their families at the state penitentiary in Lincoln, Nebraska.

A special thanks to my parents, Frank and Gertrude Fleming.

Dr. Frank Fleming, a psychologist with an active clinical practice, writes a newspaper column called *Psychology Corner*.

INTRODUCTION:
BEING BETTER
THAN YOU'VE EVER BEEN

What do the self-help experts say? Depending on your choice of guru you could be told that the true path to fulfillment is primal screaming, meditation, relaxation, transactional analysis, jogging, or avoiding your erroneous zones. The presence of so many options is confusing. And if you are like most people, you don't want to become a believer or a fanatic. You simply want some clear, practical, common-sense guidelines to help you become more comfortable from day to day.

Being Better Than You've Ever Been provides the information you need to help yourself in any of the major areas of human functioning in which you feel underpowered. It is the ultimate self-help book because it contains no pet theories, philosophies, or ideologies. The information it offers is not the opinion of how a single author believes you should go about improving your coping skills. As a result of in-depth interviews conducted in more than 50,000 miles of travel ranging from Tokyo to Amsterdam, *Being Better* is able to bring you face to face with the most successful people in every area of coping.

Be prepared to find this book lacking in complicated psychological terminology. Obsessional compulsions, defensive avoidances, pathologies, and dysfunctions simply have no place in this book. *Being Better* is written for ordinary people. Plain talk is the only language used.

Shakespearean quotations are used to introduce Chapters 1 through 13, each of which deals with one of life's fundamental problems. The quotations are presented because I have been impressed that the problems you and I deal with most of the time are not unique to us, nor are they new. There is not one problem described in this book that was not well known and causing human unhappiness when Shakespeare was writing.

As a psychologist with an active clinical practice, I am convinced that the future of the mental health field, in terms of significant help for the mentally ill, lies in the realm of chemistry. Freud's work was based on the assumption of an organic cause for mental illness. Research moves daily in the direction of ultimately proving him correct. Yet the greatest majority of those seeking mental health services are not the mentally ill. In the private offices and public clinics throughout the United States, the bulk of time is spent consulting with those who can only be described as the "normals": ordinary people like you and me.

This book is a manifesto. It is not productive at this stage in the development of the science of psychology to focus on the sick. For the researchers in biochemistry and neuropsychology concerned with the mentally ill, such work is justified. That fight must continue. For the rest—the mainstream psychologists, psychiatric social workers, and psychiatrists serving the community at large, as well as the predominantly normal people they serve—trying to learn meaningful lessons from the mentally ill is a serious mistake. Yet, when you read the average book designed to help, you will usually discover an emphasis on psychological problems.

If you picked up a book about learning to play better tennis, a learned skill just like better coping, what would you look for? Abstract theory wouldn't help much. And it would be laughable to round up the worst tennis players in the country and discuss their behavior. You would want to know about what the best players were doing. The same is true for learning better coping. Coping cannot be learned from theories. Coping with life's difficulties is not a problem of chemical imbalance. Coping well cannot be learned from people who cannot do it themselves. Coping well requires the acquisition of specific learned skills. The best people to learn these skills from are the experts who possess them.

There are a finite number of coping skills; thirteen, the way *Being Better* is designed. Visualize an individual with thirteen dials on his or her forehead to measure each major area of coping. The hypothetical expert of all experts would be a person whose gauges all read "full." But such a perfect individual does not exist. All of us have our own particular combinations of strengths and weaknesses. You probably read "full" on one or a few of the coping scales, "average" on most, and "low" on a few more. At different times and in different situations the proportions vary.

To provide healthy models in each area of coping, individuals have been sought out who, although they may be predictably and humanly deficient in many areas, are masters in their featured areas. None were born as such experts. Some learned their lessons brutally and at great cost. Some acquired their wisdom early; others found it quite late in their lifetime. R. Buckminster Fuller, an "expert" quoted in these pages, has observed that a disproportionately large share of the nation's top performing artists and scientists appear to be products of a fortunate early pairing with a master in their field who became their mentor. They have been guided, encouraged, and assisted in their budding development by those whom Fuller termed "Great Inspiring Teachers" (GITs). This is the term that this book uses to designate the experts: "GITs." If you are seeking to strengthen your coping skills, turn to these thirteen GITs. The description of the behavior of the GIT designated for each of the thirteen "Fundamental Problem (FP)" areas illustrates successful coping as it takes place in the real world.

The use of experts or masters to learn a skill is not a new idea. It is a description of what has long been known as "the tutorial method," a system of education practiced by Socrates and Pythagoras and those before them. The original system involved seeking out a master in one's chosen field. A student proceeded to live with the master until he or she had sufficiently obtained the information that was sought. You have certainly used variations of this system before in acquiring other learned behavior.

Being Better is a tutorial in the subject of living. Without requiring of you the time, money, or means to find your own master teachers or GITs, it provides them. Listening to them and witnessing the lives they are leading is the first step toward changing your life. The existence of the GITs confirms that people like this really exist. There is nothing suggested to you in *Being Better* that isn't already being done.

It is by no means certain that each of the GITs is conscious of all of the reasons he or she is successful in coping with his or her featured FP. For this reason it was critical that a psychologist, trained to identify and evaluate behavior, conduct the interviews. Abbie Hoffman, one of the GITs in this book, was particularly aware of this. We were talking about the special difficulty of interviewing media-wise public figures. The names of Castro, Begin, and Reagan, among others, were raised. Abbie said, "Oh, they must be so laid back that they are lobbing the ball from center-field to home plate. Their defenses are so strong that you get only sterile answers. It is only someone trained in psychology and who is actually listening, as opposed to just hearing himself talk, who could do the interviews necessary for this book."

It is through observing the GITs and asking the right questions that the nuts and bolts behind the coping skills of each personality are uncovered. Again borrowing from Bucky Fuller, the specific coping skills the GITs have to teach are termed "Fundamental Wisdom (FW)." In his novel *Herzog,* Saul Bellow writes about people in our lives who, in our chance contacts with them, teach us "lessons of the real." He terms these individuals "reality instructors." The GITs are your reality instructors. You can expect their lessons to be immensely profitable.

I asked the world-renowned psychologist Carl Rogers, another GIT in *Being Better,* if he believed that the simple reading of a book could have serious impact on the lives of those who read it. He was convinced: "Yes, I do. This has been brought home to me because I get letters from people who say, 'I read your book, and it just changed my relationship with my family.' I'm glad to have you ask that because I know it's true. But there has to be something receptive in the reader. It's because they've had experiences which they don't quite understand or don't quite trust but then they find 'My God, you're saying what I've always believed, but never quite thought could be true. And now I realize, yeah, maybe it's true.' It's one of the strangest things to get a letter from some woman in the outback of Australia saying how much her life has been changed by reading some book of mine."

You can find bona fide GITs all around you if you look for them. GITs are found among musicians, theatre people, professionals in the world of athletics, and school teachers—in any place or field in which people are found doing their best to deal with what life presents them. You might easily be a GIT in one specific area, while hopelessly inept in others. GITs have no particular training or background and are as easily discovered among the ranks of eighty-year-old grandparents as among university professors.

This book makes use of GITs who are well-known personalities. This is not because celebrities have cornered the market in FW. They are used only because their value for demonstration purposes is undeniable. We are all naturally interested in the people we know. Sociologists tell us that on an unconscious level we consider well-known personalities to be acquaintances. We are interested, therefore, in what they do. Why else the undying popularity of fan magazines and celebrity gossip columns?

Put out of your mind any doubts you may have that the problems of the famous and successful, and the coping skills necessary to solve them, are in any way different from your own. Dr. Rogers again: "I've known a few great and famous people, and known them well. Not very many, but a few. Their problems are just like mine, and mine are just like everybody else's. I feel that the fundamental problems of relationships and love and friendship and dying and illness and obstacles and frustrations and joys—everybody experiences those. It may be in the limelight, or it may be where nobody knows anything about it, but the situation is very much the same."

F. Lee Bailey, another GIT, puts it his own way. "It is a challenge that I faced when I came in as a legend in one's own time, which is corny, but a fair commentary in some respects; to take a jury in a community of which I am not a member and make them, to a degree, my friends to the extent that they trust me. I want them to understand my trousers go on one leg at a time and I've got the same problems that they've got. What your readers ought to believe is that their structure and the basic structure of celebrities are identical."

Over the three-year period that the interviews for *Being Better* were conducted, significant events have taken place in the lives of many of the GITs. Art Buchwald was awarded the Pulitzer Prize for columns that "made the entire English-speaking world laugh—and ponder." Abbie Hoffman has been paroled. Senator S. I. Hayakawa, at age seventy-five, decided against running for re-election to the U.S. Senate and retired. Hank Aaron was elected to baseball's Hall of Fame in his first year of eligibility. In Nassau, Muhammed Ali lost a unanimous ten-round decision in his bid to attain the heavyweight title for the fourth time. Norman Vincent Peale celebrated fifty years in the ministry and released a new book. In Tokyo, Fukujiro Sono has been elevated from president of TDK to chairman of the board. F. Lee Bailey successfully defended Lt. Christopher Cooke on charges of passing military secrets to the Soviets. Until his death in July 1983 at the age of eighty-seven, Bucky Fuller continued to tour the world speaking brilliantly before standing-room-only crowds. Former astronaut Harrison Schmitt was defeated for re-election in New Mexico in 1982. Jim Lovell's *Apollo XIII* Crewmate Jack Swigert won a congressional seat in Colorado in 1982, but he died of cancer one week before taking office. The public victories and defeats that have taken place just during the months I have been writing about these individuals demonstrate emphatically that although each is a Great Inspiring Teacher in a particular area of Fundamental Wisdom, they are, foremost, human beings like you and me.

Many people have asked me, when they stand back and look at the vast array of major problems in modern American society, how the answers to coping with them all could possibly be placed between the covers of a single book. The fact is that the practice of psychotherapy would be impossible if the hundreds of patients each therapist sees yearly presented vastly different problems requiring unique solutions. This is not the case. Despite wide individual differences in character and plot, most of the basic complaints seen daily, year after year, fall into the thirteen categories.

Each of the next thirteen chapters deals with one of the thirteen. This is your menu. The chapters begin with a brief description of the FP itself. This is followed by the body of the chapter, which is an in-depth view of the GIT. The chapter culminates in the how-tos, the practical information you need that has been gleaned from the GIT and summarized for you.

You may now be visiting a clinician's office regularly. Unless you belong to that small "chemical" group, your path to the doctor's couch began with your particular combination of high, medium, and low areas of FPs and FW that are as unique to you as your fingerprints. You are one of us, a normal. But life has increased its demands on you to the point of overtaxing your coping skills. Or perhaps you are not in therapy. You may belong to that large group that has been turned off by the idea of professional help. Let's not kid ourselves. Psychological treatment still carries a tremendous taint. So you may be holding it together as best you can with alcohol, overwork, or other forms of escape or cover-up. Your reserve, too, has been found wanting. Whether you are in therapy or not, *Being Better* offers you help.

How do you know which FPs you have? How can you determine which particular FW is likely to be the most meaningful to you? In my office I have a stack of index cards. Each card has the name of one FP. I deal one card at a time to a new client while I give a quick description of each. The client's job is simply to pick up any card that bears the name of an FP that he or she feels strongly about. Then the client is asked to put the cards in order, from the most critical FP down to the least serious. At the end of this first session the client walks out the door with an entire treatment program in his or her pocket. And *the client* put it together.

You can do the same thing by skimming the "Fundamental Problem" section at the beginning of each chapter. This will enable you to quickly and efficiently identify your areas of faulty coping. It will transform what might still be, at this point, undefined needs and vague feelings of discomfort into an exact number of specific problems. Putting the FPs you identify into the order of their intensity lets you begin with those that are the biggest for you. This is how you can do the most good, right away.

The most difficult aspect of the preparation of this book was deciding when it was finished. This edition of *Being Better* is part of an evolutionary process, much the same as adopting new coping techniques is only a stage in your personal evolution. My plans for future editions will be unlikely to identify additional FPs. Progress will reflect my attempts to continue to present the best models available to help you more easily experience that unmistakable flash of insight that leads to personal growth. But you can go beyond this book yourself. There is an endless parade of GITs. They are everywhere, available to anyone who looks for them. As you discover them and find them to be coping in ways that are personally meaningful, you can use them to replace the originals provided here.

You have the ability, using the information provided here, to define for yourself the specific FPs that are generating most of the unhappiness in your attempts to cope with life. In the real world such detachment and clarity, without the type of coaching that *Being Better* provides, is relatively rare. The actual number of men and women who accomplish this on their own, a significant portion of the time, is exceedingly small. So avail yourself of the opportunity presented in this book through the GITs and the FW they impart. This book is intended to be a source of hope, insight, information, and inspiration for us, the "normals," who are doing our best yet feel we might do even better. Using this book wisely will truly serve to make you better than you've ever been.

1/ Art Buchwald

COPING WITH
AN IMPERFECT WORLD

O world, thy slippery turns!

"Coriolanus"

FUNDAMENTAL PROBLEM

Of the thirteen fundamental problems that account for the predominance of human unhappiness, the addiction to a perfect world is unlike all the others. It is the most primitive. The affected individuals engage in no introspection. They are at the mercy of the world around them.

If this FP describes you, your attention is fixed completely on your environment: the people and things around you. You view life as occurring almost totally outside yourself. You are labeled by professionals as an "external." It is in your environment that you perceive the problems responsible for your unhappiness; therefore it is outside yourself that you seek solutions.

If you and fifty others with this FP were gathered in a room, you would marvel at the unusually high number of heavy smokers, problem drinkers, and obese individuals. But there is never enough tobacco, alcohol, or Boston cream pie to make this group happy for long. You will see that they are lacking something not found in the kitchen but in the soul.

If you believe that your problems and their solutions lie outside yourself, you naïvely insist that the world around you, including the people in it, live up to your expectations. Compounding the problem, you back up these childish demands by holding your own happiness as hostage. Barely an hour passes that you are not complaining, "Look how miserable he/she/it has made me." In plain language this means, "I will not allow myself to be happy until things go as I think they should."

If you have fallen into this trap, then you have a Disneyland view of the real world. Your thoughts and speech are sprinkled with "It should," "They ought to," and "Wouldn't you think?" This language reflects the demands you are making and reveals your distress that the world is not adequately living up to your expectations.

The psychologist Carl Rogers, one of the GITs in this book, depicts a person caught in this FP in his analogy of a man attempting to preside over the sunset as a conductor over an orchestra. Perhaps a little faster or slower, he commands. Let's have an extra dash of crimson in this part or perhaps a little less gray in another. It is at once comical and sad to clearly see the predicament of the outwardly directed perfectionist futilely attempting to direct what "ought to" take place.

ART BUCHWALD

Great Inspiring Teacher
Spreading out the Bradenton *Herald*, the local daily in my small Florida town, I am faced like my neighbors and most Americans this day with these stories crying the loudest for my attention:

- From Joan Beck, "Teen pregnancy: growing crisis."
- "Scientists' study links tampons to vaginal ulcers."
- "Commuters seek new transportation during transit strike" (the plight of 400,000 commuters stranded in Philadelphia).
- Two-thirds of Alabama's counties are under alert for forest fires.
- "Pesticides polluting state's residents." Almost all Floridians, we are told, have dangerous chemicals in their tissues. This follows last week's suggested link between drinking two daily cups of coffee and pancreatic cancer.
- "Demonstrators from across U.S. rally in Atlanta" (in reaction to the unsolved murders of children in their city).
- The futility experienced by parents attempting to monitor marijuana use by their teenagers.

In the same newspaper on that same day, opposite the editorial page, above the picture of a smiling, chubby face wearing dark-framed eyeglasses, the headline challenges: "If you think you can deliver the mail faster, do it." The author of the column suggests, tongue in cheek, that poor mail service is the fault of the nation's letter writers. He helpfully explains that the new nine-digit zip code is the postal service's one last chance to us all before we are forced to deliver our own mail.

In a reality so filled with horrors that it is surprising that anyone anywhere in the world is ever able to sleep at night, this is the voice of Art Buchwald. His column is carried in 525 American newspapers and, Art offers, "it is occasionally picked up by *Pravda* and *Izvestia*, although I've been told it loses something in the translation." Art always writes like the voice of one of us, the little guys, as we struggle to cope with kids, pay toilets, sports, Washington politicians, war, sex, TV, and middle age.

On a bitter cold Manhattan morning we sat by the window in his penthouse suite at the elegant Hotel Pierre. A waiter had just brought in a silver carafe of coffee for me and two cans of Tab for Art. Knowing that he is one of the few people in the public eye who is routinely described by others and themselves as "satisfied," I was intent upon seeing how he went about accomplishing this. He settled back comfortably in his armchair. Dressed in a starched white shirt, gray flannel slacks, and well-shined conservative shoes, he lit his trademark cigar and eagerly began.

"Why the hell should the average person have to worry about Afghanistan, have to worry about this and that, particularly when he can't do anything about it? If you're going to take on the woes of the world, you're going to be a very unhappy person. In our family we assign each member one thing to worry about. If there is nothing on the front pages that day for them to worry about, they have the day off. I don't want to be completely facetious about it. There are areas where you can get concerned. You can get concerned about all this stuff that they're burning now in the air. And you certainly can get very concerned about something when it's happening to you. But you can't deal with everything."

There is a waggish saying making the rounds to the effect that if you aren't worried, then you don't understand the situation. But if anyone is aware of what is going on in the world, it is Artie. I sat at a front table one night as he addressed a group of top corporation men following a sumptuous dinner that featured poached salmon and rack of lamb. This was not the rubber chicken circuit. Finishing his prepared remarks to thunderous applause, he said, "Since things have been moving so fast, you probably have a lot of questions which I'll be very happy to answer because I do know everything that is going on." Intended as just another throwaway one-liner, it brought laughs. But around the room there was also a barely perceptible movement of heads in Art's direction. With his Pennsylvania Avenue office located just down the street from the White

House ("I am against whoever is in power. I consider myself the cruise director on the Titanic.") Buchwald has always been one to have his ear to the ground. His typical column begins in the tone of, "Something is happening in America that I think you should know about." But in spite of his insider's edge on reality, he says, "We don't have to wait for everything to get straightened out to relax."

I asked, "But how can you sleep at night being better aware than most of us of all the world's problems? How can you be satisfied or even happy?"

"Because"—he paused to fire up the cigar again—"I know that everything changes. There's nothing gonna stay the same. You have a ten- or twenty-minute attention span in this country on any issue. You get the Moral Majority and everybody's worried about the Moral Majority one week. The next week they're worried about something else. Having lived through what we have, I know problems are not as important as we or the media make them. Problems resolve themselves.

"I think the unhappiness in this country—and it showed itself in Reagan's election—is because people feel they're not in control anymore. And they certainly aren't in control of their kids and they aren't in control of the bureaucracy, whether it's the Social Security office or the driver's license bureau or anywhere. This can happen at the post office." Art's eyes light up at this idea. He changes position in the chair. It is easy to see that he's just struck paydirt, a funny angle to cope with the tyranny of life.

Says the orphan from Queens, New York, "I guess I've always thought of myself as being a Charlie Chaplin–type of character. I still have paranoia about the fact that when I arrive at an airport they always put my plane at the last gate. My luggage is always the last to get off the plane and I know there is going to be a foul-up with the hotel reservation. I ascribe this to a syndicate. This is not an accident. There is actually a syndicate working that finds out when I'm traveling. They're responsible for all the bad things that happen to me." He is waving the cigar now, and delight is apparent in his nasal, New York–accented speech. "There's not one man. It's a group of people who are out to get me. If my American Express card is spit up and rejects me, *they've* done it. I think that's a good way to cope. One of the reasons why you can't cope is you don't know who to blame. So if you don't have anybody to blame you can invent your own syndicate and say, 'It's the syndicate that did it. They're out to get me again.'"

I asked Art if his celebrity made controlling his own life easier or more difficult.

"I did some maturing on several scales. I'm very much at peace with myself now. Success is very difficult to deal with. We prepare ourselves for failure. Most of us can handle failure because we rehearse for failure, you know. As a kid they told me I'd end up no good. Success to most of us is a fantasy, and when you achieve this fantasy it's a very frightening thing because everything has changed. You're the focus of attention all of a sudden. There's a tremendous lot of bullshit that comes with it and you can't handle the bullshit. There's a price for everything and the price of success is that everybody wants a little piece of you. Your friend from college days wants you to do his son's graduation speech. Your sister wants you to do the B'nai B'rith. Everybody's calling in their due bills on you, or what they think are due bills, and all of a sudden you find yourself in a position where you lose control. You lose control of your own options and then you get mad."

"What about the old idea that happiness really does come from the inside rather than from what is going on around us?" I asked. "Have you found it to be true that the unending chase for food, sex, money, and power is fruitless?"

"It is fruitless to a certain degree, but it's not a bad thing. If you decide that sex, food, and good living are all bullshit you might fold up your tent and die. You need stimulation. I particularly need stimulation because I'm doing three columns a week. My stimulation comes from people. I can talk to you now and maybe get stimulated into an idea, a thought process, just because I'm talking to you. So I feel it's not wrong to enjoy those things. But going after them is really more important than getting them. Otherwise you reach a point where you don't want anything and you sort of become old. We all have to live in a fantasy world and we have to believe that we don't have it all. My fantasies now are concerned mostly with writing something that might last. I know this political stuff is very fragile."

Art gazed at me intently through a cloud of smoke.   said, "I think that most people would be quite surprised to find out about the serious side of Art Buchwald. Are you basically a serious person?"

"Yeah, I imagine I am. I think you have to be serious to write humor. In fact, not in all my columns, but in a tremendous number of my columns, people aren't reading them and saying, 'That's funny.' They're reading them and they're saying, 'That's true.' And they're laughing because it's true. I did one, I don't know if you saw it, about the guy who had to vote?"

"Yes, he was going into the booth as if it were his execution."

"Well, people laughed like hell because the underlying thought was true. Nobody wanted to go to the polls.

"Seeing things with humor is a very good way to survive. I have a relative and she prepares herself for unhappiness. And she finds it. She actually looks for unhappiness. She knows it's coming or she thinks it's coming and if it doesn't come she invents it. I'm the type of guy who looks for happiness and I find it in everything."

"Last week I saw the interview you did with Mike Wallace on CBS's *60 Minutes*. The pivotal fifth game of the World Series was opposite on NBC. As it turned out, the game ended just a few minutes before your segment began. Were you in a panic for fear they would overlap and the game would pull viewers away?"

"No, I looked at it differently. Tug McGraw got the third strike in the World Series five minutes before I went on. So people switched to *60 Minutes*. If anyone saw the *60 Minutes* show they saw my segment. I just took the attitude that McGraw was working for me because he got the third strike."

"Do you mean you knew it would turn out that way all along?"

"No, I didn't know it all along, but I was rooting for it very much." He gives a hearty, head-back laugh. "I lucked out in terms of picking up a big audience that might have been watching baseball if the game had gone into extra innings."

"But what if you don't find happiness? What if things work out badly?"

"If I don't find it, at least I find the humor in it. And that is a great formula for coping and surviving." A laugh starts deep inside and Art bursts out with, "When anything bad happens to me I say, 'It's the column.'"

"You depersonalize it?"

"That's right. I use humor as a weapon. You use it and it helps you. It's a weapon in life and I don't know anybody it hasn't helped.

"Look, you work in an office and the guy above you is a first-class son-of-a-bitch. You can either go into a depression or you can see the humor of it. If you can, you feel better. Everything is comparison, isn't it?"

Buchwald threw out the phrase "Surviving in a world you didn't make." "We're all in some way survivors. My philosophy is you only go around once, as it says in the Schlitz commercial, and you can either have a good day or a bad day. A lot depends on you.

"You can make your own luck. I've been doing it all my life. Luck is not something that happens to certain people. The thing is to recognize luck and to take advantage of it. Then everybody says, 'Boy, are you lucky.' But fifty people may have seen this or had the same thing happen to them but they didn't recognize it. I think I learned as a kid to take advantage of a situation. It's sort of a streetwise thing."

Art did not have a storybook childhood. His mother died when he was an infant. His father, a curtain manufacturer, was unable to care for him and his three sisters and placed them in a Jewish orphanage. This was followed by a series of foster homes before Art returned to live with his father at age sixteen. The same year, 1941, he left to spend the next four years in the Marines. Upon discharge he enrolled for a time in college, but the veterans bonus from the state of New York gave him the means he needed to seek excitement in Paris. Originally catching on as a *Variety* stringer, he soon talked himself into a reporter's job with the European edition of the *Herald Tribune* that lasted sixteen years.

"It's what I tell kids in school. Let's say it's in journalism. They say, 'How do I get a job?' I tell them that there are no jobs. But somebody's going to get one. Someone always gets it. Out of this class of 100 kids, fourteen of you are going to get jobs. They don't exist. But you're going to get them. And it won't be the ones who say, 'I don't have a chance.'"

As we talked, Art expressed a very genuine interest in me. He asked questions about my family, my schooling, and my present life that went beyond simple politeness or small talk. I began to suspect that this might be a key to one who can live as comfortably and as satisfied as Art does in this world we all share. I asked him about it.

"Yeah, but it has to be the real thing. It can't be phony. You can't fake it. A bully is a guy who is nice to the guy on top of him and doesn't give a damn or is mean to the person below him. A secure person, and I think I can put myself in that category, is interested in people. I'm as interested in the elevator operator or the chambermaid as I am in you. I want to know what the lady who fixes this bed does at night. Does she go home to Harlem? Does she get to keep the champagne if somebody leaves it in the room? I'm curious about all those things. I'm fascinated with the taxi driver and I'm very impressed to meet the chairman of Morgan Stanley [the firm that was hosting the financial program at which he was to speak]. Here's a guy who is running an empire and I don't know how it works and I want to know how it works. And people get this feeling back.

I can go anywhere and people are not ill at ease with me and I'm comfortable with them."

AT HOME IN AN IMPERFECT WORLD

Fundamental Wisdom
Any man who can look over his shoulder at the Nixon years with a sense of nostalgia ("Nixon was my Camelot") is obviously an individual with an exceptional ability to make the most out of the world in which he finds himself. Art Buchwald recognizes that the world, not infrequently, appears to run amok. He loves to point to a news story and drolly challenge: "I could not make that up." In fact, he has a name for those who are less at home with the reality of life than he: "the uptight society." In spite of his shaky beginnings, or, as he prefers to put it, "because of them," his life has personified the ability to make friends with his environment. Art has a custom of ending his talks by saying, "Any country in the world that lets a guy like me say what I do can't be all bad." He is right, of course. The world around you and the people in it are not all bad. In fact, the world can be a warm, supportive, and nurturing place if you know how to let it. Here's how.

Internal. The best messages are sometimes found in the oldest of wisdom How many times have you heard it? Happiness comes from the inside. Try to grab hold of this simple idea on a level that makes sense to you. Once you can see that your happiness does not come from, nor depend upon, your environment you will find it possible to use the remainder of the Fundamental Wisdom in this chapter to make major changes in your emotional life. If you suffer from this first Fundamental Problem, a change in perspective right here frees you, and your capacity for happiness, from the tyranny of a world that can seem unfair, inexplicable, unpleasant, and uncomfortable. Don't participate in a system in which your happiness is at the mercy of what is happening around you. You can't win. Why not set up a system that works to your advantage? Operating in this manner, you will be one of a minority of people who actually understand and profit from a concept that everyone claims to believe in: that happiness comes from the inside.

Square One. "All right," you say, "separating my chance for happiness from this crazy world makes sense to me. Where do I start?" Begin by remembering the words of our GIT: "I tell myself they are out to get me."

Art Buchwald is expressing his recognition and acceptance of a Murphy-type process that describes the joker in every deck. The unpredictability factor is present in even your most carefully planned activities. Once you open your eyes to it you can start each day forewarned that by bedtime perhaps 20 percent of your efforts, on average, will not turn out as planned. Why? Because in some situations, such as a canceled dinner date, another's actions will be the determining factor. Or, the unknowable can strike. Even while taking your vitamins and exercising conscientiously, you may get the flu. And your tire can blow out, light bulbs will burn out, and the IRS may randomly choose to audit your return. And, of course, you too will make mistakes from time to time. Perhaps hurriedly reading the recipe you will pour a half-cup of salt into the quiche when a half-teaspoon was called for. The sheer quantity and variety of situations in which we find ourselves will defeat us if we cling rigidly to pre-formed ideas as to how each event "should" unfold. Do you recall the performer in the early days of TV who kept us on the edge of our seats watching the number of saucers he could keep whirling atop sticks? He ran wildly from one to another, just managing to restart the slowest ones before they crashed to the floor. The individual who tries desperately to make the environment conform to his or her expectations is constantly faced with taking care of too many plates at once, and life will be filled with broken china. But you can refuse to be overwhelmed and continue to stand your ground. Don't be pessimistic, but do be realistic. Facing an empty gas tank with "Well, there's part of my 20 percent" brings understanding to confusion and thereby creates order out of chaos. This allows you to withstand, with a minimum of distress, those events that would flatten the less expectant.

Luck and Chance. One piece of good news is that some of these unforeseeable events will turn out unexpectedly good. Lucky pennies are found in the street all the time. However, nature being what it is, these happy events often make less of an impression on us than life's pies in the face. But if you keep light on your feet you can tip the odds in your favor. Keeping your balance in this imperfect world frequently involves coping with that biggest portion of the unexpected that is neither good nor bad until your reaction makes it so. Opportunities will automatically open up to you that are completely unavailable to those who refuse to forge ahead and adapt because events didn't unfold as they had supposed they would. This rigid reaction occurs in people whose plans do not include the element of chance—that uncontrollable 20 percent. If you are wiser and stay alert for the unexpected, you may begin to hear others speak of you as "lucky." You will know better, that you make your own luck. Buchwald calls it the art of surviving in a world you did not make. This flash of insight hit a beautiful young patient of mine. She was recently divorced and unhappy working as a receptionist in a pediatrician's office. The following week she brought a miniature plaque for me that she spotted at a sidewalk craft show. Shortly afterward she moved away. At this writing she is a professional athlete whose name is known in half the households in America. And what was on the plaque?

> When Life Gives You Lemons,
> Make Lemonade

Satisfaction. Once you recognize that you are solely responsible for your happiness and you face up to the role of chance, it is a pleasure to learn that it makes little sense to wait for life to become perfect before allowing yourself to feel relaxed. I actually had the conversation that follows on the day I began to write this chapter.

> *Me,* to a physically and emotionally worn patient: "When do you have time for the things you enjoy?"
> *Patient,* guilty and flustered at the idea of pleasure and self-gratification in the face of a chaotic and harried life: "I have no time for that now. I have too much to do."
> *Me:* "Why not schedule a half hour each day, just for yourself?"
> *Patient:* "I couldn't. I'd just spend the time worrying about everything I was supposed to be doing."

It is sad to say, but I have had many similar exchanges both before and since. Be honest with yourself and recognize your own mortality. If you are postponing the enjoyment of your life until all your problems are resolved and everything is in order, you can expect to run out of time. Will they chisel this on your tombstone?

> *He planned life long to relax*
> *When he got the world running good*
> *He suffered two heart attacks*
> *Because plans don't go as they should.*

Day Off. Well, why *does* the average person have to worry about Afghanistan? It is only smart to pick your own fights. Don't let the fights pick you by passively falling emotional prey to whatever issues are blowing in the wind. Everything that you do in your lifetime, considered as part of the vast panorama of human history, is almost certain to be relatively insignificant—except to you. How well you cope determines the quality of your life. Therefore, sacrificing your emotional stability indiscriminately over the unending parade of situations in the world that are not going as you would prefer is exhausting. Why abandon your equilibrium over such myths as "righteous indignation" or "justifiable anger"? In such instances of psychological headbanging, people rationalize literally raising their blood pressure to the point of a self-induced stroke over such insignificant events as a driver who "cut right into my lane," or a bank statement that "really is wrong." You are not required to respond to the people and things around you with such knee-jerk emotional reflexes. "But I have enough problems right now, fighting day and night to keep the lid on. How much worse will things get if I let my guard down?" The answer is that with you no longer pushing and straining to make the people and situations around you conform to your belief as to how they "ought to be," little will change. You were never controlling events in the first place. If you can knock down your own sense of self-importance and abandon your demands as to how the world "must" behave, the one significant change will be the increase in your own happiness.

Try this experiment. Give it one day. From the time you get up until bedtime, vow not to stand guard. Declare a moratorium on standing vigilantly and reacting explosively when transgressions occur. You may state your opinion when appropriate and do what you reasonably can as a responsible person, but stop there. Let go and permit nature to take its course. When the day is over, if things are not measurably worse, you must conclude that you have been wasting a lot of your own life generating some very unpleasant stress for no useful purpose. If you pass the test, you have, like Art, given yourself a day off. Start to make it a habit.

Friendly World. If you view the world as a combat zone, you will forever feel that you inhabit a hostile environment. In turn this perception will justify selfish and aggressive behavior on your part in "self-defense." Your world reflects your view of it. When you develop an authentic interest and delight in the people around you, the world becomes awash in a friendly light. In genuine friendships we are always willing to tolerate a great deal of behavior that we might otherwise find bothersome. Carrying these feelings of affability with you in the world creates feelings of comfort and support within you that will have a permanent and stable nature. Being able to create such stability will give you a measure of healthy control that you have previously lacked. But do not unthinkingly pay every due bill dropped at your doorstep. If would-be controllers attempt to make *you* part of *their* fantasy as to how the world ought to be, it may be necessary to resist firmly. Nothing is gained if acting in another's script causes you to be robbed of your happiness.

Hunger. When you do your utmost, hope for the best, and the outcome is still unquestionably a poor one, there is still a bright side. Getting everything you want, were it remotely possible, is probably not good for you. If we have nothing to chase, it is human nature to make up new challenges. As most people's first thought turns to money when having all they want is mentioned, look at the Kennedys and the Rockefellers. At opposite extremes politically, they are both families in which the children in the current generations have had wealth almost unimaginable to the rest of us. What would you do if you had such a fortune? Would you buy cars, houses, and clothes? Would you then give huge amounts to your favorite charities? Take a year or two to criss-cross the globe? Now what? You still have so much money you can never hope to spend it, and your life is still before you. Whether you admire or despise them, if you look at the lives of a large portion of the members of these two families you can see that they have gone to spectacular lengths to create opportunities for life to both reward and to rebuff them. Human beings thrive on action. Stagnation does not wear well with us. We are said to have our origins as hunter-gatherers. We run and we chase. We are problem-solvers. We must be continuously tested and we continuously test ourselves. This is a process to be enjoyed at its best and coped with at its most disappointing. We do not get past it. It will not end until our lives end. It *is* life.

Gravity. The most obvious aspect of Art Buchwald's FW is his use of humor. In fact, this quality, although perhaps most noticeable in Buchwald, is found in many of the GITs. To paraphrase Art, there are few human situations that cannot be enhanced, improved, or at least made more bearable through the use of humor. The ability to view situations on the light side is unique to man among all living things. Applied humor is the closest man will ever come to the discovery of the mythical anti-gravity device. Humor lifts great weights from our shoulders. In this briefest of Buchwald samplers you can see how this elevation of weighty issues takes place:

The saccharin scare: "We need to develop stronger rats."

The MX missile system: "Give the contract to Amtrak and the Russians will never find the missiles."

Reaganomics: "For millions and millions of people, nothing beats Reaganomics—although herpes comes pretty close."

Gun registration: "My neighbor can't even water his lawn straight."

Computers: "Do you know it's impossible to get out of the Book of the Month Club?"

Medical costs: "Hospitals should go condominium. It's cheaper to buy a room than stay three weeks."

Right-to-life groups: "Every time I do a piece on abortion they write letters threatening to kill me."

Ronald Reagan: "The most amiable president we have had in a long time. Also, the most rested."

Arabs: "Blame the Harvard Business School. If they went to Cal Tech they'd all be surfers."

It is quite true that when the laugh has passed, the reality remains the same. But problems often seem less forbidding and more bearable, if not nearly conquerable.

Lifespan. Actuarial tables indicate that the present average lifespan for women and men is something less than eighty years. How many years do you have left? No matter what the answer, spending this precious time attempting to force the people and things around you into scripts that you have created would seem like an ineffective and unenjoyable way to spend your remaining time. Art Buchwald stated that all is comparison. After Art finished his after-dinner talk to a standing ovation we chatted as he idly shuffled through the deck of yellow index cards on which had been typed notations for his address. The speech itself and the audience reaction did not entirely satisfy him, although I had detected nothing less than overall enthusiasm. "I'm trying out some new material tonight," he said. "I still have to tighten it up." But then he walked off past almost the entire audience, which had lined up single-file to retrieve their coats from two feverishly working coat-check women. He moved down the line shaking hands, taking time to accept earnest expressions of appreciation, and frequently sharing a laugh. His eyes twinkled behind the glasses. The cigar was stuck in the broad smile. Here was Art Buchwald, contentedly living the FW from this chapter. He obviously did not feel the need to get his material perfect or to elicit exactly the audience reaction he would have liked in order to thoroughly enjoy the moment. He wants more. He said so. He is still reaching, and the idea of permanence for his work is presently on his mind. The way he adeptly balances his needs from his world with his happiness of the moment is the message. Perhaps his wisdom displayed here will not contribute one bit to the permanence he seeks. If not, Art will find a way to deal with it that will allow him to be happy anyhow.

2 / Hank Aaron

PERFECTIONISM

But no perfection is so absolute,
That some impurity doth not pollute.

"The Rape of Lucrece"

FUNDAMENTAL PROBLEM

Although the addiction to a perfect world is the most basic Fundamental Problem, there is another side of perfectionism that can be even more self-defeating. Although the potential to be perfect is no more within the range of human functioning than unassisted flight, many people create a daily hell for themselves over their own shortcomings.

The semantics concerning perfectionism are treacherous. It can be quite healthy to aspire to be a perfectionist. A desire for excellence is a creditable quality. But if you cannot accept your own flaws, even though you may be tolerant of nature's capriciousness and the foibles of others, an FP exists.

The addiction to your own perfection can be easily recognized. Do you become genuinely down and disheartened over trivial lapses such as burning the toast or misplacing the car keys? When you are meticulous in your work and even double check it, only to have your boss find an error or point out someone who did better, are you crushed? Do you believe that in spite of all this, if you are just careful enough, you will make no miscues tomorrow and all your efforts will be successful? If it sounds like I'm describing you, an FP is likely.

Samuel Johnson described the second marriage as "The triumph of hope over experience." If you are addicted to your own perfection, this is also a good description of you. Whether you are consciously aware of it or not, you hold the belief that you are capable of performance at a level unrealistically above the rest of us. You blindly accept the fallacy that failure "ought not" occur where you are concerned. Anything short of constant success is an unending source of distress.

Clients seeking psychological consultation over the unhappiness that results from being caught up in such a cycle often rebel when the FP is laid out for them in this manner. Their protests are usually voiced as, "Should I lack goals?" Or, "Why should I settle for second best?"

Resolving this FP does not require that you abandon your goals nor shorten your reach. The athletic success of Henry Aaron, the Great Inspiring Teacher in this chapter, has never been matched in the history of baseball. Yet Henry Aaron is a healthy perfectionist. Record-breaking achievement, happiness, and healthy perfectionism are all compatible.

HENRY L. AARON

Great Inspiring Teacher
We were in his office high up the circular canyon that is Atlanta–Fulton County Stadium. When the national anthem is sung here the fans tack on a final *s;* it is the home of the Braves. Henry stood next to the picture window that overlooks home plate. The blinds were pulled up to reveal a panorama of the field where Tom House, a Braves pitcher warming up in the bullpen between the left-field fence and the stands, caught Aaron's home run number 715, which broke Babe Ruth's record. Twenty-five thousand dollars had been tendered by Sammy Davis, Jr., among others, for that specially marked ball.

"Have they got a plaque out there to mark the spot?" I asked.

"No, they don't have anything out there." His strong voice is deep and rich, but he spoke these next words quietly. "It wasn't that important." It was hard to tell whether he was being humble or a little resentful. It was raining steadily, and I would have liked to walk the ball's path with him from home plate. He pointed out over the natural grass field. "See that 385 in left field? It was about fifteen feet to the left of that."

As a disciplined hitter, Henry Aaron was known for never distracting himself by eyeing the flight of a long-hit ball. His style was to run first and hear about it later. "Did you watch that one?" I asked him.

He laughs his rumbling laugh. "I don't know whether I watched it or what. I did know when I hit it, it was going out of the ballpark. I had that feeling. I guess after hitting so many home runs you kind of get a feeling when you hit one, that it's going out of the ballpark." And of course, Henry Aaron knows that feeling better than anyone.

The press coverage of Aaron over the years is a permanent record of his consistency. Issues of *Look* and the old *Saturday Evening Post* from the mid-1950s describe the young hitter, who was to outlast them, with adjectives like *self-respect, quiet confidence, discipline,* and *class.* He never changed. In his press clippings from the frantic years of 1973 and 1974, when the pressure from his chase after Babe Ruth was so great that many predicted it would break him, the descriptions remain exactly the same.

The life and career of Hammerin' Hank is a tale of consistent excellence. In 1957, at the age of twenty-three, Aaron led the National League in home runs, runs batted in, and total runs. He hit a game-winning run after eleven scoreless innings to bring the pennant to the Milwaukee Braves. That same stroke of the bat brought the Most Valuable Player Award to The Hammer and landed Henry Aaron in his first World Series. Seventeen years later, as he verged on breaking Ruth's record, he had become the object of relentless pressure from the world press, "Dear Nigger" letters, and threats that he would be shot down from the stands. But Bad Henry, still a Brave, hit home run 714 in Cincinnati with his first swing of the year. This tied the one "unreachable" record in baseball; Babe Ruth's 714 career home runs. Four days later, on April 8 in Atlanta, he hit 715 to break the record, and the world breathed a sigh of relief.

"Henry, did you set high standards for yourself even as a youngster?"

"Well, school was secondary, I am sorry to say. I graduated from high school and my parents really wanted me to go on to college. However, the only thing for me, thinking back, was sports. I always wanted to be the best regardless of whether it was stickball, football, running track, or playing half-court basketball. I just always felt that if anyone else could do it, I could do it better.

"I didn't live the life of a hermit, let's face it. I did things. I lived a normal life just like any other boy. But back early, and then as a youngster away from home in the minors, I felt that when things like staying out late got in the way of my success as a baseball player, I could easily put those things down. But even at a younger age—I'm speaking about twelve or thirteen years old—I had some direction as to what I wanted to accomplish in life. Although the doors were not open for black players at that time, my goal was to play baseball and do the very best I possibly could even if it meant that I had to spend my next ten or fifteen years in the Negro American League.

"It was a job, but how many people in this country—in the world, for that matter—can enjoy doing what they do? I was never pushed into playing baseball. Even in my son's case I'm pushing him and wanting him to succeed. But my father never pushed me. I played baseball because I loved it. I played baseball because I was very successful at it. I played baseball because it afforded me a chance to escape the ghettos. It afforded me a chance to make a darn good living and it took care of my family pretty well, you know. I have five kids and they've all been well taken care of."

"Hank, how would you answer people who would say you are just some sort of freak and write off your twenty-three years of exceptional play as simply the result of natural ability?"

"Sure, a lot of it was natural ability and a lot of it I had to work at. I have seen many, many men who have played this game who have had much more ability than I had. Yet they went on to abuse that ability. This holds true in baseball and also in anything one might try to accomplish. You have to incorporate other ingredients. If you do not have a desire to go out and—I hope this is the correct word—'punish' yourself, you might as well stay home. When I say 'punish' I'm not talking about jumping off a tall building. I'm talking about working extra hard to accomplish something. Sure, certain gifts were given to me by God. But I had to meet Him halfway in order to make all of my dreams come true.

"I've always said that, and I try to relate this to the kids in the minor leagues. Some of these kids just feel like, 'Oh, I've got the natural ability to do this or do that.' We've got about ninety-eight players on the board there. Most of them are gifted. If they weren't then we wouldn't have drafted them. I tell them this: 'God gives you a gift like the ability to play baseball which He hasn't given everybody else. So you're blessed to be able to play baseball. But if you abuse that privilege by not going out and giving it all you've got, you'll be stripped of your gift.' And I don't expect all ninety-eight of these players to get to the major leagues. I don't expect half of the kids up there on the board to even reach triple-A ball [the highest-level minor league teams]."

"So you are saying that mental factors such as the attitude of being willing to punish yourself determine who will be successful?"

"Right. That's what it is. For example, we drafted a kid last year named Ken Dayley from Portland, Oregon. He was in junior college there and he was our number one draft. He was the number three player taken in the country and he was our pitcher. We started him out at the Savannah club and moved him to Richmond. I've gotten to know Ken pretty well since we drafted him, and I was talking to him just recently, about three weeks ago, in Richmond. We had a rain delay so I stood up and talked to him. I was wondering how he managed to throw such a good curve ball. In my own mind I knew that he didn't just come up with that. I knew he had to be throwing it all his life. And he came up with an interesting answer to me.

"He said, 'Mr. Aaron, you know what? When I was a ten-year-old kid I used to go down in my coach's basement and practice.' And he described the things his coach had him do. He put up a dot for him to throw the curve ball at and certain other things. Here is a kid who has been working at this ever since he was ten years old.

"Now if you talk to some of the players on the same team who are much older than this boy they'll say, 'Oh, it's just natural.' That's a lot of baloney. He was blessed with ability but he's been working with that ability all his life. That's the difference between a guy who achieves something and a guy who doesn't achieve. The others get to a certain status where they stop working at it, and they're just like stagnant water."

"I know that success in terms of public recognition for you was very slow in coming. For your first sixteen years in the majors, in fact, you seemed continuously overshadowed by other players. Did that cause you to get down on yourself?"

"I felt that if I did my job, regardless of whether I went out there and got four hits for four or not, and as long as I approached the game the way it was supposed to be, getting to the ballpark on time and doing my job, one day somebody was going to recognize the fact that Henry Aaron was a great ballplayer. Every dog has his day, as the saying goes. Thirty years ago when I started out in Jacksonville, Florida, every time I left the ballpark we [the black and the white players] went in different directions. When we finished playing a game at night if we were in Columbus or Montgomery, we would go in one direction and my teammates would go in the other, although we would play together on the field. When we were in Jacksonville I stayed on one side of the town and they stayed on their side. I guess I'd use the old slogan one of the automobiles dealers used. 'When you are second best you try a little harder and stay a little longer.' That's what kept me motivated. That part is something that blacks in this country, unfortunately, have to do all their lives. They have to work harder to achieve the same status as their white brothers.

"I just kept pushing and plugging away and then one day, of course, I thrust upon the record of Babe Ruth and everybody started looking at me as a superstar. It was too bad it had to happen that way, but that's what carried me on, you know? After sixteen years it's kind of frustrating when you are doing the same thing as other players are doing and yet you're not recognized for your feat. Everybody else is carrying the status of 'superstar' and you are living in the shadows. But they say if you don't play in New York or California or the largest cities then you don't get the status that some of these other players get. You can't make some writer in New York write about you. They had three ballclubs there to write about and certainly their paper was filled with making their own players superstars."

"Henry, I think it is important that people realize you were not born a great baseball player. Early in your career you didn't hold the bat as well as most Little Leaguers. You batted cross-handed and you were notorious for swinging at bad pitches. I'm interested in how you went about becoming the premier all-around player of whom Tug McGraw said, 'You pitch to him just the same as anybody else—just don't let go of the ball.'"

Hank allowed a chuckle and moved across his desk closer to me. Low country music played from the novelty sparkplug radio on the bookshelf behind him. "Well, if I walked up to the plate and I popped up with the bases loaded, I didn't blow it out by throwing a helmet or cracking a bat. I went out to the outfield with my head held high and I'd try to figure out why I popped that ball out. And there's always an answer. You must have swung under the ball or you took your eye off it or something. I feel like that's a man's weakness when he gets angry. You can't think. Even as a youngster the thing I had going for me was the fact that I could always keep myself under control. So I would always be in control of Henry Aaron. That's number one. I couldn't think by crushing my helmet down or hitting my fists up against a brick wall. What is that going to do? That's only going to keep me out of the game for the next two weeks. I've seen a lot of players do this.

"I hate like hell to lose, yeah. I like to be a winner all the time. But I'm not that naïve and I'm not that foolish to believe that I'm going to always be a winner. I accept defeat but I'm not going to accept it to the degree that I'm not going to try to do something about it the next time. I realize that if two teams are playing a baseball game or if we are arm wrestling or whatever we're doing, somebody's got to lose. But as I said, no matter what you're doing, if you go out there and give it 100 percent, when you stand before the mirror, defeated or not, you have nothing to be ashamed of.

"I have always felt that although someone may defeat me, if I strike out two or three times in a particular ballgame, that pitcher on that particular day was the best player. He was better than I was. But I know if I see him again I'm going to be prepared. If he struck me out on three good curve balls I'm going to be ready to wait for a curve ball. I think that failure is a part of success. If a person has not failed he doesn't know what it is to be successful. In order for anybody to be successful at what he's doing he's going to have to fail. There's no such thing as a bed of roses all your life and you're going to have to live like that without letting failure stand in your way.

"I could very easily have given up when I was growing up in Mobile. We were the poorest poor anybody could be. There were times when we didn't have meat to put in our beans or greens. We were vegetarians before people knew what vegetarians were. But I didn't let that keep me down. When I was hounded by people when I was going after the record, I could have very easily folded my tent and said, 'Well, I don't want it anymore.' That was related to failure, but I didn't let it stand in my way. It's very easy for anybody, adults or kids, to sit back and say, 'I can't, I can't, I can't,' because that's easy to say. But it's hard for a person to say, 'I can,' and hard for a person to be knocked down and then get up off the floor and be the champ again."

"As a perfectionist, were you ever able to finish up a season and say to yourself, 'I had a good year and I'm satisfied'?"

"Never. I've never been satisfied. I've had some decent years in the big leagues but I always look back over the 162 games and I think, 'Well, I could have done better.' Each time I went to the plate and went three hits for four I felt I should have gone four for four. One year I hit 358 and I've always thought that if I had tried a little bit harder I could have hit 368 or close to 400. If I had tried a little harder."

"This situation is the downfall of so many perfectionists. They never achieve quite enough to please themselves so they are never very happy."

Another deep laugh from Henry Aaron. "Well, I haven't reached that point. I may make an error in the outfield but I'm not one to go home and brood about it. But on the other hand I feel that there's always room for improvement and I should know why I made that mistake. It doesn't make me unhappy, but given a second chance I will do better. I didn't think I was somebody godly or something. Even though I expected a lot out of myself, if you cut me I'll bleed and if you abuse me enough I will cry, you know. When I say I had a special gift, I always felt I was a human being. I just felt I could do something a little bit better than some of the other players but I don't think I ever expected any more out of myself than what I could do if I tried a little harder."

"Does that mean you can be serious about improving without taking your work home with you?"

"I do take it home with me, but not to my family. For example, if I was in some kind of batting slump I would wait until everybody was sound asleep. That's when I would do most of my concentration. I would stand in the mirror like I was ready for the ball. I'd swing again and again at that same pitch that I popped up with the bases loaded."

"As you approached the record under all that mounting pressure from every side, you didn't fold as many so-called experts in the media predicted. How did you manage to stand up to it all?"

"There was nobody on this earth that could put enough pressure on me to make me fold, because I had my own way of escaping it. I had many ways to relax and get out from under that kind of pressure. It was usually a matter of going someplace. I could catch a flight and go to Mobile and stay with my mother and nobody knew where I was. Twenty-five miles from here I had a very good friend with a resort and that was another place I went to get away. I could relax as well as anybody. I had so much fan mail that I got to the ballpark at 3:30, which was early enough to get things out of the way. So by the time five o'clock came around I would have nothing to do but concentrate on the game."

"With reporters asking you non-stop when you would reach the magic number, you often answered that one home run was just the same as another and your goal was to simply hit the next one."

"Well, it would have been foolish for me to be looking ahead when I was ten, fifteen, or twenty home runs behind Babe Ruth. If I did, I wouldn't have been able to concentrate. You know tomorrow is promised to none of us. My job was to hit a home run or do whatever I could do that day. I let tomorrow take care of itself. When I got down on my knees to pray I didn't pray about tomorrow. I said, 'Give us *this* day.' I didn't say, 'Give us *tomorrow*.' I can't worry about the next time at bat. I've got to make sure I do a good job this time, and I can't if I am worrying about next time. If I'd really wanted to push myself I probably could have broken the record in 1973. But that would have been playing strictly for Henry Aaron. I wanted to do everything I possibly could for my team. If you look at my record in 1973 I ended up hitting about 301 with close to one hundred RBIs and I scored a hundred and some runs. So I was concentrating on being a team player.

"When the season ended in 1973 I left with one home run behind as far as tying the record and two behind as far as breaking it. Somebody asked me if I was going to hibernate for the winter. I said, 'No way. I'm going to live my life the same way I always live it. I'm not going to try to walk across the street when the red light is on but I'm going to do everything I usually do and if I've got to go to California I'm going to get on a jet and fly to California.'"

"Stars come and stars go, Henry. But the record book shows that no one who played the game of baseball ever had such a string of exceptional seasons lasting over twenty years. It seems like your approach of taking one hit, one game, and one season at a time is the attitude that made this consistency possible."

"Well, you're absolutely right. I've seen it happen in my time and it's happening now where a player will come up and will be a 'great superstar' for a year or two years. Then pretty soon he fades away and everybody starts wondering what the heck happened to him. I've always said that yesterday's news is good for only one thing and that's wrapping dead fish in, you know. So when you start looking at what you did yesterday or two days ago or even what you achieved last time at bat, then you're in for serious trouble. And that goes for any sport and that goes for life, no matter who you are. If you stop reaching for the top and you get conceited, you have nothing to keep you going.

"I'll say for any professional player to have superstar status put upon him he has to hold on and do something consistently. I mean one year, even five years don't prove anything as far as I am concerned. Not in the major leagues. The only one to reach superstar status is the guy who can do it over and over and over again."

Along the broad walk that circles the stadium and allows the fans access to the upper deck, sits the life-sized bronze head and shoulders of Henry Aaron on a marble pedestal. Henry Aaron is only forty-seven years old. He looks playing fit even in the three-piece business suit he wears in place of the uniform with the number forty-four on the back. On the occasions when he comes to work dressed more like a golfer than an executive, Henry's short-sleeve sport shirts reveal what is perhaps his most unique physical attribute. I've been with Muhammed Ali and I've been with Henry Aaron. Aaron's wrists, the wrists that powered so many balls over outfield fences, at eight inches around, are bigger than Ali's.

"How does it feel, Hank, to be the proverbial legend in your own time? What is it like to come to work past a statue of yourself?"

"Well"—Henry sat way back, relaxed and smiling—"I want people to know I'm still living. It makes you feel good any time people remember you. A dead man smells no flowers, you know. So I like receiving all my accolades while I can still walk around and enjoy them. And I'm still a loner. Many celebrities, be they movie stars or professional athletes, when they reach a certain pinnacle in life, I see them stringing with a lot of people behind, you know. I just never had that.

"Of course I have my own scholarship fund here through the city of Atlanta. We have about $100,000 in that plan and we use the interest to help motivate kids. Black and white, it doesn't make any difference who they are, if a kid is poor and excels in certain things. Say for example he excels in music. If his parents can't afford to buy him his own horn, music or music lessons we take some money and buy the musical instrument. And we give enough money so he won't have to work after school at the grocery store and can stay home and work at his studies. I set this up myself when I retired. I didn't want a scholarship that could help only one student. This way we can help fifteen or twenty students at a time with their interests. All we're trying to do is get those kids started in the right direction."

He pointed to the blackboard next to his desk with five vertical columns labeled Atlanta, Richmond, Savannah, Durham, and Anderson. Neatly printed down each column were the names of the players in the five teams of the Braves' organization. Most of the names in the Atlanta group, of course, were familiar. Few of the others were, as yet.

"I'm in charge of the whole board. All except the Atlanta ballclub. I'm in charge of signing, the managers, the coaches, the instructors, and the players. I make changes moving one from Richmond to Savannah or from Durham to Savannah. Just flip-flopping them around like checkers, making sure they're in the right place. Basically my job is farm director but it's nice when they say, 'vice president in charge of player development.'

"The job here calls for patience. You just have to be patient waiting for some of these kids to come around and show what you drafted them to be—that is, to be major-league baseball players. You can get a little edgy at times. You wonder why a certain player is not living up to his capabilities. One of my goals now is to one day see the Atlanta Braves win a championship with these minor leagues here. Everybody has to have something. If I were just sitting back here saying, 'Well, I'm satisfied,' I wouldn't have any motivation to push these kids."

Following our first talk, Henry was planning to attend a meeting for coaches and staff with the team's owner, Ted Turner, or "Captain Outrageous," as Atlanta's boy wonder is often called. I asked Aaron if he didn't feel a special kinship with the young man who is pioneering cable news, owns Atlanta's "Superstation" WTBS, and had captained his yacht *Courageous* to an America's Cup win.

"He and I are very similar in some ways. Although we're both in different areas—he's in the business world and I played professional sports—they relate to each other. After knowing Ted Turner, money doesn't mean anything to him. He could sell this ballclub tomorrow. What I recognize in him is that determination. He has that inner drive, that feeling within himself that he wants to be on top. He's got the biggest news network, cable news was born right here in Atlanta, and he wants the Braves to be the best." Henry smiled. "That sounds very familiar."

When you sit across the desk from Aaron you cannot help looking past his shoulder to that unmarked spot over the left-field wall. After playing out the 1974 season in which he broke Babe Ruth's record in game nineteen, he returned to Milwaukee to play for the Brewers as a designated hitter. In two years he pushed his career home run mark to 755. I asked him, "Do you think we will ever see that mark touched by anybody on the scene now, like Reggie Jackson or Bob Horner?"

"I don't know. Reggie probably won't have a chance because of his age. And Bob Horner would have a chance but he's been plagued with injuries. And you know, every day counts and every year counts." Here is the consistency factor that finally wore down every player but one. "I know a lot of people said 714 would never be broken but I think all records are made to be broken. The kids that are coming along today are much stronger. They can hit the ball further. The game is played a little better and I'm happy for it, you know. But in order to break the record we're talking about, the 755, you've got to play for a long time. These kids today are making these astronomical salaries and they're just not thinking about playing for twenty-three years. I can't blame them. If you sign a contract for twelve or fifteen million dollars like a Dave Winfield, why should you go out there and sacrifice and play? Why not just make your investments and cool it?"

Henry made this last statement in a voice tinged with a hint of resignation. It wasn't surprising that during the long July of the 1981 baseball strike the man for whom every playing day was precious would break his silence and uncharacteristically speak out against both sides. He said the strike had gone on long enough and that the people getting hurt were twelve- and thirteen-year-old boys. And he decried the fact that the players might make a sudden return to the diamonds in less than top condition.

The night before our last conversation I sat in Atlanta–Fulton County Stadium or "Henry's launching pad"—watching a game between the Braves and the Dodgers. Some words caught my eye as they flashed on the message section of the scoreboard. They remained for just a few minutes without attracting much attention and were soon replaced with information about purchasing tickets to upcoming games. The message read:

> On this day in 1935, Babe Ruth hit his last 3 homeruns,
> 712, 713, and 714, as a Brave.

Those runs were a feat by a different kind of figure. As an aging player Ruth hit these last three home runs in Forbes Field after carousing with a reporter until five o'clock the morning of the game. When I mentioned it Henry said, almost to himself, "And I was one year old."

During his final years, Henry Aaron, like Ruth, was baseball's highest-paid player, at a then-phenomenal $600,000 over three years. More than thirty endorsements came his way, and the one with Magnavox for one million dollars over five years made him the highest-paid individual on the Magnavox payroll, including the company president. On April 8 in Atlanta before 53,775 fans, Dodger pitcher Al Downing put himself as well as Hank into the record books with a fastball Aaron describes as "just a little too fat." The fans screamed themselves hoarse for a period that lasted in excess of ten minutes. Hank circled the bases uncustomarily smiling and was met at homeplate by his mother and father and his wife, Billye. He was hoisted on the shoulders of teammates as dignitaries, including then-Governor Jimmy Carter and Atlanta Mayor Maynard Jackson, and celebrities the likes of Sammy Davis, Jr., and Pearl Bailey joined in the mid-game festivities. For at that point, Henry Aaron had defined excellence in the game of baseball. He has given future generations of players the yardstick against which they must measure themselves.

HEALTHY PERFECTIONISM

Fundamental Wisdom
Henry Aaron's broad smile and relaxed manner are proof that the perfectionist need not be a strung-tight bore who is never pleased with personal efforts and carries the air of a "genius at work." Perfectionism means doing your best and refusing to coast. But high expectations and extra

effort do not require an emotional atmosphere of tense and furious activity. Such self-imposed pressure *decreases* efficiency; it does not improve it. In twenty-three years of sustained effort, Hank Aaron was considered to possess such a relaxed demeanor that some found it unsettling. Pitchers alleged that he slept between pitches because he showed none of the bat flailing so many less powerful hitters affect. Catchers swore he decided whether to swing after the ball went past him because, waiting until the last millisecond to commit himself, he seemed to pick the ball from out of their gloves. Never a kidder when in uniform, he spent his time in the dugout studying the pitcher and he moved about in such an unconcerned way his teammates once took to calling him "Snowshoes." Perfectionism takes place in the mind, and Henry Aaron knows himself so well that he can clearly describe the mental processes behind his superstar performance. These ingredients of healthy perfectionism follow.

Humility. Hank Aaron said he was always aware that if he was cut he would bleed. Being a healthy perfectionist means maintaining the awareness that you are not aspiring to perfection. Living with such an impossible goal will make your human best appear disappointing and cause you to feel defeated. Fundamental Wisdom first requires the internalization of a concept perhaps most clearly embodied in a kind of folksy utterance I first heard from a very down-to-earth lady sent to me from a rural area. Following the illustration to her of a GIT, and a brief mention of the FW involved, she was electrified. "In other words," she sat straight up, "I'm no better or worse than anybody else." She played with this phrase, rolling it around on her tongue and repeating it several times. "I am enough," it spoke to her. Her phrase represented an internalization of FW that would ever remain clear to her. This insight is based in a quality I found in Hank Aaron that may be out of fashion in the "Me Generation." The quality is humility. Hank Aaron is a humble man.

Impotence. You can accept that occasional failure is inevitable and must be experienced by all who aspire to success without being demoralized. Neither must this reality cause you to lower your standards or develop a defeatist attitude. Emotionally alive and healthy individuals will always weigh the available alternatives and make rational choices based on their best estimate of the most likely means to success. Yet all but the most imperceptive and naïve will admit that we are rarely in full control of unfolding events. There is never certainty in applying for a job, making a sales presentation, or proposing marriage. Our efforts constitute but one of the factors that tip the scales. An addiction to your own perfection and thus an unwillingness to accept the failure that you constantly risk is simply a lack of recognition of this reality. You are refusing to recognize your own impotence.

Execution. You must play with the cards you are dealt. Nature deals all of us an ace or two, and you will find your aces if you look. But whether yours are special talents, a quick mind, good looks, quick wrists, or a family fortune, personal success is still not guaranteed. Success depends on how well you execute—the energy you expend in developing whatever resources you may have. Aaron stressed the willingness to punish himself. He is referring to the perfectionist's willingness to habitually put forth a little more effort than is comfortable. The fabled overnight success is a myth.

Striving. A perfectionist by definition is never easily satisfied. Always willing to give more than enough and ever intolerant of performance that is less than ideal, he is a constant striver. But there is an emotional balance that eludes perfectionists of the less healthy variety. The drive to perform at your peak does not necessitate carrying negative emotional baggage. If falling short of a goal becomes cause for self-rejection, you have failed to grasp a key item of FW. You are lacking the ability to handle the consequences of your best efforts. Self-acceptance and happiness with yourself come from trying harder and staying longer. This is all that is necessary to be happy with the face in the mirror. Al McGuire, a former NCAA-winning Marquette basketball coach turned NBC-TV sports commentator, was supplying his unique brand of color to a nationally televised Duke–Marquette contest when Duke player Michael Wilson crashed violently to the floor. With little to go on, McGuire recklessly commented that Wilson may have suffered cracked ribs. A short time later viewers were no doubt astonished to hear McGuire make a heartfelt apology for "having put fear into people." "I'm still learning my trade," confessed the media rookie to announcer Billy Packer, "and I need you for a security blanket." Flustered, Packer attempted to drop this hot potato with a soothing, "I'm sure you were hoping they [ribs] were OK." McGuire, case closed, self-accepted, and unaffectedly back to the game, gleefully shouted, "What a shot! Did you see that?" How much would you be willing to bet that McGuire lost little sleep over the incident *and* got it right the next time around?

Recycling. Al McGuire is unlikely to repeat his mistakes because healthy perfectionists do not react to the fruits of their best efforts gone awry with anguish, self-recrimination, or fits of temper. They use these incidents to educate themselves. Our GIT said, "Once I lose my temper I lose control of Henry Aaron. That is the weakness of a man." What will be your chosen response to failure? Pitchers often comment that Aaron would never make the same mistake twice. He laughingly added, "And I tried never to make it once." But he acknowledged that while other erring players might be kicking the water cooler, he was simply making another entry in his catalogue of experiences. Recycling mistakes into profitable lessons takes away the sting of failure because it puts you back in control of the situation.

Determination. You must combine the new learning made possible by failure with a determination to make the second effort. When Hank was talking about the similarity between batting problems and problems in life he said, "You have to attack the problem before the problem attacks you." If you are scared off easily, you will fail. Victory comes to the person who pushes past the barriers that defeat others. Aaron stressed that it is easiest to say, "I can't." "You can't imagine the things I went through the last four years of my career chasing Babe Ruth's record while listening and reading everything about Babe Ruth and why I wasn't as good as he was." But Aaron's own respect for Ruth, and the generally held conviction that Ruth's record was invincible and any attempt to touch it sacrilegious, did not lessen his determination.

Instant. The American society has also become the "Instant Society." The artisan laying brushstroke upon brushstroke with precision and care is now rarely seen. Yet excellence, success, and superstar status in any endeavor can be created with only one brushstroke carefully placed upon another. You may have noted that none of the GITs in this book have an instant flavor to them. One year or even five years, Aaron said, really proves nothing. Excellence over time: This is an attribute the healthy perfectionist cannot do without. A quick success, said our GIT, followed by a loss of determination and the failure to create new goals is like so much stagnant water.

Roses. Maximum effort will require periods of intense concentration and single-purposeness. Remember Aaron's "Give us *this* day." Dealing at once with today and all the tomorrows can be overwhelming and will dilute your power. The future is your lifetime before you. Don't rush to it or hurry through it. Even while we talked, Hank took time to smell the roses. He had just finished telling me about the Atlanta scholarship program of which he is justifiably proud. "In fact, I got one started in Milwaukee too. I was just reading about it in the *Sporting News* here." He thumbed back through the pages until he found what he was looking for. Then he read the piece to me about the planned Salute to Hank Aaron Night to raise funds for the Aaron Youth Leadership Fund. Ten thousand tickets were to be sold to raise money to help deserving youth in the Milwaukee area. "It's a great thing," said Hank, savoring the moment. "I'm grateful to the Brewers and the Brewers' Organization." Take your best shots in the present and smell your roses in the present too. The present is where you live.

Fitness. As a healthy perfectionist you will be pushing yourself hard. If you expect your body and mind to respond, it is important to knowledgeably maintain your sharpness. Most athletic trainers advocate a hard/easy regimen. Follow all-out effort with a period of less demanding activity to allow the body time to recover and strengthen. Mental effort is no less demanding. You will use your head better if you seek out opportunities for mental refreshment. Life is anything but a single event and is coped with best when you plan to sustain your performance over time. Hank Aaron, for example, did not play every game on the Braves' schedule. He was quite adamant in his insistence that if he played a night game he would not play a day game if it immediately followed. He added, "I played tennis yesterday and golf is a very relaxing game for me too. But I don't approach them the same way. If I took golf as seriously as I took baseball I'd have challenged Jack Nicklaus and the other guys on the tour a long time ago." Take your days off too and develop physical and mental diversions. The best-performing perfectionists expect a lot of themselves. In return they are generous to themselves in allowing opportunities to step back and regain strength for the next push.

3/Norman Vincent Peale

SELF-CONFIDENCE

I had rather be a dog,
and bay at the moon,
than such a Roman.

"Julius Caesar"

FUNDAMENTAL PROBLEM

Do you regularly feel that the attention of your conversation partner is wandering just as you are expressing your most deeply felt convictions? While you admire other trim-figured women, does self-consciousness about your own unabundant bust size cause you to walk stoop-shouldered or to avoid the swimming pool? Do you sometimes feel you are invisible to people, and at other times wish you were?

A Fundamental Problem in the area of self-confidence is the opposite of the FP in the previous chapter. Whereas individuals addicted to their own perfection harbor the belief that they are capable of unrealistically perfect performance, a deflated self-esteem originates in the conviction that one is capable of significantly less than most. If this describes you, you are displeased with who you are. With your self-worth sagging, you are fearful in situations that could be occasions of enjoyment and satisfaction.

There is a feeling of worthlessness present, although the label "worthlessness" describes a trait that many people will not admit to. The Declaration of Independence, they seem to feel, is quite specific on this point. All men are created equal. But while you may be quite willing to fight for the equality of the underdog with the last breath that is in you, you may be carrying around, closer to home and possibly unrecognized, the unfaced conviction that all men are created better than you are.

This debilitating FP centers on one or both issues of appearance and competence. Appearance issues are, of the two, the most irrational. Did you ever try to convince a friend that her nose really wasn't too big? Anoretics—typically intelligent teenage girls—starve themselves to 70 percent or less of their recommended body weight while remaining unshakably convinced that they are fat.

Those experiencing the conviction of worthlessness in the competence area frequently remark, "I can't do anything." Their loss in the semi-final round of the tennis tournament seems to cancel out the memory or significance of the games won in earlier matches. Burnt apple pie at a dinner party negates the marvelous hors d'oeuvres and entree. Try to tell *them* it doesn't matter!

If you are among those most seriously affected by this FP, you may be past the point of being willing to try. When you are forced to function, your expectation of defeat results in a half-hearted performance. Even what is seen by others as an acceptable appearance—"I like your hair"—or performance—"You bowled great tonight"—is interpreted far differently by you. "I don't, but there's nothing I can do with it." Or, "I let the whole team down in the fourth frame. I'm going to quit this game."

A seriously impaired self-confidence resembles a house built on a foundation of mush. It often originates within those most sensitive to the daily ration of "hard knocks" that pound us all from childhood on. Teachers helpfully point out each child's homework mistakes. Later, spouse and employer alike, with the best of intentions, never fail to comment when we make an error. They never realize how defeating the cumulative effect of their "constructive" comments may be.

NORMAN VINCENT PEALE

Great Inspiring Teacher

Flanked by two associate pastors, he enters the sanctuary from a side door. The three gowned-in-black preachers are seated, the choir is singing, and the show begins. From the outside, on the corner of Twenty-ninth Street and Fifth Avenue in Manhattan, the old brown church, which shares the block with Jack Gell & Co. Wholesalers and an interior design concern, is unpretentious. The message board declares that at 11:15 A.M. Dr. Norman

Vincent Peale will encourage the congregation to "Stop Worrying and Start Living," a very Peale-ish topic.

"I've advertised this as my annual sermon on worry," he soon tells them. "But when I looked it up, I find that I have usually given two such sermons every year. So, over a period of years, I've preached about ninety sermons here against worry. I've really laid it on the line," he thunders, with a humorous twinkle, "but you know something? There are still a few people around here who worry!"

His sermons are gently humorous and often poke fun at himself. They are never boring. My describing the scenario as a show rather than a service is not out of disrespect. His participation is encased amidst a properly reverent Sunday-morning rite. But more than this, it contains all the trappings of a media event. Admission to the service is strictly by reservation, and the reservations are much in demand. The large overflow crowd is accommodated in several large halls where the service is televised live. Upon entering the sanctuary, the first-time visitor is startled by the blinding TV lights. Propped upon the pulpit is a card displaying metallic bars in various shades of silver, gray, and black—an aid to the camermen stationed at strategic points in the gallery aboye. The decor inside is as remarkably warm and plush as the outside is drab. Ushers in formal attire and festive carnations seat the worshippers in swing-doored pews leading to thickly cushioned seats. Celebrities on the Sunday I visited were generously represented and ranged from twenty members of the South African Parliament to a former beauty queen/TV personality.

The name of Norman Vincent Peale is the most recognized among the world's clergy. *The Power of Positive Thinking* is only one of his best-sellers, among many. He has two newspaper columns and a radio program reaching tens of millions each week. A movie has been made of one of his biographies, *One Man's Way,* he is a friend of presidents, and he receives thousands of letters each week. Peale's *Guideposts* publishes two-and-a-half million copies monthly, and his Foundation for Christian Living sends out thirty million pieces of literature annually. Even at the age of eighty, Dr. Peale makes personal appearances across the country each week. week.

The day after the service I met with Dr. Peale and Mrs. Ruth Peale, a columnist and author in her own right, to find out more about Norman Vincent Peale's own struggle to gain self-confidence.

"Dr. Peale, in reading about you I was very interested to learn that your father, the Rev. Charles Clifford Peale, was the former health commissioner of the city of Milwaukee. And your great-grandfather was also both a Methodist minister and a physician. The core of your message is that the ills of the flesh are often closely related to the ills of the mind, heart, and soul. Does this viewpoint have its roots in your dual theology/medicine lineage?"

"I never could tell for sure when my father was a minister and when he was a doctor," Dr. Peale replied. "I grew up in this atmosphere, so it was a normal relationship. Later, when my brother Bob was in the Harvard Medical School I was, at the same time, in the Boston University Theological School. He would come over one night to my area and have dinner with me and my theological friends. The next night I would go over to the Harvard Medical School and have dinner with him and some of the medical students." With this connection behind him, Peale was to later seek out Dr. Smiley Blanton, a psychiatrist. Together they became cofounders of what is now called, forty years later, The Institute for Religion and Health. The merger of these two disciplines in 1940 was a radical one. Proven prophetic, many of the self-help ideas preached for years by Dr. Peale have now become solidly respectable in the practice of humanistic psychology.

"I must say first of all that there will be few readers of my book who won't be surprised to learn that someone so heavily involved in appearing before the public might not be the pinnacle of confidence."

"Well, from the time I was quite young, a young boy, I was very shy. I was what they called in those days 'bashful,' which I always thought was a very good word. It meant, I imagine, that you were abashed in the presence of other people and situations. I was very reticent. I didn't believe that I amounted to very much and I was easily overawed in school by the bright and articulate students. When I would be called on to say something, I felt an inability to express myself. I was tongue-tied, and very embarrassed, and I would get red in the face. This is a miserable way to live. And right now, for example, I'm in what you might call the speechmaking business and I've got to confess that I still go out there at times feeling inadequate. When you go on a platform to make a speech, it doesn't make any difference whether you've made 10,000 speeches beforehand. This is the one that counts."

"So you came to this prestigious Fifth Avenue church as a young man not exactly brimming over with confidence?"

"I was a pastor in the church here at the time of the Great Depression, and I had not been trained to deal with people who were beside themselves mentally. It's hard to reconstruct the atmosphere that existed in those days. People's savings would be wiped out overnight and they were desolated; they were in utter despair. Not theoretical despair—they would threaten to blow their brains out, jump out the window. It was frightful. And they would come to see me and I was unable to cope with it because I had nothing but academic training in the theological seminary."

"I think that it is important to hear that others find themselves in situations for which they do not feel entirely prepared yet survive and thrive. Does the fact that you still must control your feelings of inadequacy mean that possessing the necessary FW is not a free pass for life? Are we required to put out effort in coping with difficult situations no matter how long we are at it?"

"That's right. I think we all can reach a higher level, but things never become automatic. I have to keep struggling all the time." He sharpens this. "When I joined the Methodist ministry, which I did before I became a minister in this church, they actually had a question that they put to the ministerial candidates. There were three things they asked them when I was a young minister: Will you avoid the use of tobacco? Will you stay out of debt? Are you going on to perfection? Now, I remember I answered the first two 'yes.' But, about the third one, I had some doubts." He laughs heartily at this. "I think you can improve humanity, but perfection is another matter. And the people that I meet, generally speaking, are people who have some desire to find self-improvement."

"You bring up the point that when we take an objective look at ourselves we find that we all do have real deficiencies. What have you found to be effective in coping with fears and self-doubts that may be quite justified?"

"Well, having had them myself, the best thing to do is to face them and think them through." We began discussing an example he had used in his message the previous day. "Now, one time I was in Chicago, and I went to the Chicago Rotary Club with a friend of mine. I should have gone anyway. I'm a member of the Rotary Club, and when you're out of town you're supposed to make up the meeting at another Rotary Club. And I went to this, which is Club Number One. It is the first Rotary Club in the world. There were maybe a thousand men present. Now they didn't all belong to that club, there were visitors, but a thousand men were in the ballroom of the old Sherman House. And a man got up to make a speech. I could tell that he was nervous because I get nervous myself. And I picked it up. I sensed it. But he really put it over. It was a powerful speech. It made sense. It was full of wisdom and full of humor. And I had never heard of this man before. And he was a farmer, I think, from somewhere in Illinois. So I went up afterwards to congratulate him. And when he knew who I was, he said, and I considered it a great compliment, 'The reason I was able to speak here today was because of something that I once read in one of your sermons.' I said, 'What wise remark did I make?' He said, 'It wasn't one of your remarks, it was something you quoted.' He said, 'It was from Basil King,' a man who wrote probably the greatest book on fear ever written in this country. It just bore that one word, *Fear*. That was the title. And he said the quotation was 'Be bold, and mighty powers will come to your aid.' Isn't that terrific? Be bold, and mighty powers will come to your aid. 'Well,' this man said, 'I always wanted to make a speech, but that was the one thing that made me quake with fear, and I determined I wasn't going to have that fear, or all the other little fears that I had. So, I decided I would start making speeches. I made them in church. I made them in local community gatherings. I finally joined a Rotary Club and I made them there. And once I made a speech at a Rotary convention and somebody from Chicago heard me and thought it was good. They invited me to speak to this, one of the greatest crowds of businessmen in the United States, and I was scared to death. But,' he said, 'I remembered that: Be bold, and mighty powers will come to your aid.' And long before Basil King said it, Emerson said it, 'Do the thing you fear, and the death of fear is certain.' You defeat worry and you defeat fear by filling your mind with the faith that you can do it. And that's about the best way I know to get rid of worry and fear about this and that—get out and *do* something about it."

Dr. Peale had arrived for the interview a few minutes late and in a rush. At first, while certainly cordial, he did not seem particularly delighted to be taking up part of his day with this talk. But as the minutes passed it was easy to read in his growing enthusiasm that this subject had deep meaning for him. It became apparent that he wanted to give me all he could. This was the substance of a struggle he had been coping with all his life while attempting to get the same insight across to his growing congregation.

"You know, I learned something very valuable a long time ago when I was in Hollywood from, strangely enough, an old character actor. He told me that what he did was to practice loving the people he was going to talk to. He would stand on the edge of the wings and love somebody out in front by projecting love thoughts to them. Well, that made a big impression on me, so I practiced that same thing—in other words, to get myself out of the center of consciousness. Self-doubt is an exaggerated self-consciousness. So any way in which that [self-consciousness] can be cut down gives you more control."

"If there is anything, Dr. Peale, that can be said to best describe what you labor to communicate to people, it is the power of the human mind to overcome the problems of self-doubt that hold us back and keep us from functioning at our best."

"I think the average person exercises only about 25 percent of his potential. If the person could release 30 percent of it, he would probably be a genius. But even geniuses, so I am told, don't go much higher than that. I know I've had experiences where I was making a talk, a speech, a sermon, and all of a sudden I've had an awareness of what seemed to be unlimited power in myself. And I find myself reaching for it, and then, like somebody had pulled a curtain, it would be shut off. I've had other feelings like that—that there was capacity. But because it was unused and unexercised and undeveloped, you got only a flashing intimation of it. And I think this is, to one degree or another, in everybody. I've told people at public speeches that this is a possibility in human nature. Now maybe they reach for this, and failing to get it, they become dissatisfied and cynical, I don't know. But I think we ought to all reach for the best that's inherent within us.

"If you make yourself sit down and think creatively and constructively, you are very likely to come out at the positive end. I am a great believer in what people can do with themselves if they will think and not react emotionally. Positive thinking tends to have an intellectual content; a cool, rational, factual, intellectual content, in my opinion.

"I also think one of the great troubles that we have today is that people do not get enough chance to be alone. You're not used to it. When you are alone, you feel uncomfortable. I am driven constantly by the clock from morning until night. I complain about it. Ask my wife if I don't complain. You never get a chance, not enough. There is such a thing called 'reflection,' where you reflect, cogitate; that's a good old word too. Now you can't cogitate dashing down the street in a taxicab, ten minutes late for an appointment. Where I get the best at being alone is in the long walks I take. I try to walk two to three miles a day, but I don't achieve it as much as I'd like. Oftentimes on a Sunday morning, I will walk a mile or two down Fifth Avenue, then my wife comes along and picks me up. I can do more with a sermon in that mile or mile and a half than I can at any other time because I'm alone, and I'm in motion. I can do better at that than sitting in a chair, for some strange reason. I think it's important."

"Dr. Peale, you are the man who made the phrase 'positive thinking' famous. What would you like my reader, the one who doubts him- or herself, to understand about positive thinking?"

"Let me describe a positive thinker as I see it. A positive thinker is a person who is tough, rugged, and realistic mentally; who sees every difficulty inherent in a problem and who sees the difficulty straight. But he is a clear thinker and he's not abashed, nor overwhelmed or defeated by these difficulties. But he knows that with the help of God, he possesses the ability within himself to meet this situation creatively. There is nothing dreamy about it, nothing Pollyannish about it. It requires intense discipline. It's hard going. Now, I've been preaching and teaching positive thinking for years and I have to work at it myself, every day, to take a positive attitude because it seems that by training we're negative. Now I don't believe we were born negative. I've never seen a negative baby. A baby fresh in this world is not a negative thinker. He or she is a normal thinker. Then they *learn* to be negative. They go to college and they sit under negative professors and they go to church and they sit under a negative preacher. So they become negative and it requires an immense change of mental pattern to get back to being positive."

SELF-CONFIDENCE

Fundamental Wisdom
Winding my way out of his apartment building, through the long, wide hallways, I felt elated about Norman Vincent Peale as a Great Inspiring Teacher. He has that hard-to-describe "sense of fit" that GITs have, which rubs off on others. Like finding a real rose at the table after weeks of plastic flowers, being with a GIT always has an awakening effect on the spirit. The following seven features of Norman Vincent Peale's Fundamental Wisdom provide the essential information for you to grab onto and to use in making concrete changes.

Complacency. Your opinion of each of the many aspects of your appearance and competence can be lumped under the term *self-worth*. Unquestionably, some areas of each can be improved. Making this effort is important. Do what you can. Your present strengths and the new ones you develop demand maintenance. Identify your present strengths, cultivate new ones, and keep what is yours in peak form.

Hard Knocks. The lessons of the real, beginning in childhood, may well leave you feeling inadequate in many areas. Worthlessness, to whatever degree you may feel it, is learned. This is good news. It means that new ideas about yourself can be learned in place of the self-defeating ones. You are not so naïve as to believe that all the unaccepting experiences you have suffered can be undone. Fortunately, this isn't necessary. A nine-year-old boy learns that the darkened room that frightened him as a five-year-old is no longer to be feared. Similarly, through internalization of the appropriate FW, and the use of the GIT as a model, you can come to new terms with how you view yourself. Make a new self-assessment. The old self-image you are carrying around may be long out of date. What is good about you?

Boldness. Rabbits run from situations in which they fear being bested. Norman Vincent Peale told me about the end of his rabbit period. "I was on the steps of the main building at Ohio Wesleyan, called Gray Chapel, and right then and there I had a discussion with a professor who saw through me. He said, 'You're a scared rabbit. Why don't you act like a man, and stand up and take your place in the world?' This angered me, but I knew it was the truth." Dr. Peale decided to be bold and do the things he feared. Your advantage over the rabbit, which behaves by reflex, is your ability to *reason*. With this power, you can as become successful as you please, almost without exception. Do you really want to become an exceptional golfer? Honestly? You can. If it is important, you can serve notice to family and friends that you will be on the links every weekend and holiday for the next year. Each day during lunchtime and after work you can hit balls and take lessons. Professionals tell us that any golfer who can break ninety, a mediocre score, can beat most golfers in the United States. You can if you want to. This is exactly how the good golfers, writers, fathers, sales managers, and students go about it. As for physical attractiveness, the same can be said for your weight, your muscles, and, with the availability of cosmetic surgery, even your profile. How much improved competence and appearance do you need? Decide how much and then use your brains to go get it.

Reasonableness. What about the things you can't have? Ask yourself how many things you must be good or best at. How many areas can you reasonably expect to be superior in? Most importantly, in how many areas can you be strong enough to tolerate being rated average, marginal, or poor? An honest assessment of strengths and weaknesses will suggest the most likely goals for you to pursue in order to experience success. It is healthy to follow some of these directions. If it isn't a beauty contest, then perhaps a poetry contest. At least enter enough of the events in life to produce some measure of success. On the other hand, if you wear inch-thick glasses and have flat feet and poor coordination, don't hold back from volleyball at the office picnic. Enjoy the freedom of not being an expert. Certainly it was a burden for Einstein to be the world's foremost physicist every day. Every now and then he must have enjoyed a Sunday during which he could be Princeton's slowest bicyclist or his family's worst turkey carver. Your competence and appearance are not your worth in the sense of "more is better." The formula is simple: Reasonable appearance and reasonable competence equal reasonable self-worth. Do what you *reasonably* can in terms of the first two, and the latter, your feeling of self-confidence, will automatically rise to a reasonable level.

Positive Thinking. Norman Vincent Peale tells us that positive thinking is not a saccharine, unrealistic "life's a bowl of cherries" philosophy. It involves clear and rational thinking. Conversely, FW dictates that you be aware of the voice in your head when it broadcasts "worthless messages." "Five frames and not a single strike! You, Judy Green, are just no good!" Do not accept this! How often do you accept similar statements? You must, once and for all, be able to differentiate between competency and appearance issues and your worth as a person.

Spotlight. Acute sensitivity and discomfort with your own shortcomings stem from an overawareness of yourself. It is uncomfortable to keep yourself center stage and in the spotlight. How do you look at your everyday activities? Is it *you* at a party? Do you see *you* at work? *You* with those you love? *You* and the world? If the emphasis is always on you, the result is excessive self-criticism. The result will be a low self-image. Practice playing down your sense of self as you go through the day. Instead of being self-involved, put more emphasis on the people around you.

Solitude. An old axiom is that the greatest decisions are made in quiet rooms. Doing your best and creatively dealing with the numerous areas that are not your forte require bold and effective behavior, devoid of emotion and soundly conceived. Positive thinking, according to the man who coined the phrase, demands time to be alone with your thoughts. Through practice, enforced periods of personal solitude will, rather than create discomfort, prove their value. Effort is required. Make time for yourself daily. Otherwise, if relegated to "when time allows," this personal debt will never be paid. Time for yourself is an important step in abandoning a lifestyle of revolving crises, accidents, and reflexes.

4/ James A. Lovell

FUTURISM

True, I talk of dreams,
Which are the children of an idle brain,
Begot of nothing but vain fantasy,
Which is as thin of substance as the air
And more inconsistent than the wind, . . .

"Romeo and Juliet"

FUNDAMENTAL PROBLEM

The future is a dream that can easily be distorted into a nightmare if you are a person who copes poorly with it. Imaginary though the future may be right now, how it unfolds is more up to you than you may realize. If you fail to give the future proper attention by retreating into the past, or if you ignore the future by attending exclusively to the present by running to one unforeseen crisis after another, you could be lacking in skills for dealing with the future to a degree that signals a Fundamental Problem.

Even for a person with sufficient awareness of the future, there remain pitfalls. "I know it won't work." Those are the words of an individual whose hands are tied by blindly accepted fatalism. "What's the use?" Those words reflect the often unnecessary surrender of one who has magnified the imagined dragons in his or her future to such proportions that the person is overwhelmed and unable to act effectively.

Do you waste your time and your creative problem-solving energies on areas in the future so remote that they are beyond your influence? Do you dwell on events for which the outcome is already determined? If so, your real power in those upcoming situations on which you might realistically expect to make an impact becomes diminished.

You may already have found from experience that there are unpleasant physical and emotional consequences that result from the frustration of being in a situation in which you are powerless to act. Perhaps the most ironic result of the incorrect application of your ability to visualize various possible outcomes is the real possibility that you may play a role in causing such a dreaded script to unfold. Self-fulfilling prophesies occur daily. A dramatic example witnessed by millions occurred on January 7, 1981, when Joseph Granville, a stock market forecaster, caused the "Granville Slide," a twenty-four-point drop in the Dow Jones, during the biggest wave of selling in the history of the New York Stock Exchange, by suggesting to his subscribers an impending decline.

Universities from Texas to Massachusetts have rushed to offer courses and even degrees in the area of future studies. It is more recognized daily in both the academic and the business worlds that accomplishment in almost every area requires sharp skills as a futurist. Unknown as it is, the future inevitably becomes the present. The future cannot be ignored.

The space program under the direction of NASA has made activities routine that a generation ago, even the agency's own employees would not have believed possible. James A. Lovell, Jr., the Great Inspiring Teacher in the area of futurism, was the first man to go on four space missions and was a member of the first crew to circle the moon and see its dark side. Now a group vice president with Centel, a fast-track Chicago-based communications corporation, he logged 715 hours in space, in excess of twenty-eight days, before leaving NASA for the business world. But for all his successes in the futuristic space program, Jim Lovell was selected as a GIT because of his involvement in *Apollo XIII*. This was the one manned mission that came closest to tragedy, yet the one that Lovell has dubbed "a successful failure."

JAMES A. LOVELL, JR.

Great Inspiring Teacher
Forward looking as were the goals and eventual accomplishments of the American space program, it would have been almost laughable, back in the beginning, to think about using one of the astronauts in a chapter on the future. As Tom Wolfe points out in *The Right Stuff*, his book about these

men, if the performance of the unmanned rocket program was to be any guide, the first astronauts were likely to have a very short future. Wolfe, in breezing through the history of these rockets, reminds us that "they all blew up."

To prepare a human being for such an unprecedented adventure, the most heavily relied-upon technique at NASA was simulation. The capsule simulators were so realistic that any situation the astronauts might be predicted to encounter could be programmed into the trainers' computers and pre-experienced by the men. The training benefits were enormous. Learning to cope with virtually every conceivable situation before the flight, the astronauts experienced little of the anxiety or disorientation often associated with entering into the unknown future.

But there had been no simulation to prepare them for what they were about to face when, on April 13, 1970, the crew of *Apollo XIII,* commanded by Jim Lovell, thundered away from the earth at 20,000 miles per hour. They found themselves in trouble so grave and improbable that its simulation had never been considered.

Lovell was a veteran of two previous *Gemini* flights and the seven-day *Apollo VIII,* the "Christmas mission." *Apollo VIII* marked the first time man left earth's orbit and had been captured by the gravitational attraction of another celestial body. Circling the moon, Frank Borman, Bill Anders, and Lovell shared the reading of the biblical tale of creation for awe-inspired listeners on earth, four days into space. Upon their return, with comic relief supplied by Lovell—"Please be advised there is a Santa Claus"—the men were feted with a ticker-tape parade in Manhattan, a reception at the United Nations, and a White House dinner. They were proclaimed by President Lyndon B. Johnson to be "history's boldest explorers."

On the *Apollo XIII* mission, Jim Lovell and Fred Haise were scheduled to be moonwalkers. Remaining in lunar orbit would be Jack Swigert, alone in the command module. Swigert was a back-up astronaut who had come aboard the mission only a few days earlier when Ken Mattingly was exposed to the German measles. Fifty-five hours into the planned ten-day mission, the crew heard a bang. Lights on the control panel signaled warnings, and the craft began to pitch and roll. The suddenly crippled craft had just passed the point of no return, and they were now committed to continuing toward a loop around the moon before they could turn toward home. Swigert calmly radioed news of the incident to mission control, and Lovell followed shortly with his own message. "Yes, Houston, I think we have a problem here."

The bang they heard was the explosion of leaking oxygen. In the early minutes after the explosion neither the crew, forty-eight hours from their lunar rendezvous, nor the controllers on the ground had any grasp of the magnitude of the crisis that would consume the next ninety hours. One-third of the world's population, the largest group ever to follow a space mission up to that time, would offer their prayers. Thirteen nations, including the Soviet Union, would volunteer planes, ships, and even the hope of a rescue rocket. This plan was found to be not feasible because the three would be dead of suffocation before any rescue rocket could be readied.

The future, you can see, is mined with surprises that cannot be anticipated. Fortunately, a human being can develop the tools to deal with such events. From what transpired aboard *Apollo XIII* in the hours between the explosion and splashdown in the Pacific, you can find examples of all the Fundamental Wisdom needed to be an effective futurist. Whether the time frame you are attempting to manage encompasses just the hours from breakfast until bedtime or the rest of your life, the approach is identical and can be learned from Jim Lovell.

At five feet eleven inches, Jim is tall for an astronaut. He has an easy smile and simultaneously conveys a relaxed good nature and a sense of high enthusiasm. I asked him about the failure to anticipate and prepare for an in-flight accident of the type experienced aboard *Apollo XIII*.

"Well, in our analysis of problems we threw out double failures because there was such a combination of possibilities that it would have been impossible to train. And with the reliability and redundancy of the systems, the chances of a double failure were very, very low. So, of course, on *XIII* we had essentially a double failure. Did you read the accident report?"

"Yes, it faulted the Beech Aircraft Corporation, maker of the oxygen tanks themselves; the North American Rockwell Corporation, manufacturer of the service module that housed the oxygen tanks; and NASA itself. It termed the accident 'an unusual combination of mistakes.' "

"The accident started five years before the flight when they didn't put a thermostat in the oxygen tank that was compatible with the power at the Cape. It's a classic airplane accident. If you analyze aircraft accidents, you see that most of them are caused not by one incident. They are caused by a series of incidents that either overcome the pilot or the aircraft. This was a classic example. The accident was built in. But we had another problem. This tank was dropped at the factory!

"This bad thermostat was in all flights starting with *Apollo VIII*. But being dropped had loosened a tube. And prior to take off there was a second incident where we had to turn on the heater in this particular tank for eight hours. This caused further damage. The combination of all these things got to us.

"In flight, the damaged tank exploded. We had redundant tanks, but the explosion from the first tank released liquid oxygen into the bay of the spacecraft, which flashed into a gas and blew the entire side of the spacecraft off. That was the explosion we heard. And that explosion either ruptured or damaged a valve, allowing liquid oxygen to escape from the second and last tank."

At the time of *Apollo XIII*, Jim was forty-two and an experienced test pilot. The early astronauts were picked from among the country's hottest fliers and a premium was placed on physical condition, quick reflexes, and the ability to think calmly in the tightest situations.

"Jim, is it true that you had just seen the film *Marooned* prior to the *Apollo* mission?"

"Just a couple of months before."

"How did you keep your mind from locking onto that film, in which a helpless orbiting American spacecraft is rescued by Russian cosmonauts, but not before the commander dies? How did you avoid panic?"

"Well, that's why the people they picked in these early phases of flight were ones who were accustomed to a certain stress factor. Testing airplanes is not an easy job. I mean it's one where you always have to be prepared. It's like defensive driving. And the space flights were just an adjunct to test flying. *Apollo XIII* was part of the job. The age-old question that occurred to all three of us, as I imagine occurs to everybody who suddenly finds himself in a position that death is a strong factor in the near future, is 'Why this flight?' Why wasn't it *Apollo XII* or *Apollo XIV*? How did I get into this mess?

"When finally it dawned on us that some of those factors that we were afraid might occur *had* occurred, we could have panicked for about ten minutes and bounced off the walls of the spacecraft. But ten minutes later we'd be exactly where we were before. When our explosion occurred, if it didn't immediately damage the pressure hull, we were still going someplace and had to determine what to do. We were some ninety hours from home by going around the moon and didn't know what had occurred. So you might as well just sit down and try to figure out how to get home right now."

"That sounds like an incredibly logical approach in such a crisis. Here was your situation. You had lost one oxygen tank and were losing the second. The oxygen tanks in the service module were not only used to provide oxygen for breathing, but in the manufacture of your other two consumables, water and electricity. The electrical shortage caused numerous dangers. You had to shut down your on-board computers, which were used for navigation. There was reason to believe you might not be able to separate your craft from the lunar module—doing this was necessary for re-entry—or get back in the slingshot orbit to allow yourselves to swing around the moon. You would have difficulty holding your course and hitting the earth's atmosphere at the precise angle required. The crew was dehydrated and unable to sleep because of the near-freezing cabin temperature. You had vetoed getting into your spacesuits because they were bulky and you felt that maneuverability was necessary. And finally, there was the real possibility that if you survived all of this, and I have mentioned only some of the biggest problems, the heat shield, which was right next to the exploding tank, might be cracked. If the heat shield failed, for all your efforts, you would be incinerated as you hit the earth's atmosphere 400,000 feet up at 24,000 miles per hour."

"Frank, we could have looked at these problems surmounting us, not knowing what caused the accident, and lost all of our objectivity, saying, 'Our problems are so great there's nothing we can do. We can't cope with a way of getting home.' But you've just got to chart a course in action, I think, maybe not even knowing which way to go at the time."

"Do something."

"Yeah, do something."

"Is this the typical approach of the test pilot?"

"Yes, I think so. He learns this by experience because he meets these kinds of criteria quite often. You mentioned Tom Wolfe. Tom interviewed me for about three hours. This was years before the book came out. He uses Pete Conrad as an entry to the book on the original seven astronauts. Pete and I were in the same class at Pax River [the Navy flight test school] and he talks about losing all these people. And we did. Probably more so than we did in the space program. But if everybody had bought the farm the way he was alluding to in the beginning of that book, there would have been none of us left."

"How does the test pilot effectively use the time he has to make the right decisions about the future?"

"Well, I think first by limiting your attention to the big problems. Secondly, the more you learn about your particular job the less fear there is. Fear is born out of ignorance. Finally, there comes a time when you've got to get down to the problem and solve it. This might require piecing together various types of training that you've had."

I asked, "So you can sit back and plan for just so long and then it is time to get to work?"

"Oh, yeah. Yeah." he replied.

"And what about this distinction between the anticipation that means healthy planning and the anticipation that is just worry?"

"Well, you have to be prepared, there's no doubt about it. You have to anticipate what could happen. I've seen cases though, where people have tried to do too much when something does happen. They get confused."

"So the test-pilot approach is to size up the major problems and take your best shot. If that doesn't work, keep trying your next-best approach."

"Right, you have to have a positive approach to things. And you keep on trying things until you run out of things to try. And fortunately we never ran out of things to try."

"Can my readers learn this?"

"Yes, I think so. I think this should be an attribute of anyone who wants to have peace with himself in life. I mean otherwise it is continual frustration. Things don't always work out the way you want them to. You've got to look at the thing philosophically, know what you can do, and train yourself to think positively: 'Well, I've got to do something else.' "

"For example?"

"Well, when I graduated from test-pilot school, I was number one in my class, just by working hard. When you were number one you could pick the part of the test center you wanted to go to. We had four areas. We had 'flight test' which was the Tom Wolfe, you know, 'flying to the outside of the envelope,' or testing the limits. Then we had 'service test' which was more mundane. Lots of flying, but you were testing how long these aircraft would last per maintenance hour and stuff like that. Then you had something called 'armament test,' which was merely to test the airplanes to see how they fired the rockets, dropped the bombs, and shot the machine guns. And finally you had a directorate [programs with openings for individuals to serve as directors] that was called 'electronics test,' which would be the most boring thing possible for an aviator. You go out and do antenna patterns, test out radars, and all that sort of thing. So when I graduated I put down that I wanted to be assigned, in this order, to flight test, service test, armament test, station laundry, commissary officer, you know. Down below was electronics test. Guess what I got? At that particular time, the captain in charge of electronics test said, 'Listen, we're always getting the dregs over here. Now let's get some other people.' So I was mandated, regardless of the old criteria, to go to electronics test. There never was a more dejected person in all his life.

"But it turned out to be really a blessing in disguise. Electronics test got the F-4 airplane and there weren't people there who knew about night fighters like I did. So I got to be the project manager. And I got to fly it. And electronics test became weapons test, a more complete directorate. And consequently it made it a lot easier for me to get into the space program, because at flight test there were dozens of guys who were all waiting to fly the F-4. I'd have been number eighty-five on the list otherwise."

"So we can't always tell ahead of time which alternative we try is going to be the one that pays off."

"That's right. And electronics test was really the way to go. But you know, you couldn't have told me that when I got selected for it."

"At least in part, then, the idea of approaching things with a positive attitude and picking the best options available at the time must be what leads you to call *Apollo XIII* a success. After all, there had probably been no undertaking in the history of mankind that had been planned with such precision. But in spite of it all, you came very close to either being incinerated or drifting off forever into space."

"Well, I dubbed it 'the successful failure.' It was a failure in all respects of what the mission was supposed to do; all the experiments and everything like that. But it was successful in the fact that given a set of circumstances, posing a problem to both the flight and the ground crews, putting them in a situation that was unexpected, I really have a sense of satisfaction that we pulled the thing off and got home safely. It's one thing to make a flight to the moon. You plan and work and you do everything down to a gnat's eyebrow. You've got a book on board like a cookbook, and if you just follow the directions and push the right buttons and you learn the basic knowledge of flying a lunar module, you can't miss."

"But your challenge was to cope with the unexpected."

"That's right. To take a set of circumstances unknown ahead of time, with all the manuals and the procedures and everything that had been carefully thought out to make the flight as successful as possible in reliability, and then say, 'Hey, that all goes by the board and now you've really got to start thinking on how you're going to get back home again.' That's what made it a success."

"I have read about taunts at that time by some members of the flying deal. Even monkeys did it.' Obviously a monkey could not have survived community not associated with the space program along the lines of, 'Big *Apollo XIII.*"

"Oh, no. There was a little bit of sour grapes there. It takes humans to take circumstances as they come, anticipate, and adjust to change. There were certain things we had to do that have never really been brought out. We were literally flying home by the seat of our pants. We went into the lunar module (LM) to fly the vehicle, to control the attitude [the position of the spacecraft in relation to the horizon], but these two vehicles were mated together. The reaction control jets of the LM were designed to operate by themselves, never with the command module attached. If you used the controller to pitch down it might go off in a sideward direction, or if you tried to pitch up you might go off in a downward direction. Consequently, to fly the vehicle to a new attitude we literally had to learn to fly all over again.

"We began to have a loss of one battery at a time, and after our speed-up maneuver around the moon we turned everything off. It took a lot of electricity to operate our guidance system and our computers, so we shut them down. But they had our attitude reference in their memories, so from then on our only attitude reference was the stars. The ground had no idea of our attitude."

"Yet, incredibly, you landed four miles from the carrier *Iwo Jima.*"

"Yes. Of course the ground was tracking us on their big radar, so they knew our path was wrong. We had to make a midcourse maneuver or we'd have skipped off the earth's atmosphere and gone out into space. The exploding tank had got us off course. To make a safe re-entry from the moon you have to hit a pie-shaped corridor, a small segment no less than 5½ degrees or no greater than 7½ degrees with respect to the horizontal. Well, we were coming in too shallow, which meant that we would skip off like skipping a stone on water."

Aquarius, the name of the LM, the vehicle that was designed to take the astronauts from the orbiting command module down to the surface of the moon and back again, was termed the "lifeboat" because this vehicle, while never to make its moon landing, made the safe return possible. "On *Apollo VIII* no landing was planned so you had no LM with you. If this accident had happened on that mission, or even on *Apollo XIII* while you and Haise were down on the moon, return would not have been possible, would it?"

"No, we'd have been in deep trouble without that lifeboat. There's an old cliché, 'The best laid plans of mice and men often go astray.' This was a case where that happened. Although you try to cover every eventuality, occasionally it doesn't work."

"This can lead to tremendous frustration. When people are watching the countdown for a space shot on TV and the clock stops, it can be agonizing. I think everyone pictures the poor guys sitting on top of that rocket. And the worst case of all, speaking of plans gone astray, as happened with the second shuttle mission, is when the hatches must be reopened and the astronauts climb back out. Do they feel this frustration just as we do?"

"Yes, there is a certain amount of frustration in that. You work hard, you get delayed." He repeated, "You work hard, you get delayed. John Glenn's first flight was tremendously so. The anti-climactic period of life in this business is when the engines ignite. Once those solids light off in the shuttle or the liquid fuels in the other ones, there is no turning back. It can go five feet and quit and that's your mission. It can make a complete success and that's the mission. But once zero comes down and they light up, you know there is no more getting out of that spacecraft. It's going to go."

"How does one best deal with these on-again–off-again frustrations? Do the astronauts try to keep busy up there to take their minds off it?"

"I think we have to cope with them just like everybody who successfully copes with frustrations. You find this not just in the space program but here in this business. You put in certain programs or plans and then they get shot down or modified. You go back again. You keep putting them in and they get modified. The attitude you have to take is one of perseverance. If you believe in something, you've got to keep grinding away at it. You've got to coax it. You get shot down once but maybe you get two feet ahead the next time. You have a certain objective and if you become discouraged you never get anyplace."

"You just keep going, staying after it."

"Staying after it, yes. You see that in a big way in the space program. The delays only mean going back and regrouping and working it again."

"You are one of a handful of people who have actually left this planet and then returned. Looking back, what strikes you?"

"Well, *XIII* was the most dangerous. But *Apollo VIII* was a unique flight. It was the beginning of the era of really going out into space and the most exciting flight that I was on. It was a feat that you don't want to underestimate. Here you are seeing the back side of the moon for the very first time. No human had seen the back side other than in photographs from *Luna IX,* which the Russians sent, and our own unmanned orbiters. So going from earth orbital flights where earth is still the dominant factor, to going out to where you could put the earth behind your thumb, was certainly an achievement that I'll never forget.

"Once you get away from the earth and you can see it as one small ball, and you have the anticipation of never getting back to it, you view it with a different perspective. Anybody who has made a flight to the moon and seen the earth as it really is knows it is a planet that is sort of nondescript. It travels around a medium-sized star in some corner of one of a million different galaxies that we know of." Jim stretches his arm straight in front of him and sights down past his upturned thumb. "And you can put it all behind your thumb. All of your training, all of your environment, everybody that you've known and loved, all of your experiences, all of your existence is now behind your thumb. It's a little mind-boggling. And when you get back down on the earth again, suddenly what was behind your thumb expands tremendously, and it is your world again."

"It sounds like you attained a heightened sense of the present, like a man given a second chance."

"Living on borrowed time. Yes, that's what it is, living on borrowed time. Occasionally I mention that to my wife and she says, 'Well, that's ridiculous.' But I mean when you get back you take a look at all those things around you, and you take a different perspective."

"How does the new perspective affect your view of the future?"

"Well, I think it comes in handy in that you don't get that serious about things. You can take life as it comes along, which is a nice attitude to take because things don't always go your way. You can take a more philosophical view of what's occurring and you can be more yourself. Like in this job. You make decisions. Some of them will be proved to be good and some will be bad. But that's always better than indecision."

"Jim, it seems like quite a few negative decisions regarding America's long-range space program are being made. I'm thinking about decisions that must be made right now about missions that will not reach their targets until years in the future and require a strong element of foresight. In contrast to the atmosphere of excitement during the race to the moon, the public seems apathetic about space. And the politicians are being very tight-fisted with NASA appropriations. Aren't people interested in the future?"

"I see these recent cutbacks of NASA as a positive step. We have to curtail spending, so we have to look at what our priorities are. I'm not in the military anymore and I'm not supported by the Navy, but I do think in the past five to ten years we have sorely neglected our defense posture. And while you might say this is an enlightened world, people listen to the strong. If we're not strong enough to defend ourselves and be a positive force in the world then we'll be a second-rate power."

"You're saying you think the cuts to NASA were a good thing?"

"Yes, because NASA had to take its share of reductions just like everybody else. The shuttle program and the earth resources program, the programs in place today, are designed to bring a quicker return on our investment. Money for these programs and the military aspects of the shuttle program have not been cut. But the rendezvous with Halley's Comet and some of the other programs that I'm not completely familiar with are designed to increase basic knowledge. And as much as I would like to see them go, because Halley's Comet comes around only once every seventy-five years, what we find out about Halley's Comet is not really going to affect the majority of the people on this earth today or in the next hundred years.

"Now the technology that came out of *Apollo* is something that is helping you and me today. The advent of computer technology, the development of new materials, innovations in management techniques and medical advances associated with supporting people going to the moon and back are helping us right now. But the basic knowledge gained from going to the moon, the scientific exploration, is not helping us. Do you know we have 800 pounds of lunar material in this country? I'm sure the analysis of it is not affecting you one bit. It might tell some scientist at Cal Tech how the moon was formed, but to help you materially today, it's not doing that."

"So again, whether we are talking long or short term, it ultimately is not an emotional decision but a question of priorities."

"Yes. I would like to see everything done, but right now our basic thrust is to help the populace. People have lots of needs today, and we should use the space program to help them."

"Since we're speaking about public concerns, I know you were the President's Consultant on Physical Fitness and Sports. What was the logical connection between the futuristically oriented space program and this one?"

"Well, if you're familiar with the Council, you know that it got started by Eisenhower. The reason Eisenhower started the Council was that during the draft they found so many young men physically unqualified for military duty. The president thought that the country was really going to pot and that there should be some emphasis on physical well-being. This was very similar to your philosophy in this book. Most people write about diseases after the fact, and what you can do about it. You're writing on the positive aspects of preventive maintenance, essentially. And physical fitness is also preventive maintenance."

"Keeping the body in shape for the long run."

"Yes. Why wait until it becomes diseased or inoperative and then all of a sudden begin? So many people wait until they get a heart attack and the doctor says, 'You should keep yourself physically strong.' Then you see them out there walking every day and they're converted. But it takes something like that to convert them.

"In 1967 we had that explosion in the spacecraft on Pad 34 where we lost three people. There was a slight delay in operations as we fell back and regrouped to figure out what to do with the spacecraft. So the president asked Jim Webb, who was the administrator of NASA, if an astronaut could take over rather than an athlete, as had been the tradition. The basic thought was that athletes are in shape because they get paid for it. It is almost part of their skills. But being in shape was not our main job. We kept in shape just like almost any job requires you to be in fairly decent condition. So I was asked and they told me it would probably be a three- to five-month thing during the refurbishing of the spacecraft. But I went on board in June of 1967 and I stayed for eleven years."

"Were most of the early astronauts fitness oriented as well?"

"Well, they selected people to be physically fit, but then they really didn't have a program to maintain that fitness. They thought they could put you on the shelf and you'd stay that way. And that when they needed you they'd dust you off and put you to work. Ed White, who was killed on Pad 34, was the fitness expert in the group and he got the physical fitness program going at NASA. He said, 'You've got us and now you're going to have to keep us in good shape.' "

"I felt that an astronaut, more than a person from any other area, would represent the ideal for demonstrating a constructive approach to the future. Are astronauts, in general, a forward-thinking group of people?"

"Oh, I think they all are. Most of us who were in the program and are no longer active are on second careers. We have the tendency to carry over the aggressiveness and the motivation we had in the program to see how well we can do in the private sector. The last thing that NASA and the Navy did for me for schooling was to send me to the Advanced Management Program at Harvard. When it came to what I should do in the future, I felt that I had done all I could do with NASA. There were many astronauts who had not flown and to wait around would not have been productive for me.

"Pete Conrad is with McDonnell-Douglas. Jim McDivitt is with Rockwell International. I've always wanted to be in an organization where I could see the results of what I did. So I chose to go the small company route, until I came to Centel, to see if I could make these companies grow. I've had more satisfaction from this than I would have if I joined something like a Rockwell, unless I was in a capacity like Frank Borman [president of Eastern Airlines] where I had complete control."

"Two from your group are in elected office, Harrison Schmitt and John Glenn. Jack Swigert ran unsuccessfully for the Colorado Senate in 1978 and it is rumored that he may run for the United States House of Representatives or for governor of Colorado. Swigert said in a political speech recently that 'it's time we took a lesson from *Apollo* and began to look toward the future.' Do you know what lesson he is talking about?"

"Well, I can't put words into Jack's mouth. But with *Apollo* being future-oriented, he was probably referring, in the context of his political ambitions, to the fact that the earth does not stand still. Yet people tend to stick to the status quo. We have that here in the telephone industry. Telephone companies by their very nature have been very conservative. There is a big segment of this industry that would rather stay just the way they were. But you know the world has changed and the whole nature of telecommunications has changed. The fact is that if we don't make an effort to anticipate these changes, then it will be too late to adjust to the change. And such people will find themselves out of a job because technology and social advances have passed them by."

"Whether we are talking about telephones or space programs, how does a person keep up?"

"In a world of change you are never completely educated. You have to keep educating yourself into the changes. And you've got to look forward to the future, as I think Jack was saying. Look at how the changes in the world affect whatever you are doing."

"Why would an intelligent businessman, like some of the people you mentioned in the telecommunications industry, tend to fall behind?"

"People tend to do what they are comfortable doing. Most don't want to change if they don't have to. Certainly when I moved to Chicago after spending eighteen years in Houston, it wasn't really my cup of tea. But I saw it as an important move in terms of the changes taking place in this business.

"Change is uncomfortable to most people. I know it myself. I like to have everything orderly, but I realize that every time I just get things running smoothly, something comes along and changes it. You have to sit back and regroup and restructure, or you get left behind. That's the world. It changes all the time."

"Do you think because of his approach to the future, the astronaut makes a good businessman?"

"Well, most of us are not really nine-to-five people, and most of us live by objective rather than by rote. I'd like to see milestones accomplished here and I try to integrate that into my people. I don't care if they go out and play golf on a Wednesday afternoon or if they show up late in the morning. If they have certain jobs to do, they do the jobs. If they've got to work here all weekend, they work here all weekend and they get the jobs done. All I'm interested in is results."

"Let me ask you what may be a tough question for you. You said before *Apollo XIII* that you regarded that mission as the climax of your career. Your whole life was directed toward that moment when you would step on the moon. But in this respect, at least, you failed. How does a person deal with a failure of this magnitude—a goal for which he or she has worked so hard and so long and yet does not reach?"

"That is the past now. The future is something else."

"That's it? You don't find yourself going over it again and again?"

"You can't. Oh, I do some speaking on the *Apollo* program and that sort of thing. But that was just a goal we didn't make."

I really believed him. His job at Centel and the prospect of his company's future are now his primary interests. Talking about the moonwalk that never took place is not something he has a lot to say about. But in talking to Jim about it, you do not sense that this is because the subject is emotionally painful for him. Just irrelevant. The past is past and that is all there is to it.

FUTURISM

Fundamental Wisdom
Jim said he takes matters lightly, including himself, and he does. In the corridor leading to his office is a wall arrangement of glossy photos depicting events from his space flights. They are the familiar shots of the crew being welcomed aboard the carrier deck, Jim sitting at the capsule controls, and the like. I had glanced at them in passing several times. "There

is an astronaut looking for his future," Jim pointed to one of the pictures as I was walking past for the last time. One of the eighteen-inch-high enlargements was a fake. "See the jar of Tang?" he laughingly added. It was a shot of a space-suited astronaut with a two-week growth of beard sitting on the steps of a skid-row flophouse. His helmet was beside him, and his feet were covered by huge moon-walking shoes. He was reading a newspaper that had "Help Wanted" circled in red. And his Tang was there too.

The future is something that Jim Lovell is comfortable with. It weighs lightly on his shoulders. It may be the moon's influence that inspired Lovell and his fellow pioneers to venture so successfully into a future unmarked by footprints. But there is nothing in Jim Lovell's method of dealing with the future that you cannot adopt as your own.

The Futurist. When I was in graduate school in Cincinnati, a new university president, Warren Bennis, was elected. He was a charismatic man who immediately began referring to himself as a "futurist." The meaning of that term soon became clear. An emphasis began to be placed upon the university as a resource for all age groups in the community. One of Bennis's first questions was why one had to be a mechanic or lawyer or a housewife or accountant for his or her entire lifetime. Why not a second career after twenty years of service? Bennis's imprint as a futurist was felt in every area. It is uncomfortable to think about change, but if you do not approach the future willingly and creatively, you will be pushed into it anyhow, albeit unprepared. As the world changes, you must change with it or be left behind. The revolution in the technology of information handling is causing the rate of cultural change to accelerate. If you are to be among the successful at living life in the 1980s, you must be among the futurists—those who allow themselves to see life as a forward-moving adventure.

Monkey Business. A chimp named Ham, who died in 1983 at age twenty-six in a zoo in Asheboro, North Carolina, was America's first space explorer. Animals were successful in space as long as nothing more was required than they be projected like living cannonballs or orbited in an automated up-around-down maneuver. But decisions about the future require anticipation, an exclusively human capability. Only an insightful human being can combine a positive attitude with the ability to deal with change and thereby adjust to the future. Almost as soon as men were introduced into the space program they fought hard for increasing on-board control, a factor that Lovell points to as an essential difference between the American and the Russian space programs. He said, "You had to anticipate problems. You had to have a good scanning of the instruments and react quickly to what was going to come up. You had to take adverse situations and try to work your way out of them."

Controlled Anticipation. Looking ahead to the future is not constructive if it is done in a manner that does no more than frighten you. The most constructive first step when attempting to anticipate a murky future is to find out as much as possible about your present situation. Then actions can be taken toward your primary objective, and unproductive, fear-breeding fantasy about the unknown can be avoided.

"Jim, did worry take a big toll on the crew? It was said that the crew had about reached the limit of their endurance by the time of splashdown. In fact, the three of you were judged to be in the worst shape of any returning crew."

"I don't believe that statement too much. I know it was made. Fred Haise had a urinary infection and he did have about a 102-degree temperature when we landed. In fact, I kept my arms around him because he had chills on the last day. Jack was wet and I was cold. The temperature got down to 38 degrees. But we could have lasted a lot longer. 'Couldn't last one more day' is not true."

"You could still keep coming up with contingency plans?"

"Yes. If we had missed coming in to land we would have run out of electrical power eventually. But certainly we could have stayed alive for another week and a half. Then, of course, our whole attitudes might have changed a little bit." He laughs. "If you came to interview me at that time, via radio or something like that, you might have found a different person."

"What do you think I'd have found?"

"Well, I don't know. We would have probably just tried to pass as much data back to the earth as possible until we had run out of oxygen, because it would have been a unique situation. Jesus, what else can you do? You're already committed. You could go out, you know, sort of in an idiotic state, but what does that get you? You're still going to go anyway so you might as well make the most out of it."

"Did Swigert have anything special to say after being put on the flight at the last minute?"

"Well, of course, when the explosion occurred I looked over at Swigert and his eyes were about as wide as saucers. His emotions probably were, 'How did I get on this flight? What am I doing here?' People in the news media and the networks already had us dead. At least Haise and I, this is our flight. I have to admit, though, that Jack acted in the same manner as we did. He didn't have any thoughts about it once we started down."

The message, of course, is to be very careful not to turn your powers of anticipation into a handicap. Utilized properly—to set goals and to provide the basis for educated guesses about the future—the ability to anticipate is a powerful tool. If allowed to carry you away in the form of negative fantasies ("What if . . . ?"), anticipation can be a powerful hindrance.

Letting Go of the Past. Your past has value. As Lovell noted, successfully charting a course into the unknown will require that you draw on the entire spectrum of your experiences. But chronic regret over missed opportunities and the excessive mourning of past failures are counterproductive. These thought processes divert your attention from the issues at hand. A good sense of the present and the real issues before you is essential to the futurist. By presiding in such fashion over the here-and-now aspect of your life, one unexpected dividend is that you will not come to the realization at some point, be it at age sixty or ninety-six, that your life has raced by while your attention was distracted somewhere else. The pathetic "Where did it all go?" is asked only by people who have lived ineffectively and unproductively in a world of historical fantasy while their lives were taking place unnoticed, right before their eyes. The FW here is that while futurists do not lack for goals, they insist of themselves that these goals be approached in terms of "What can I do *now*?" If your goal is to have $5,000 in a savings account, the answer as to the totality of what you can do about it now, in the present, might be limited to opening a savings account and depositing $200. No amount of worrying about how you should have started sooner can improve on this. You can most profitably forget the issue until next month. Until that time, unless your financial situation should change and require more action of you, your time will be most profitably spent in dealing with other issues that could logically benefit from your attention.

Priorities. Looking ahead to your future, you see many goals. Although your goals are targets on which you set your sights, you cannot aim in two directions at once. The totality of one's goals can appear contradictory when looked at *en masse*. This fact has caused many who were attempting to cope with the future to become overwhelmed and sink into inaction. For this reason, priorities must be established before you act. It is a matter of priorities that enables an astronaut to say that cuts in NASA's budget are a good thing. Lovell would be in favor of all space missions *if* he could have everything. But he knows that the United States literally cannot be chasing Halley's Comet and simultaneously accomplishing other goals that Lovell feels are higher on the list of priorities. Only by setting priorities among numerous desirable goals will you put yourself in a position in which you can consider action.

Objectives. Management by objectives (MBO) is a strategy which dictates that once your goal is selected, it must be stated in terms that are specific and measurable. If you determine that physical fitness is your highest priority, restate this in a form such as this: "I will lose ten pounds and be able to run an eight-minute mile by my next birthday," and there will be no doubt about whether this goal is reached. Such an approach also requires that you continue to work toward your goal until the objective is reached or it is changed. This type of results orientation will allow you to consistently produce results in your future by taking the focus off peripheral issues and keeping your goal in sight.

The Unexpected. As true as it is that your goals for the future are quite susceptible to taking some unexpected directions, take some delight in the knowledge that these surprises are just as likely to be pleasant as not. I asked Jim Lovell about surprises that affected his own early plans. "You said you were firing rockets as a teenager at a time when the word *astronaut* had not yet been coined. Did you honestly, in your fantasies, see yourself blasting off for the moon?"

"Oh, no, I didn't see that. I read an article by Wernher von Braun in 1946 about how you could go to the moon. I was taking speech class at that time and gave the class a talk concerning that. But even in this article, it was never contemplated to do it in such a short time period."

The lesson speaks for itself. When you take steps toward the future, why worry that things might not work out as planned? They will frequently work out better.

Frustration. There will be times, of course, when an unexpected outcome is decidedly a setback: a frustration in your efforts to reach your goal. At such times, says Jim Lovell, you must regroup, rework, and try again. The important point is to keep at it by continuing to do something. You may be surprised to learn of the many setbacks and detours in our GIT's career.

"The real reason I wanted to get in the space program was that I had been interested in the technology of liquid fuel as a kid in high school. I had read everything from the fiction of Jules Verne to the publications of the American Rocket Society. I even went to the point of trying to build rockets in high school. Some of them were pretty interesting. Some of them blew up.

"At that time none of the schools had much in the way of curriculum or courses specifically designed for space flight, and I didn't have money to go to places like MIT or Cal Tech that might be the best. So to get an education I changed goals. As a psychologist you realize that you frequently have to change goals. Although my first goal was to become a rocket engineer, it was obvious that I couldn't do it at that time, even though I was very interested in it. I applied to the Naval Academy. The reason for it was that I had an uncle who was the 58th Naval Aviator, a graduate in 1913 of the academy, and this was an alternate goal.

"And I didn't make it on the first try. But I did get into what was known as the Holloway program, which was a naval aviation program that was started after World War II. It sent you to college for two years, then down for flight training, and finally back to college as a commissioned officer for two years. I went a year and a half at the University of Wisconsin and I started flight training. But at Wisconsin I applied for the Naval Academy for a second time. And when I was going through pre-flight in Florida, my appointment came through. I was the first alternate. The principal either bilged [failed] the physical or the mental, I'm not too sure which, so I was transferred to the Academy from Pensacola and graduated from the Naval Academy.

"I was still very much interested in rockets, and in my first class year, 1951, I wrote my term paper on rocket technology. In 1958, after becoming a naval aviator and graduating from test-pilot school, the closest I thought I could get to rockets was a modified fighter plane with a rocket engine that the Navy was testing. Didn't get that either. But then when the opportunity came to join NASA, I took it. NASA was looking for the original astronauts to fly the *Mercury* project on top of the *Atlas* rocket and they picked 110 names from computers of both the Air Force and the Navy. They gave us secret orders. We all went to Washington and got briefings on what they planned on doing, and then they picked 32 out of the 110 to go for physicals and other testing. Then they picked the original seven. And, of course, I didn't get in.

"I was very much disappointed. I became the program manager on the F-4 Phantom airplane, as I mentioned. But the opportunity came again in 1961, when they asked for a second group. At this time I took a more cavalier attitude toward it. I said, well, yeah, I'll go. I'll give it a try. So they sent my name in. And I was picked as one of the second group of nine.

"I had a medical problem with what is known as a high bilirubin. They found out I didn't have yellow jaundice and I didn't have malaria or things like that, but I had this thing that probably helped drop me out of the program originally. But I had it checked by a flight surgeon for two years and sent the report back to NASA just to clear my record. That helped on my second physical.

"It is interesting to note the difference in the selection criteria between the first group to the second group. In the first group psychologists played a big part in selecting the criteria for what might make a good astronaut. They looked at combat duty, feeling that that would give the necessary stress. They looked at physical condition as tremendously important. But there were a lot of things they guessed wrong on. I think motivation is the most important quality. You can overcome a lot of difficulties if you have motivation."

Where would you have been beaten by frustration into abandoning your goal? At age fourteen when your rocket blew up and singed your eyebrows, as happened to Jim? When you didn't have the money to study in a good engineering program? When you were turned down by the Naval Academy? When your blood tests yielded inexplicable results? When you finished first in your class at flight-test school but were not selected for the first group of astronauts? When both of your oxygen tanks were lost halfway to the moon? Frustration can rob you of your future. Only a high level of motivation to keep moving toward your goal will enable you to create the future you choose. Healthy futurists deal with setbacks in the manner of the test pilot. They keep their eyes on their goals and keep working on alternative courses of action. They keep moving by continuing to select the next best option. If option number one meets with a roadblock, go to number two. When that has taken you as far as it can, jump to option three. Just as this strategy keeps the pilot alive in the literal sense, it will keep you alive in your progress toward your goals.

Pushing the Envelope. An aggressive style of dealing with the unknown future was referred to by Jim Lovell, in test-pilot jargon, as "pushing the outside of the envelope." Pushing the envelope is what those in test flying do when they take their machine past the point where it has ever been before. As always, when dealing with the future, the results are never completely predictable. "If in testing an F-4 we went out to a point where the wing fell off or the engines flamed out or you got into a flat spin and you couldn't recover, you bailed out and the plane splattered on the ground. Then you wrote your report. You fall back and either say, 'Listen, fix the aerodynamics so it doesn't get in that spin,' or you put it in the flight manual that you don't want to get in that spin and you go on to something else."

When you meet a stranger, say goodbye to a lover, or put yourself into any interaction with human or machine, you are never certain what the results will be. In human interactions the predictability factor is always low. But pushing the envelope, risking the unknown, can be as exciting as a ride in an F-4, and attempting to control every aspect of your future can be limiting. By overcontrolling you will never find the best you are capable of. Sophisticated futurists know that problems lie ahead. They plan for the big ones and use their problem-solving skills to cope with the rest. When Jim got into his problem aboard *Apollo XIII* he mentioned that he could have bounced off the walls (he literally could have, considering his weightlessness). Instead, he charted his course from where he was. Your future, by testing the limits through action, is to a significant degree yours to determine.

Simulation. "Simulations help and that was a big part of the training. You build skills in simulations and there is a stress factor trying to cope with the problems thrown at you. But at the same time you know that you can just go back to zero again and start all over." Simulation is an effective technique to use in preparing for events in which your performance is critical. Simulation allows you to pre-experience upcoming events and will help improve your performance by creating that "I've been here before" feeling. It shortens decision time because you have already learned to deal with similar choices.

Simulation is not worrying. Lying in bed and scaring yourself into a sweat by going over and over your fears about giving a speech the next day is not simulation. In contrast to worrying, you begin a simulation by getting relaxed. This can be easily accomplished by focusing all of your attention on your regular breathing. See in your mind's eye, the air as it enters your nose, travels down to your lungs, and exits again. As you do this for a minute or so, allow your muscles to go limp. A little practice will allow you to reach a relaxed state by this means very quickly.

Once relaxed, mentally place yourself in the situation you want to prepare for. In your imagination, use all five senses. The more detailed you can be, the more successful your simulation will be. Are you simulating asking your boss for a raise? Are you preparing yourself for the moment you will drive your ball off the first tee at a crowded local golf tournament? Ask yourself what you see, hear, taste, smell, and feel. Still relaxed? If not, return to the relaxation step until you can visualize the situation completely and remain relaxed. Next, always returning to relax when necessary, visualize your way through the entire event. Whether the request for the raise or the golf swing, take care to always visualize the ideal. This is another important difference between simulation and worry. You are not, after all, interested in practicing failure. Anticipate any snag that could conceivably come up: the boss asking you why you feel you merit a raise, telling you why you don't need it, or saying no. Rehearse all the possibilities and picture yourself dealing with each situation exactly as you would like to. Simulation will help you with your golf game, but don't limit its use to golf. Pre-experience any tough situation that you can see coming your way. Simulation will tip the odds in your favor.

Psychosomatics and the Future. Your vision of the future can actually make you sick. Shortly before my interview with Jim, a friend made an appointment to see me professionally. He complained that he was tired and cranky, always felt he was on the verge of "coming down with something," and couldn't concentrate on his job. We went over the important factors in his present life, such as family, job, and financial condition, and no problems were apparent. Nor could he think of anything in the future looming on the horizon.

Before his second visit, he met me for breakfast and pronounced himself "cured." It seems that months before, his company had been tapped for an IRS field audit. He hadn't mentioned it to me because he had confidence in his bookkeeping department and felt that everything would turn out all right. I questioned how he was so sure this had been behind his difficulty. He answered that as soon as the IRS auditors told him that everything looked fine and walked out the door, he jumped up in the air and let out a whoop, and every symptom he had was gone. He then admitted that from time to time, upsetting fantasies about the future had crossed his mind: "What if they find a big error?" "What if they know something I don't?" "What if I go to jail?" Although when thinking logically he knew that these fears were unfounded, he was poisoning his present with his unhealthy view of the future. He did not act to help himself. He did not specify objectives. He was simply worrying. This specific incident passed through my mind as I was talking to Jim. "Test pilots are oriented toward an approach of 'What can I do now?' and 'What's my next option?' This gives them a sense of control over their future. Are the astronauts and test pilots you know fairly immune to ulcers, high blood pressure, and other worry-induced disorders?"

"Well, I have to guess. Of course I don't have all their medical records. But I don't think there are too many around, none that I know of, with these type of problems."

With the stringent screening procedures, it is likely that would-be pilots who are susceptible to such problems are eliminated early, but there is reason to believe that being a futurist carries physical as well as mental benefits.

Savoring the Moment. Your efforts to shape the future should never be allowed to deter you from experiencing the present moment. In the hours of feverish activity when the lives of the men aboard *Apollo XIII* were hanging precariously, Jim tells of looking up to find Haise and Swigert, both novices at lunar flight, taking pictures of the moon through the window. Man's ultimate priority is always to experience the real present no matter how compelling the imagined future may be. The comment by the veteran Lovell? It was an understanding reminder that unless the translunar tourists resumed planning for the immediate future, there might be no opportunity to have their film developed.

5/Samuel I. Hayakawa

MANAGING YOUR EMOTIONS

. . . for there is nothing
either good or bad,
but thinking makes it so . . .

"Hamlet"

FUNDAMENTAL PROBLEM

A bolt of lightning always precedes the thunder clap. A thought, too, must occur before emotion can be experienced. Over the last twenty years the psychologist Albert Ellis and his colleagues have developed this relationship into an orderly collection of literature and technique termed Rational Emotive Therapy. Jargon aside, this is simply a recognition of the connection between thought and feeling. The relationship is one of cause and effect. If you want to control your emotions you must know that your thoughts cause your feelings.

Semantics, the study of the meaning of words, is at the very heart of why we feel as we do. How we talk to ourselves determines the type and intensity of our emotional response. Talk to ourselves? Sure—through the ever-present and familiar voice in your head that can be termed the "self." It is a voice that you can readily recognize as having been with you from your earliest memories. Have you ever tossed in bed at night, unable to sleep, with thoughts tumbling and churning? Who or what was it that observed and thought about those thoughts? Your self. Most of our thinking happens in just this way, with our self talking to us.

Your self, the voice in your head, observes, reasons, and narrates. It employs certain characteristic words, phrases, and emotional tones peculiar to you. This self may be said to have developed a certain learned attitude or personality.

For some of us, our selves possess a perspective on life that creates the Fundamental Problem of gloomcasting. Poor copers develop the tendency to view the events around them, too often inaccurately, as unpleasant. This is an easy trait to recognize in others. We describe those possessing it as "pessimists" or "sour on life." Experience has shown, however, that this is a particularly difficult FP to recognize within ourselves.

Imagine the therapist in consultation with a gloomcasting patient as a deeply distressful problem is unburdened. Should the therapist respond with a negative exaggeration such as "That's the worst problem I've heard in all my years of practice," he or she would be unlikely to get an argument. Similarly, your answer of "How absolutely awful" to a gloomcasting friend would also be considered by that person to be appropriate. Curiously, naïve attempts to cast sunshine with "Things could be worse" or "Everything will be fine" or even a more realistic "Let's try and look for a solution" will probably be spurned. While the gloomcaster is quite willing to accept negative exaggeration, almost everyone feels too worldly to fall for any amount of sugarcoating. We resist excess in the positive direction.

Truth telling is at issue. The concern is not about telling the truth to another. Few people, for example, are likely to go to the trouble and expense of weekly psychotherapy in order to sit with a therapist and lie to him. The challenge is *self*-honesty. It is often a painful effort to look within yourself and admit to the hard answers. It is easier to quickly come up with the responses you would like to believe and that are therefore seductively easy to accept. It is personally dishonest to live through a routine, uneventful day and yet be constantly accompanied by unpleasant, negative, emotional responses. Your feelings are counterfeit. There is no ring of authenticity. This is thunder without lightning and nature is askew.

Emotional thunder, justified or not, can be considered among the most sensuous and luxurious of emotional experiences. Many have described a binge of body-wracking crying or a dish-hurling rage as having been a rather pleasurable emotional experience. Jim Fixx in his *Complete Book of Running* reminds us of the fine line between pain and pleasure, both of which are well known to the distance runner. Adjectives such as *unendurable* and *exquisite* are commonly used to describe both pain and pleasure. Yet a totality of days and years filled with inappropriately negative emotional responses is self-destructive. It calls to mind the forlorn and perplexed cartoon character walking through life with a rain-spewing black cloud overhead while those around him bask in sunshine.

You definitely have a choice in the emotions you will experience. But if you are deep in the throes of negative emotion, this may be a particularly difficult point to appreciate. The usual tendency is to defend and justify emotional distress through rationalization. "Well, how would you have felt if your child had just told you that he hates you?"

How *should* you feel when a supervisor offers a critical opinion of your job performance? What *would* be the appropriate response when another person unfairly receives recognition for work that was yours? The answer, no matter how disconcerting until you become accustomed to it, is that your feelings are entirely a matter of choice: yours. It is within your range of control, quite literally, to decide exactly what your emotional responses are to be.

Are we to be happy robots, going through the motions of our daily routine in a state of hypnotic bliss, oblivious to life's real pain and suffering? No. At the death of a loved one it is healthy and appropriate to grieve. If the sound of a train whistle pierces the silence as we stand on the train tracks it is healthy and appropriate to experience fear. The immediate release of adrenalin, the flow of blood to the muscles, and the sudden ultra-acuity of the senses all work in such a situation to assist us in the matter of survival. To suggest that we should always choose to be calm, relaxed, and happy is preposterous.

The question you must attempt to answer honestly is: How much of your day is spent jumping from railroad tracks, grieving for deceased relatives, and dealing with other events that truly call for appropriately negative emotional responses? Should you determine that these occasions are relatively few, the next question to be answered is how much of your day is flavored with negative emotions. If there is a disparity between the two you are not managing your emotions as effectively as you are capable of and a FP may exist.

SAMUEL I. HAYAKAWA

Great Inspiring Teacher

> *On the Panama Canal: "We should keep it. We stole it fair and square."*
> *On a Senate Budget Committee expenditure of $2 billion: "I never realized it could be so easy. It's all simple addition. You don't even have to know subtraction."*

On his conviction that the poor don't require gasoline: ". . . these people waiting in the long lines at gas stations are people who need gas to get to work. And they need to get to work in order to pay their taxes so that the poor will be supported."

Whether you agree with such statements or are enraged by them, they are clearly the product of a man who understands the power of language.

S. I. Hayakawa was elected by the voters of California to the United States Senate at the age of seventy. He had already had a distinguished career as a semanticist, helping to popularize this science of the meaning of words with his classic *Language in Thought and Action*. His career as an academician reached its zenith when, as acting president of San Francisco State College in 1968, he was vaulted to hero status by the bewildered and beleaguered middle class. In an internationally publicized incident, he jumped to the bed of a sound truck, familiar tam-o'-shanter jauntily in place, and pulled the microphone plug on the militant dissidents who had been disrupting classes with their non-negotiable demands and had driven his two predecessors from office within the previous seven months.

The senator appeared to relish his role as lawmaker. In *Through the Communication Barrier,* a book he sent to me when I invited him to participate in this book, he remarked "For the first time in your life, people begin to treat you as being as important as you always thought you were." Dwarfed as we talked by his oversized, book-lined, memorabilia-strewn office on the sixth floor of the Dirksen Senate Office Building, he was immediately attuned to the Fundamental Problem of gloomcasting.

"Senator, you were among the first to popularize the science of semantics. I would like you to show people reading this book what is causing their emotions and how they can use that information to manage their feelings."

"Well, all my life I've been concerned with the relationship between emotional distress and the language people use to talk to themselves. If I were to greet you by saying, 'I hear you're one of those quack psychologists,' " he offered mischievously, "then your blood pressure starts to go up." With semantics, "that rise in blood pressure itself is part of the meaning. The meaning is a reaction, a semantic response to a body of words. The meaning is more than the definition in the dictionary."

"How do people avoid getting trapped in what you have called 'the pitfalls of language'? You have said this occurs when we misread what is going on around us and you have noted that people would do best trying to think by report, rather than with inferences or judgments."

"I just want to give you a little example to show how hard it is to make a distinction among the three. Some years ago at an airport lunch counter, I saw a man leave a dollar tip after having had a cup of coffee and walk out without even waiting for a smile from the waitress. I didn't realize until she punched up ninety cents that he had left her a ten-cent tip. My conclusion that he had left a dollar tip was an inference, but I didn't know it was an inference. I thought it was a report."

"And to cover the field, the waitress probably made a judgment that he was a cheapskate? So in order to keep on the most even keel emotionally, and to avoid introducing error into the process, it is best to think in terms of reports, just the facts, as much as we can?"

"Of course. This gives us our best view of what the world is really like. I mean if a guy left a ten-cent tip or whether it was a dollar tip is a trivial matter. But nevertheless, the world is full of these trivial matters about which we may lose our tempers or give undue credit to somebody for something he didn't do and so on."

Hayakawa stresses changing our thinking from inferences and from judgments to reports whenever possible. Such a deliberate change of perspective when we feel ourselves approaching the boiling point is often sufficient to regain emotional equilibrium. He terms this strategy "keeping a semantic scheme of things in mind." In an analogy for which he credits his wife, Margedant, he equates this strategy with driving down the highway, keeping safely to the right of the vaguely perceived but ever-present white line. It is unnecessary to concentrate on the line to follow it. Neither in managing our emotions must we constantly examine our thoughts and conversation as we attempt to interact with our environment as objectively as possible. However, when we find our emotional stability threatened it is usually appropriate to re-orient ourselves. Not as difficult as it may at first appear, this is done by examining our language to determine whether we are accurately reporting or simply reacting to unexamined inferences and judgments of questionable validity.

"So in a practical sense, Senator, what do you do personally when you find yourself in a situation that has the potential of being very upsetting?"

"When I am in great distress I consciously search for other ways of looking at the same problem. If someone has disappointed me severely, are my impressions about his behavior or about his motives trustworthy? I try to work out other ways of explaining what it was that caused the disappointment. Was the disappointment in my unrealistic expectations or in his behavior? I just toss things around. I regard that as a reasonably normal process for anyone."

A testimonial to the effectiveness of the senator's strategy was offered by Janice Barbieri, then his press secretary. We were discussing the volume of his mail—an unofficial Capitol record at 12,000 pieces each week—consisting of requests for assistance and information and the registering of opinions. Directing his staff in handling these requests, meeting with the press, making addresses, and listening to special interest groups make up the typical workday. Yet all of this is subordinate to the actual business of being a senator. Barbieri pointed to the special wall clock. Through a system of coded lights and buzzers it summons senators for floor votes, demanding that they drop everything for the sixty-second subway ride to the Capitol. Votes can be called as frequently as fifteen times in a single day. She threw up her hands, saying, "I will go crazy before he will lose his temper!"

Later I asked him. "Senator, do you ever lose your temper?"

"Sure."

"How do you bring yourself back?"

"Well, sometimes I don't bring myself back. I give vent to my temper. There's nothing wrong with losing your temper as such; it's just losing your temper on the wrong occasions. Like, for example, when they started tearing down that beautiful college of mine. I was Goddamn mad. They weren't going to stop the war in Vietnam by disrupting the chemistry class."

"So people can be assured that negative emotions like fear, grief, frustration, and anger are legitimate in the appropriate context?"

"Yes. Of course they are. I was mad enough so that I could stick to my guns. I said, 'I'm going to call the cops and have every one of those bastards arrested,' which is exactly what I did. In those situations people say, 'Well, now, can't you reason with the kids?' Well, I'm not going to reason with them. My predecessors already tried that—and it didn't work."

I brandished a copy of a Mervin Field poll from a San Diego paper that claimed an extremely negative voter reaction toward Hayakawa over another of his patented statements that, on the surface, appeared outrageous. He had told the press, in response to a question about the number of bills he had introduced as a senator, that he saw his job as not to pass bills but rather to get people to think. The press was incensed.

Such fare is a steady diet for those in public life. "How, on a human level, do you deal with this sort of thing? How do you keep from getting very down and black about it on the one hand while avoiding rationalizing by passing on the blame?

"I had a reason for the statement. At that time there were more Democrats in the Senate than Republicans. As a member of the minority party, very few of the things I wanted to get done I had been able to get done, because the Democrats sat on my bills and wouldn't let them through committee. And when I did get into floor fights, I lost them. The press reported, in a very condescending kind of way, that I said I regard it as my job to bring up difficult issues that are still controversial and attempt to bring people around to my point of view."

"But don't such slanted writing and other attacks make you feel stepped on and unappreciated or misunderstood?"

"No. I want to show you something." He got up from the living-room-like section of his office, walked around his desk, and pulled two legal-size manila folders from the high bookshelves. "I said something that got attacked terribly in the papers. During the hostage situation I said, and this is not an actual quote, that the Iranian students ought to be rounded up like the Japanese were in World War II. Well," he continued, holding up the thinnest folder, labeled "anti" across the front with a marking pen, "these are the letters I got in criticism of that position. These," he said, holding up a bulging folder four times as thick, "are the letters I got saying, 'You're quite right; that should have been done long ago.' It all balances out. On the whole, the intellectuals, including the newspapers, are much more critical than the general public. The thick folder indicates an awful lot of patriotic sentiment like, 'A Goddamn little country like Iran can't do that to us.' So I don't worry too much about the press, unless it's a totally false story, as it often is, because I take it as part of being in politics."

"If we could take a public opinion poll on how we lived our life it would be helpful, in one sense, because we could see that unfavorable opinions, while maybe the loudest, represent only one point of view."

"Yeah, that's exactly right."

"You said you don't ignore criticism that is totally false. How do you deal with it?"

"I can write some pretty strong letters." Turning impish again, he said, "I wrote to one guy who criticized me in a magazine article, and I said, 'It's clear that you get your political information from the Johnny Carson show.' I got back at him."

"Senator, you have mentioned several areas of FW. Staying to the right of the line by thinking in terms of reports helps us keep a semantic point of view. You spoke about balancing criticism with other points of view. You point to the logic of tolerating unhappy feelings only when they are justified on the basis of the facts. But here is the problem. The behaviors you recommend require breaking the habits of a lifetime. How is that done?"

"Well, I'm reminded of someone who was giving a prescription on how to cure people who say 'ah, ah, ah.' He told them to turn on a tape recorder and listen to themselves say this, for example, during the course of a speech. I think of something similar myself. People don't know. They haven't heard themselves. If they knew that in nine cases out of ten, or ninety-nine cases out of a hundred, they react negatively to life, they wouldn't do it. 'These eggs are fried too hard.' 'The coffee is cold, for Christ's sake!' 'The train is late.' Some people just react like that all day long, but they haven't heard a record of themselves doing this. It would help if people were made conscious of the degree to which their language is full of negative evaluations. And if your language is full of negative evaluations, no wonder you're so damn miserable."

"So you believe that the simple awareness of this trap is therapeutic?"

"That's right. That's exactly what *Language in Thought and Action* was written for. To create that awareness.

"I use an analogy about three baseball umpires: 'I call 'em like they are,' 'I call 'em like I see 'em,' and 'They ain't nothing till I calls 'em.' Now the first one, 'I call 'em the way they are,' that's a kind of naïve realism. I saw it go over the plate, therefore it's a strike. Just the way it was. The second, 'I call 'em the way I see 'em'—it's a realization that there is a subjective element. Just possibly I didn't see it right. But when you say, 'They ain't nothing till I calls 'em,' that is really very profound." Hayakawa wrote about the last ump, "He is no grammarian, but he can be said to be a semanticist, deeply aware of the way in which the reality we experience is largely created by the language with which we describe it."

"But often, we aren't sure whether a negative emotional reaction is justified or not." I asked, "How does the wife whose husband says, 'I want a divorce,' or the salesman whose boss says, 'You're not doing the job,' apply this? How can they see that events have only the meaning we attach to them, no more and no less?"

"Well," said Senator Hayakawa, "if the boss says your work is not satisfactory, it sure isn't satisfactory to him. And if he's the boss, you have every reason to reexamine your own behavior."

"But how do I avoid taking this personally and attaching more to this than there really is? If you are not managing your emotions, the line between 'You are not very good at selling refrigerators' can very quickly blur to 'As a person you are no good.' "

"It's getting back to self-acceptance," said the senator. "I am who I am. If the boss says my work isn't adequate, well, all right. There may very well be ways in which he's right. It's not satisfactory to him. Therefore, I can revise my behavior correspondingly." [Examine the real issue—selling refrigerators—objectively and avoid gloomcasting by introducing a different issue—your overall self-worth].

As with all of our GITs, managing emotions in Senator Hayakawa's life is more than just theory. The ability to control his own life by refusing to react reflexively has helped Hayakawa cope in exceptional fashion to a tragedy that has struck and devastated countless families—the discovery that his son Mark was afflicted with Down's syndrome. In *Through the Communication Barrier,* the senator wrote, "It was a terrible blow for us to discover that we had brought a retarded child into the world. . . . His retardation has brought us grief, but we did not go on dwelling on what might have been, and we have been rewarded by finding much good in things the way they are."

"You did not choose to look at this as the end of the world. What semantic technique enabled you and Mrs. Hayakawa to see past what must have seemed at first to be an endless darkness?"

"I don't know whether we ever used the word *semantics,* although with our both having studied a lot of semantics, that sort of thing comes naturally. We have found Mark to be someone to love and someone to care for, someone to watch the development of; he developed so much slower than other children. I just learned to accept him as he is. Who is it that said this?

There are so many people who spend their lives
Wishing the world were otherwise.

They waste a lot of emotional energy. Insofar as I am concerned, if Mark is retarded, okay, he's retarded, and let's make the best of it."

"It is obvious that parents in a similar situation could look at such a thing in a lot less healthy manner."

"Well, I think that my wife and I are a lot less affected by the way others think. That is, hell, we wouldn't have even got married if we weren't independent in our thinking. In 1937, an oriental-white marriage was a damn rare thing. They became common only after World War II. We both looked in ourselves for the decision as to whether it was right or not."

"How do you get like that?"

"It's hard for me to say. I don't know how you get like that because I've always been like that. So has my wife. I suppose it is very largely because of the way in which we were brought up. I was the oldest son and like so many oldest sons, I was thought absolutely wonderful by my mother. She was never censorious, never scolding, and she accepted me the way I was. My wife received much the same treatment as a child."

"Based on what you have written, I know you don't believe that one must either be brought up this way or there is no hope for him."

"No. That's right. I know people can change. In fact, one of the things you do as a successful psychologist is to help people produce those changes."

Hayakawa is a slight man and speaks so softly he is difficult to hear at times. He looked at home in the Senate, professorial in this three-piece suit. While the Senate is in session he lives with his sister and his administrative assistant, preferring to spend much of his time reading. He is, however, not unknown at Washington discos. Musically inclined, he once wrote a jazz column for a black newspaper *The Chicago Defender,* and he also served as a director for the Institute of Jazz Studies in New York. He keeps fit with tap-dancing lessons and attends all the parties given by his staff, to whom he enjoys a genuine closeness.

"Do you feel, looking back over your life, Senator, that you have lived with a semantic point of view?"

"Yes. For example, all the time I was working for an M.A. and a Ph.D. in English, people would say to me, and in terms of the 1930s this makes perfectly good sense, 'Why do you want a Ph.D. in English? No one's going to hire a Japanese to teach English, unless you plan to go back to Japan.' And," said the Canadian-born senator, "I would say, 'Well, maybe you're right,' then pay no attention, and go right on. And, maybe, they damn near were right. I had a hell of a time getting my first job. I wouldn't say it was because of racism. The word *racism* was hardly known then. You look into a 1939 dictionary and you'll find that *racism* isn't even there. All I'm saying is that I knew what I wanted to do. I wanted a Ph.D. in English, I wanted to become a writer, I wanted to become a poet, and I was determined to go ahead and do that. And, you're able to do that."

EMOTIONAL MANAGEMENT

Fundamental Wisdom
In one of his regular meetings with the California press, an interesting
undercurrent could be noticed as the senator fielded questions ranging from
predictions on the upcoming 1980 presidential race ("Trendiness leads you
astray ideologically"), the military draft for the handicapped and elderly
("I'll register myself anytime they want"), to the Carter administration's
handling of the Afghanistan situation ("Fine, once they woke up"). The
undercurrent had to do, naturally, with words. Hayakawa would regularly
challenge reporters over the use of certain words in phrasing their questions. At least once he jumped up to grab a dictionary. "Just for your
education," he told the reporters, "I'm going to read you a definition of
viable." He had previously been asked about the viability of a certain
politician, to which he responded, "Don't use the word *viable* in that silly
way." Then, when it was repeated, he mocked, "Yes, I think he'll live
until election day." Senator Hayakawa is the GIT in this chapter because
he clearly acts on his recognition of the impact our words have upon us.
As important as the correct use of words is to this semanticist, their correct
use is no less important to you. Care and accuracy with words in your
thinking and speech is the key factor in the overall accuracy and stability
of your emotional life. Before reading this chapter you may have viewed
your emotions as autonomous entities functioning according to their own
rules. With the information provided here, it is unlikely that it will ever
again seem reasonable to you to blindly accept unmanaged emotional
thunder.

Nature's Law. Difficult though it may be to find professional agreement
among psychologists in most areas, few would argue about the cause-and-
effect relationship between thought and the emotions that our thoughts produce. No particular event carries with it a preordained emotional response.
How do we feel when it rains? A drought-plagued farmer is likely to tell
himself something far different about the rain from what the host at a
backyard barbecue has to say. You are the missing link between your
world and your emotions. What you choose to tell yourself about an event
at any given moment determines your emotional response. Recognizing
yourself as this link puts you in control, master of your own emotional
life.

Perilous Pitfalls. Beware the treacheries of language, your language, advises Hayakawa. Are you a gloomcaster? What would a playback of your thoughts and speech reveal? Do you use the same pat phrases like "This is the worst day of my life," "I wish I were dead," or "That was the nastiest person I ever met" for *any* adverse event, ranging from the trivialities of burnt toast to those as substantial as family crises or national emergencies? Distinctions must be made.

Whitelining. Taking control of your emotions requires that you deliberately search for alternative interpretations of events before giving yourself over to the clutches of emotional turmoil. The view must be experienced from where others are standing. Says Hayakawa on anger, "When you find yourself losing your temper, there is your little white line. Say, 'What am I getting mad at?' " This ability requires a larger perspective than the immediate situation. Our GIT has a perspective-gaining prescription. "You cannot be completely absorbed in your job, your children, or whatever it may be to the exclusion of all else. Each one of us has to have a private life, whether it's a passion for Beethoven, or a passion for the poems of Shelley, or whatever it may be—but it must be a life in which you cultivate a set of evaluations that are independent of the immediate society around you."

Reporting. Gloomcasting can be eliminated by insisting of yourself that you think by report rather than by judgment or inference. A report, as in reporting the news, is based entirely on fact. It is as uncolored and accurate as we can make it: "My date is ten minutes late in picking me up." If we go further and rely on inference, we take one dangerous step out on a limb. We attempt to reach a conclusion through logic and assume more than the facts. We say, "It's rush hour on Friday night and it's raining, so he is probably held up in traffic." We may be right acting on inference more often than not, but errors are bound to be made. An infinite variety of alternative explanations are possible. Your boyfriend might have left with the company funds for South America. Graduating to the judgment puts us on the riskiest ground of all. Moving farther away from the facts, to a judgment, we take on the role of judge. We presume to approve or disapprove. It is from the judgment that sparks most frequently fly. They can be reeled off in strings: "He's a bum." "He lied." "He doesn't care anything about me." Each one serves to fan emotional fires.

Umpiring. Recognize yourself as the link between your world and your emotional reactions to it. Determine to promote accuracy in your use of words. Be willing to search for alternative explanations. Become the wise umpire who knows, "They ain't nothing till I calls 'em." You give the meaning to your environment, and this takes a fine hand. Recognizing the distinction between one's view of reality and reality itself is the mark of those who cope well in their emotional life. Hayakawa illustrates this point further with a statement made by A. E. Housman, and a retort by Alfred Korzybski, the founder of general semantics and Hayakawa's mentor.

Housman: I, a stranger and afraid, in a world I never made.
Korzybski: Don't be afraid. With your evaluations you made that world. With different evaluations you can make another one.

Righteousness. If your best analysis of a situation leads you to conclude finally that frustration, rage, shame, guilt, fear, humiliation, loneliness, or any other feeling from the long inventory of negative emotions is appropriate for the situation, don't hold back. All emotions are legitimate. No one is constantly happy and tranquil. Negative emotions are often called for. Expressing them constructively can make you feel cleansed and can be highly productive. His fury at the efforts of militants to disrupt his campus led Acting President S. I. Hayakawa to the permanent presidency. This position was given to him as a vote of confidence by the San Francisco College Board of Trustees following, and largely in appreciation of, his indignant response.

Relearning. It may seem artificial and ponderous to take time and examine your thoughts before embracing a given emotional response. Be confident that this is quite possible. If at present it appears "automatic" or natural to produce negatively slanted emotions, this is simply a learned response. A certain amount of deliberate effort will be required to produce the new learning that in the future will cause you to "automatically" employ honest, nonflammatory language. This management of your emotions will ensure that they accurately reflect your experiences.

6/ Russell Means

RESPONSIBILITY

. . . we make guilty of our disasters
the sun, the moon, and the stars . . .

"King Lear"

FUNDAMENTAL PROBLEM

"I am steadily employed, I pay my bills on time, and I never forget to send a Mother's Day card." So you are certain that irresponsibility is one Fundamental Problem that does not require a second look. Be careful. Consistency and reliability are not automatic indications that you are unaffected by psychological irresponsibility. I am not referring to the shiftless character who throws away the family grocery money on gambling. The FP of irresponsibility describes the inability or unwillingness to exercise the real control we possess over our own intellectual and emotional functioning and our behavior. It hits at the heart of how we live.

The irresponsible blame you if they feel irritable or have a headache. It is another's fault, rarely theirs, if they make a mistake. Operating with a psychological blind spot, they engage in a myriad of behaviors that, at their worst, destroy them. Often, those close to them are destroyed as well.

"I don't like to drink, but I can't help myself."

"I didn't want to kill anyone, I just needed money."

Most of those possessing the FP of irresponsibility are unlikely to be involved in behavior so melodramatic as alcoholism or armed robbery. Yet, the effect of this FP may be no less destructive. The hallmark of the problem is the need to blame anyone or anything handy, reason often to the contrary, when things do not go as you believe they should. Little else matters as long as you can make it appear that you are blameless. You shrug your shoulders: "Don't blame me." If you are irresponsible, you will be able to benefit from little of the Fundamental Wisdom in this book unless this FP is resolved. All other FW requires the commitment to personal responsibility.

The irresponsible are children in the coping sense. They do not recognize their personal power any more than they see their potential for self-destruction. Not recognizing or fearful of their ability to act, they remain sleeping giants, psychological Gullivers bound by fine Lilliputian threads of fear, doubt, and imperception. Ironically, were they to recognize their strength and their power to act, there would at once be nothing to hold them. They would be free.

The mind each one of us possesses has been described as a billion-dollar biological computer. We possess this marvel without benefit of an operating manual. In terms of effective human functioning, the irresponsible can be said to know the least about the effective operation of this bio-computer. Again, the program, or our language when we talk and think, is at issue. But unlike the gloomcasters who use negatively exaggerated programs to worry and frighten themselves, the irresponsible use marshmallow language. They are masters of equivocation and non-involvement with their "maybes," "I can'ts," and "I don't knows." They would actually have us view them as aimless billiard balls, rebounding from rail to rail, with you, me, the weather, their own body, anything but themselves, responsible for the events in their life. They are playing a cameo role in their own movie.

One great fear that you will recognize if this FP is yours, and it is in itself a valid perception, is that responsibility places you at risk of being challenged. It does, to be sure, create the very real probability that not everyone will agree with you and that not all will judge you kindly. Yet irresponsibility, a path at times euphemistically termed "tactful" or "diplomatic," describes a life based on a philosophy that can be defined only as the fear of taking a stand. Living such a life is to exist in a shadowy no-man's land of half-truths in order to escape the need for commitment. Earth-shaking atrocities have been committed by those who were "only following orders." Smaller-scale tragedies occur because of all those who would like to help, "But I can't. I have to think about my family."

Fundamental Wisdom demands a semantic shift, a literal change in both the language you use with others and the language you use to think. "I think so" is replaced by "Yes" or "No." "I should" gives way to "I want to" or "I will not." The conscious decision to abandon functioning as a slippery, amorphous person brings with it the gain of spontaneously improving your interpersonal relationships as people begin to discover someone easier to grasp and truly know.

Early in my psychological training at the University of Cincinnati, Professor W. Bruce Welch continually commented to his graduate students on their need to "be a man with a point of view." For many years I was wary of this, fearing such a posture necessitated intellectual rigidity while precluding openness to new ideas and the freedom to change. I have come to believe, however, that taking positions on issues in life is an important ingredient of responsibility.

Spoken at a church discussion group: "I am for abortion." Directed at a boss: "I can see you're in favor of the change, but I'm against it 100 percent." While discussing politics: "Yes, I voted for Smith four years ago and you're right, I blew it!" Such refreshingly responsible statements allow us to learn from the consequences of taking stands. If you equivocate on issues, tell people one thing while believing another, or explain away rather than admit mistakes, you blow smoke in your own eyes. You become blind to important lessons. Wasting intellectual and creative energy weaving excuses and impressive rationalizations creates impotence. You find yourself unable to bring to bear the full force of your problem-solving abilities on fashioning effective solutions to real problems. Often you create illusory reasons for failing to act. After all, should you succeed in convincing yourself that events are not your fault, and you are not central to them, it follows that there can be little reason to act. This pseudo-logic, built upon a foundation of dishonesty, generates pseudo-facts that will inevitably misdirect you.

RUSSELL MEANS

Great Inspiring Teacher
The response to my invitation was neatly penned on a sheet of yellow legal paper and mailed in a pre-stamped envelope.

Dear Dr. Fleming,
Thank you for honoring me with your request for my participation in your preparation of a book.

With due humbleness, I confirm my willingness to participate in your work. May the Sacred Mother-Earth win her struggle to stop her continuing rape!
Russell Means*

The tale of the struggle of the Native American People against the invading Europeans is a long and painful one. This history of attempted genocide begins with Columbus and was articulated by Thomas Jefferson. It reached its peak under the banner of Manifest Destiny in the Civil War period when General William Tecumseh Sherman was quoted as saying, "The only good Indians I ever saw were dead."

For 400 years the North American tribes, by one anthropological estimate originally totaling 10 million people, attempted to co-exist with the white people. The basic Indian philosophical-religious orientation revering "mother earth," eschewing the individual ownership of property, and dictating the sharing of wealth was incompatible with the European thirst for conquest, conversion, and the acquisition of riches.

The two cultures were destined to clash bloodily. The Spaniards taught ruthlessness and torture to the Apaches. Scalping too was a European practice that originally involved returning home with the heads of the enemy. As a result of this fighting, and through treaty, entire Indian nations were relocated from lands they had occupied for centuries to one remote and presumed worthless geographical area after another. They were promised each time that the move was in perpetuity, only to be moved again by the "Indian-givers" as the economics of an expanding frontier dictated.

The last Indian treaty was the Fort Laramie Treaty of 1868 between the United States government and the Sioux, Northern Cheyenne, and Arapaho Nations. The Black Hills of South Dakota, considered worthless by the U.S. Government, and a tabernacle by the Indian, were set aside for the Indian people. Government troops were assigned to keep white people out.

From this day forward all war between parties to this agreement shall forever cease. The government of the United States desires peace, and its honor is hereby pledged to keep it. The Indians desire peace, and they now pledge their honor to maintain it.†

---

*Russell Means (unpublished letter, Kyle, South Dakota, March 11, 1980).

†Dee Brown, Bury My Heart at Wounded Knee: An Indian History of the American West. New York: Holt, Rinehart & Winston, 1971.

Yet, in less than ten years the white people, several times illegally led by General George Custer, had discovered gold in the off-limits Black Hills. Finally, in 1875, President Ulysses S. Grant withdrew the last of the troops assigned to enforce the treaty. In 1876, when Custer and his Seventh Cavalry once again ventured into Indian territory, they found that after 400 years of backstepping, the Indian would move no further.

But any satisfaction the Indians may have felt in their victory over Custer at Little Big Horn was short-lived. Severe punishment followed in 1890, again in the Black Hills. Most of this land had by then been taken away from the Indians. Only a few reservations remained to dot the area. A few days after Christmas, Custer's old Seventh Cavalry surrounded a migrating band of 350 Sioux at Wounded Knee on the Pine Ridge Reservation. In *Bury My Heart at Wounded Knee*, Dee Brown describes how the cavalry guns were trained on the camp. Reinforcements arrived as the soldiers drank through the night. In the cold morning a scuffle broke out. The soldiers' Hotchkiss guns, which could hurl explosive shells for three miles, began to fire. When the smoke cleared, as had happened so many times before, 300 Indian men, women, and children lay dead. For almost the next 100 years, the American Indian was scarcely heard from; not until seventy-one days in 1973, again at Wounded Knee.

Russell Means easily one-handed the wheel of his low-slung aging T-Bird around the curves and over the hills. Driving the reservation roads in the Black Hills means frequent, sudden swerving to avoid the ubiquitous potholes. These hills, the setting for so much glorious and then tragic Indian history, are low and roll gently. Along the roads of the 2500-square-mile Pine Ridge Indian Reservation there are no billboards. "The top-soil is thin," Russell said, "and there is only so much you can grow." He told me the hills were primarily used for grazing, but they were brown and dry in May, and few head of cattle could be seen.

His gesture, with cigarette in hand, was casual, but the voice and the words are powerful. The rage seems always just contained. "For seventy-one days the most powerful military machine in the history of mankind lay siege to us. They would not allow in medical supplies or food. We were shooting with 22's, shotguns, handguns, one AK47, and a few 30-30's. We had to have ammo because we were in fire fights night and day. And we had to have food for the three to four hundred people that were inside 'The Knee.' And we whipped the United States of America at Wounded Knee because they acceded to all our demands before we stood down arms."

Means, just forty, is tall and in good shape. His black hair is long and held by the headband he always wears. He and his brothers, in the traditional way, had cut off their braids in January when their mother died. He wears traditional Indian jewelry: rings, earrings, and a bear-claw choker. The American Indian Movement slogans on his jacket patches and AIM belt buckle complete the picture. He is, as he says, a full-time Indian.

"Full time" to Russell does not simply describe the person with the Indian clothes. It describes the one who maintains close focus on his goals, without letting up. Means's goal is to do all he can so that his people prevail. Secondary to this is a strong feeling of support for "all people of color" who are struggling to be free. Being full time means responsibly living your life consistent with these causes. As I gave my order to the waitress for a beer with my hamburger one night he good-naturedly announced that I could have any label in the house—except Coors. Coors, at that moment, was being boycotted by the Chicanos over labor practices. When the order arrived he carefully checked the bottle. Had it been Coors, you can be sure it would have been politely but firmly sent back. That is "full time." That is responsible behavior in a small but constant way.

Russell is not without rancor for the less than dedicated. In what he sees as a clear-cut struggle for survival, with the stakes genocide, the loss of identity of the American Indian people, he scorns the part-time Indian. "If they are not traditional, therefore spiritual, they are not Indian in my book. They're just a waste. There are a moderate amount of allegedly full-blooded Indian people who are genetically Indian, but spiritually, in their heart and mind, they're white. They're apples, you know? Red on the outside but white on the inside." On the reservation, a division clearly exists. Means and the AIM loyalists are opposed quite violently by Indians who identify with the reservation bureaucracy. The official reservation governing system is headed by the tribal council, the local arm of the Bureau of Indian Affairs in Washington. Russell's son Scott told me that the long hair of the children from AIM families is frequently taunted in the BIA-run reservation schools. This long hair signifies that a child is receiving a traditional upbringing with instruction in the Indian language, history, and the wisdom of the great chiefs. Means considers the hope of the survival of a living Indian culture to rest primarily on the shoulders of these young people.

You may be surprised to learn that Russell Means is not a two-dimensional, fire-breathing automaton, but a complex man who displays an appealing readiness to break into a booming, whooping laugh. He never seems happier than when finding a chance to talk about his children. He can often be overheard talking about a son's Junior Olympic boxing medal or a daughter's accomplishments in school. One cassette tape made on a Saturday morning as we sat with coffee cups across the round wooden kitchen table contains a passionate discourse by Means on the traditional role of women in Indian society, peppered with his pauses to shout instructions to the three teenagers leaving on a school bus trip.

The warm and comfortable Means home is filled with memorabilia. Gods' eyes and blankets adorn the walls, one portraying, close to life size, a buffalo. On another, wall is an equally large banner proclaiming the "Longest Walk, 1978, S.F. to D.C." A plaque hangs in appreciation from the Cleveland American Indian Center, and another in Middle Eastern script is adorned with an engraved likeness of Yasir Arafat, for whom Russell holds undisguised admiration. Under the plaque hangs a commemorative license plate from the Pueblo Revolt. A typical Means humorous touch is the prominence of AIM-brand toothpaste in the bathroom.

"I know that when you were five years old your family took you off the Pine Ridge to live. This had to give you a perspective that the reservation Indian doesn't have. Do you credit that experience with making you as effective as you have been in taking the Indian struggle to American society?"

"The first five years of my life were highly influenced by my mother and her folks in terms of being proud to be Indian, and only Indian; to be spiritual. They were the foundation for my pride. I never lost that pride of being Indian.

"I moved into an integrated town, Vallejo, California. We were the only Indian family, period, in Vallejo. We lived in the projects. I went to elementary school with blacks, Filipinos, Chicanos, and whites, poor whites. I had to fight every one of them just because I was Indian. So I got to wondering, 'Well, what have they got against Indians?' In grade school I found out as much as I could, with the books available, about Indian people. I grew up hating—yeah, I was going to qualify that and say not really hate—Kit Carson, Davy Crockett, Daniel Boone, the Lone Ranger because he never gave credit to Tonto, Roy Rogers, and all the westerns. It was this involvement and education that got me beyond the community. I wasn't isolated like the reservation Indian, put out of sight and out of mind. When a person grows up in a concentration camp"—the phrase Means usually substitutes for "reservation"—"he doesn't have any options except either to totally sell out and try to become a two-bit facsimile of a white man or, in frustration, give up and find methods to escape, like with alcohol or dope."

"What did you do after quitting high school?"

"All during that time I was drifting around, getting an education, working, drawing unemployment, hustling, putting scams on people, and whatever. Then I went back and graduated. It took me ten years to get four years of college, and you know, that's when the white man almost got me. Because I went to college to become an accountant. I wanted to be rich and I figured that the best way to be rich was to find out all about the white man's money. But thanks to Dennis Banks and the American Indian Movement I was literally saved."

"You returned to the Plains in the late 1960s to work in tribal affairs and then relocated to Cleveland, where you met Banks and opened the second AIM chapter in the nation. What made you decide to push the Indian cause into high gear through maximum visability?"

"When you're in a fight for the liberation of your people," he states simply, "everything is necessary for that liberation." On Thanksgiving Day 1970, he led the capture of the *Mayflower II* in Plymouth Harbor. He clearly had a flair for the symbolic. He next staged a prayer vigil atop Mount Rushmore, the landmark in the Black Hills that AIM followers consider a desecration. He and Banks reached national prominence when they led the takeover and sacking of the hated Bureau of Indian Affairs in Washington. The BIA, the last colonial bureaucracy in the U.S. government, holds a position of omnipotence over the lives of reservation Indians through the administration of education, health care, local tribal councils, and land allotment.

Means's final thrust on the warpath to Wounded Knee came from Cleveland Indian baseball fans. As leader of the Cleveland AIM he went to court over the degrading image of Chief Wahoo, the comic-book Indian mascot of the team. The case, Means notes, is still in the courts, but Cleveland fans hounded him out of town. Shortly afterward, on February 27, 1973, Means and Banks grabbed front-page headlines away from Watergate, the Vietnam POW release, and the Daniel Ellsberg trial with their armed takeover of Wounded Knee. In the end, two Indians, Pedro Bissonette and Buddy Lamont, had been killed by government bullets. They were buried in the Wounded Knee cemetery alongside the bodies of the 300 government victims from earlier times.

"What did Wounded Knee accomplish for the Indian people?"

"Wounded Knee was effective because it embarrassed the United States of America internationally. The whole world saw that they'd been caught with their pants down. They realized the government was wrong. Everyone in the world knew that. In the Harris or Gallup poll only 24 percent said we were in the wrong; 76 percent of the people in this country were behind us. That's a hell of a majority, you know?

"I would say what Wounded Knee '73 did for the Lakota [a branch of the Sioux] people is put us back on the road to self-dignity and self-pride.

Especially among our young people. The benefits are immeasurable. The key to our survival, the key to anyone's survival, is the dignity and pride that comes from self-awareness and the realization that being Indian is not a degradation. But we didn't say, 'Wow, what's going to be the end result of this?' Because we thought we were going to be wiped out. When we went into Wounded Knee, man, we didn't expect to come out alive. The press is partly responsible for saving our lives, I believe. I mean there wasn't any press in 1890."

AIM and Russell Means are attempting to create an Indian renaissance. "We sit down and we say, 'Hey, we're oppressed, we're suppressed, and we're a depressed people. So how are we going to liberate ourselves?' And first of all we to look in the mirror to find out and recognize our own imperfections, our own colonization, and attempt to decolonize ourselves."

When Means looked in the mirror he saw trouble with booze. "I had problems with alcohol from the very first moment I took a drink when I was fifteen years old, to the time I quit. The problem was that I was not a twenty-four-hour-a-day Indian. I was still colonized, and this is part of looking in the mirror and decolonizing oneself. You must respect yourself. I am a leader and therefore an example to my people. I have to maintain that example, and not on a part-time basis. Even though most never saw me inebriated or gassed, still some of them did whether it was in another part of the country or not. It was detrimental not only to the movement, but to me, to my family, and my people. It's a spiritual thing. If you have respect for all green things, and the winged things of the air, and the four-leggeds, and the things that crawl and swim, if you have respect for all of life, then you should have respect for your body. And if you can treat your body with respect, it's that much easier to treat all of life with respect."

Watching Russell Means cope with the little and the big challenges of life, one realizes that unlike the irresponsible, who hide behind every manner of excuse to justify their failures, he recognizes no boundaries whatsoever. I saw this at three o'clock one morning as we made the long drive home after a speaking engagement. It was still two hours to the Pine Ridge, and the fuel gauge was reading empty. The gas pumps don't stay open all night on the two-lane roads that angle across the plains of Nebraska and South Dakota. Most, in such a spot, might be content to pull into a service station and salvage a few hours' sleep until the town stirred. But Russell plunges ahead with enthusiasm. He lustily storms the police station and then politely inquires of the young and sleepy desk sergeant about the availability of gas. He believes in action in the face of potential defeat. Because of this, things seem to work for him. In just a few minutes the town's gas station/bowling alley/health food store was opened up, gas was flowing, and the attendant was happily checking the oil and wiping the windshield. You will be amazed at what can be accomplished if only you avoid excuses.

"In 1977 you served time in jail as a result of Wounded Knee. Now, ten years since the takeover, what are conditions like on the reservation?"

"The first thing I realized when I was in prison was that I had to acknowledge the wall. And then, after having experienced prison, it was very evident that prison life is no different, absolutely no different, from reservation life today. The horrendous statistics on the deprivation of Indian people in this country attest to the fact that the reservations are concentration camps. Goddamn it, less than a half-million people live in those concentration camps throughout America, and the United States of America cannot justly deal with those half-million people. There are twice as many Chicanos in East L.A. than there are Indians in the concentration camps. Yet, we are at the bottom rung of the ladder on any scale of measurement in every aspect of life; education, health, socio-economic, etcetera."

The facts bear him out. Of the 840,000 Indians in North America, those on reservations experience:

- the highest infant mortality rate of any group in the U.S.
- a life expectancy seven years short of the U.S. average.
- rates of alcoholism and suicide at twice the national rate.
- deficient education in reservation schools.
- dangerous medical care from the Indian Health Service under the BIA.
- astronomical rates of sterilizations and infant adoption into white families.
- a higher incidence of arrests and an underrepresentation on juries.

The historical approach in this country has been to "de-Indianize" the American Indian. It is only since the Indian Reorganization Act of 1934 that speaking the Indian languages in reservation schools has ceased to be legally forbidden and severely punished. Many charge that in fact, these practices have continued until very recently. "The typical response when hearing about the disgraceful reservation conditions would be to ask why the Indians don't leave the reservations."

"We don't want people leaving," says Means. "That's exactly what the white man wants."

The AIM's present efforts are focused on undoing the damage that has occurred over the last several hundred years to Indian society. The AIM seeks to strengthen Indian identity and culturally disassociate Indians from American society. "We would like a cultural leave-us-alone policy implemented by Western civilization, industrial society, and the white man." The AIM has applied to the United Nations for recognition and has already been granted Special Observer Status. "We're into community development and the international community. If you want to be sovereign you have to act sovereign." The Indian position is that secession from the United States government is unnecessary since, under the 1868 treaty, the Sioux never gave up their status as an independent nation. "Secede? We never have been part of it according to treaty law, constitutional law, and international law. They [the U.S. government] have never recognized that fact. We're not going to secede from anything. We're just going to self-determine with what we have."

"As leader of the South Dakota AIM, what are you trying to accomplish right now?"

"Our primary concern is instilling discipline within our ranks, which requires no drinking and no doping. The short-range goal is community self-sufficiency. We're rebuilding our nation so that Indian people can remain in the community instead of going out to work in the other world.

"You see, the first thing the government attacked of the Indian people was our *tiospiya*. If you attempt to translate it into English you can say it means 'village' or 'camp,' but it's more than that. It's everything that we were as a nation. So what the Dakota American Indian Movement is doing is recreating the *tiospiya,* which will be our self-sufficient community, without any government handouts. Totally independent: energy independent, economically independent, socially independent, and legally independent. We will police ourselves. And we hope that once our people see the self-sufficient, independent Indian community right in the middle of this reservation, it will get other communities to do the same thing.

"It will be on Pine Ridge, on my Dad's land that he left to my brothers and me. We have donated that land, 160 acres, to the Dakota AIM. First of all, we start with alternative energy and appropriate technology. We're going to build underground homes, which, by the way, have more window space per square foot than a conventional home. We'll be using solar and wind power. Here on the Northern plains we have plenty of wind. At the very minimum we will provide for 70 percent of our energy needs. Under Pine Ridge there is geothermal water, another resource. But that's down the road. Technology has to improve to where the cost isn't prohibitive to recharge the underground water formation, because we don't want to rape our Mother Earth and take away from her.

"We're going to have wood stoves and water wells. We'll have community showers, separate for men and women, and a laundromat. One does not go back to total self-sufficiency all at once when you've been colonized for hundreds of years. It's a step-by-step procedure. After we have solidified our base we have a number of economic enterprises on the drawing board. One is a dairy. It's the closest thing to depending on the buffalo by hunting them. We're going to establish a chicken farm and a rabbit farm. Eventually we're going into the export business. We'll produce Indian goods, star quilts, beadwork, and jewelry, and export it to Eastern and Western Europe."

Modern Western society, in Means's view, is on the brink of certain disaster. He has made it his mission to ensure, through a return to traditional Indian life, that Indians avoid the same end. "Industrialized society is destroying itself. I don't give a damn if only one village on a mountaintop in the Andes survives. The Indian people, the red people of the western hemisphere, will survive and prevail. Whether it happens during my lifetime, my son's lifetime, or his son's lifetime is not a matter of importance. We will prevail. As long as we struggle to that end, we are one with everything that is sacred and holy and good. The whole duty, as we see it, is that during our minute lifetimes on the face of this earth, we should try, at the very least, to maintain the world as it was when we came into it so our unborn will have the same chances at life that we were given. If, when we leave, we have either maintained that or improved it, then that's the purpose of life."

Of all the people I might have chosen to represent the FW underlying effective coping in the area of responsibility, I can imagine none better than Russell Means. To many of his people, those who support him, he is considered a patriot. After the hundreds of years that the Indian has been oppressed by the Europeans who migrated to his land, Means says, "I want to be a free man."

I said to him, "Being a twenty-four-hour-a-day Indian has its price. You are neither without controversy nor without enemies. How do you feel you are generally viewed among your own people?"

"There have been five attempts against my life, but it wasn't my time to go. Some of my people see me as a troublemaker and some as a hero. Some hate me and some love me." He points out his living-room window to the house across the street. The woman living there, a tribal council worker, had passed around a petition, unsuccessfully, to have him put out of the neighborhood upon his return from prison. As a result of Wounded

Knee he served, he says, one year, three days, and twenty-two-and-one-half hours in the South Dakota Penitentiary for riot to obstruct justice. The law under which he was convicted has subsequently been repealed by the South Dakota legislature, but with no retroactive provisions. Although Means is still on parole for the offense, the judge who sentenced him was arrested for shoplifting, is receiving psychological help, and was forced to resign his judgeship.

RESPONSIBILITY

Fundamental Wisdom
The Fundamental Wisdom in this chapter is based on the undeniably logical argument that you are irresponsible if you approach life with the attitude of "Don't blame me, what can I do?" If directly or indirectly you chronically disavow responsibility, then you are, by your own admission, irresponsible.

I lived and traveled with Russell Means. His teenage son shared his bedroom with me. We argued and laughed together and pooled our money for a speeding ticket in Grand Island, Nebraska. We sat on his car in front of the Longhorn Saloon just outside the reservation. He was amused by my naïveté as I stared in disbelief at the two-foot letters across the roof proclaiming, in 1981, "No Indians Allowed." We never got to jog because it always rained. He kidded about hearing from his teachers that George Washington was the father of his country. He raged at anthropologists, "the U.S. government's official grave robbers," as we drove past one of several digs we were to see at Indian burial grounds. I learned that Indian fetuses are dying before birth in horrifying and disproportionate numbers, and that Indian women have an exceptionally high rate of hysterectomies for cancer. Both problems stem from the reservation water. It is radioactive. The AIM is attempting to solve this problem.

Never in our time together did Russell Means ever speak the word *responsibility*. He talked about dignity. He speaks often of pride. "How does one grab onto that first handhold?" I asked him. "How do we begin to deal responsibly with issues, large and small?"

"You have to live it a little bit," he said. "You learn it by living it." The FW at its heart requires you to recognize, where it exists, the strength you do possess: your potential to act and effect changes in your life. The resolution of this FP is basic to all great stories in which the hero, underdog at the outset, conquers adversity and triumphs in the end. It is a theme running deeply through adventures as diverse as the Resurrection, the Wizard of Oz story, and the struggle of the American Indian. To be found in the resolution of this FP are the ingredients for triumph in the adventure that is your life.

Self-Respect. The key, says Means, to anyone's survival is the dignity and pride that come from self-awareness and the realization that you don't have to apologize for being who you are. The first step in the direction of responsibility demands this insight. As a moving, striving, growing organism you have a right—yes, a right—to be responsible. You can hold up your head and actively seek what you want and what you believe in. So the first act, when peering into the mirror under the harsh light of self-honesty, is to respect the person you see. "Draw strength from who you are," says Means. Only then can you plot a course of purposeful deeds. At this point the need to blame, excuse, equivocate, and mire in indecision becomes obsolete, and responsibility makes sense.

Colonization. Colonization is the control by one power over a dependent other. The irresponsible have allowed themselves to be colonized. While standing before the mirror, a personal critique is required. This will be for your eyes only. Neither is it a time for modesty nor flattery. Think of the figure you face as though it is that of another person whom you are free to be objective about. In what way is that person colonized? Locate the areas of irresponsibility that have insidiously become almost forgotten and tolerated parts of yourself. "No one's perfect," the irresponsible whine to themselves; "that's just the way I am." These personal myths are simply unscrutinized fallacies that serve to help you co-exist with your irresponsible self. Write them down. Do you drink too much? Are you allowing your waistline to expand while pacifying yourself with "It's just middle-age"? Are you nasty to your wife while excusing yourself because "she's just a bitch and gets better than she deserves"? Are you going to let your children grow up before you get around to being the type of parent you know you should be? Do you fail to stand up for what you believe, letting things pass because "nobody understands anyway"? From this hard look at yourself you may have concluded that someday you should become assertive, be able to get closer to others, or revise your feelings of self-worth. To make "someday" today, commit a list of these needed changes to paper as you work your way through this book. When you reach Chapter 13 you will find the techniques you need to make these changes.

Blame. Blame is a cardinal feature of irresponsibility. Through its use you tie your own hands. If you convince yourself that problems are not your fault, it becomes extremely difficult, even nonsensical, to act. While in the short term it may feel good to be uninvolved, the pervasive feeling that events are beyond your control quickly becomes a burden. Your personal power is blunted and you become ineffective in coping. If you see the need for change, do what you can to make changes. When things turn out badly, do what you can to fix them. In life a winner is rarely declared. Life is not a trial in which you will be judged innocent or guilty. Ultimately we all die, and we die alone. Why accept boundaries? Don't wait for an invitation to get involved, and don't allow yourself to look the other way. Always put yourself in position to act. This is impossible with a posture of "It's not my fault" or "He did it, not me." Such irresponsible thinking creates defeat. Responsibility sets the stage for success, and success stems from your realization that what you do on your own behalf and for others is all that ultimately matters.

Buts. Says Means, "When I give talks at universities around the country the reaction I get is often 'Yeah, but . . .' It is only a few minutes in their total life that they have allowed themselves to listen, and then their old brainwashing takes over." You have now looked into the eyes of the enemy and recognize that it is yourself. You accept responsibility, you have identified the issues, and you are ready to act. Then, as Russell says, the obsolete thinking begins again as you start to talk yourself out of changing. Beware of excuses. Change is painful. The organism fights hard, through twisted reasoning, to maintain the status quo. How much discomfort and inconvenience are you willing to endure to quit smoking or to get on better terms with alienated relatives? Means again: "The Indian says that man is cursed with the power of reason."

Diplomacy. What does the tactfulness you're so proud of really mean? What's behind it? What is so hard about saying "I believe . . ." or "I'm against . . ."? Rather than open-mindedness and flexibility, sympathizing with both sides of issues may signal confusion, disorientation, indecisiveness, and a lack of commitment. I have a friend who describes himself as "often wrong but never in doubt." He is no less frequently wrong or right about life than anyone else, but he is always sure where he stands. Most responsible people are like this. When Russell Means states with conviction that modern industrial society is going to go up in smoke any minute, he is putting himself on the line. Whether he will be proven correct does not matter. Look around at the issues and cut out some definite opinions for yourself. Firm stands become ignorance and prejudice only if you remain closed to change in the face of new information.

Selling Out. Responsibility means being the person you want to be. You must resist selling out. Russell Means is attempting to restructure Indian life because, as it exists, Indian youth has no opportunity to be responsible. The few choices he sees for young men to express their manhood, for example, are through drinking and taking drugs, beating their women, engaging in athletics, escaping into the military, or becoming imitation white men. To Means and other responsible Indian leaders, these choices are absolutely unacceptable. They are determined to create additional alternatives. Draw on your pride, your intelligence, and your anger. You do not have to become what others expect of you, what is forced upon you, or a pale copy of someone else. There is no need to knuckle under to values and a lifestyle with which you are uncomfortable. Do not escape to the security and imprisonment of your private reservation, whether it may be your job, your friends, or your present pattern of living. Open your eyes and, like Means, get an education. There is a real world around you, and you are in a fight for your own liberation. Everything is necessary. Russell spoke of the meaning of life as he sees it, and his actions reflect those beliefs. Do yours?

Responsible Living. An action approach to life makes life work for you. You will be amazed at the results when you begin to face life without excuses. You must begin with very concrete steps. Early in his tribal work, Means confesses, he was sidetracked into imitating the white man. He tells of traveling to national meetings smartly dressed in European tailored suits and white shoes. "I thought I was a dude," he says, self-mockingly. "And I was embarrassed by those I saw dressed in the traditional Indian way." His own switch to such Indian dress was a tangible outward signal to himself and others of his rediscovered commitment. To paraphrase his statement about sovereignty, if you want to be responsible, you must act responsibly. Put yourself on the line. If you are going to stop abusing your body and finally lose weight, tell everyone about your commitment to eat sparingly. Be willing to discuss how you reached your decision and why being thinner is important to you. Then live it. You will be proud of yourself, and others will respect you.

Full Time. Responsibility is not an occasional proposition. Means says, "There were Indians who went through Wounded Knee. They came in, got their glory, and left. They didn't want to die." Responsibility is the concept of full-time commitment, not the commitment of convenience. Do you believe in God? Clerics have always been frustrated by the masses of irresponsibly pious who proudly walk down the church aisle on Sunday, yet manifest no apparent carry-over of spirit on Monday. A responsible Christian probably runs the risk of being considered a religious fanatic. A responsible vegetarian does not eat steak on Saturday night nor sneak a Big Mac when the mood strikes. In the process of becoming responsible, these may be tough words for you to hear.

Bio-Computer. It is said about computers, "garbage in—garbage out." Responsibility requires the responsible operation of your own bio-computer: your mind. Your mind can only be as good as the program it uses. The language that you select when you think and speak is that program. Make a list of the irresponsible words in your vocabulary and learn to use their responsible translations. I have a client who began to pay a fine to her fiancé whenever he could catch her speaking irresponsibly. Responsible speech is unmistakable. Discussing life and death, and the risks he has taken, Russell Means remarked, "Don't misunderstand me. I don't want to die. I love life. Yet when it's my time I am ready to go." Are you becoming sensitive enough to catch the strong ring of responsibility in that statement? It is clear and direct. It is free of "yes, but," "I'm not sure," and "maybe." Stop living life in a half-hearted way. Train yourself to think and speak in a fully alive manner. You will find that among all FW, responsibility is the area of coping most closely allied with the successful attainment of all your personal goals.

7/Fukujiro Sono

DECISION MAKING

. . . there's small choice in rotten apples.

"Taming of the Shrew"

FUNDAMENTAL PROBLEM

"I've been feeling sort of flat." "I'm a little down." "I just haven't felt right." A close examination of the daily coping of people who describe themselves in such terms often reveals a Fundamental Problem in the area of decision making. Many have developed a pattern of avoiding even simple decisions. Others make choices that too often show poor judgment.

The predicament caused by avoiding decisions can be best understood by visualizing yourself perched atop a barbed-wire fence. Until you decide which way to fall, you are destined to experience ongoing discomfort. Not all choices must be made among rotten apples. Even when torn between alternatives that are pleasant enough in themselves, as whether to buy your brother a tie or a shirt for his birthday, you find that making a decision produces a clear feeling of emotional relief.

Whenever you experience a reluctance to make a choice, fear is what inhibits you. Do decisions create the possibility of failure? Are your decisions too often poorly made? Does a choice mean an irrevocable commitment? The fear of making decisions has many possible origins, but indecision always represents a choice in itself. Often, it is the least satisfactory alternative.

For the woman agonizing over whether to try to improve an unsatisfactory marriage through marital counseling or seek divorce, there looms a third alternative. If she postpones matters too long and allows the months to turn into years, she has, in effect, selected the alternative of remaining in the marriage as it is, for perhaps the rest of her life. If she had clearly seen this alternative for what it was she might have immediately rejected it. Passively choosing what appears to be the status quo may even result in problems of increased severity and precipitate additional complications. Failure to decide to diet is, in reality, a choice to continue eating inappropriately. Rather than simply resulting in a prolongation of the problem such a choice will result in increased problems, as sustained overeating causes additional weight gain.

The inability to deal with choices is based in a misunderstanding of how it is that life, the process, really works. You don't have to look hard to see that real life is not as it is presented to you on television. On the TV screen you can witness life's deepest problems arise, decisions made, and either a clear-cut success or failure result, all in the course of an hour with three breaks for popcorn. While most of us prefer some degree of order in our lives, reality is neither compartmentalized nor simplistic. Results can rarely be anticipated with certainty, and there are few guarantees. You can help yourself by learning all you can about a situation in the time available. But the time to make a choice always arrives. Avoiding decisions until the last minute will increase your proportion of poor choices and may lead you into being more hesitant in making decisions the next time. There is an art to decision making. Using the time that you have available before making a decision, in an effective and purposeful fashion, is the essence of the Fundamental Wisdom in this chapter.

At this moment the United States is under economic attack by the Japanese. The Japanese are inflicting heavy damage with their automobiles and electronic products. Our balance of trade weighs heavily toward the Western Pacific. An educational stampede to the Orient has resulted, and it is focused on studying the methods of those called the "samurai businessmen," the powers behind the success of what has been termed "Japan, Inc."

From our thirst to uncover their secrets, *The Book of Five Rings: A Guide to Strategy* by Miyamoto Musashi, said to heavily influence the Japanese management style, has become an improbable bestseller. Musashi, who died in 1645, writes about the ways of the ancient samurai warrior. Modern texts on the subject of Japanese management techniques are also being rushed into print, and their conclusions appear unanimous. The

Japanese management system is distinguished by consistently superior decision making, which results in products of extraordinarily high quality at a very competitive price.

Japan's present status as a high-tech superpower is not the result of that nation's ultra-modern industrial complex but the expertise of the decision makers behind it. For this reason I traveled to the islands called Japan to find the Great Inspiring Teacher in the area of decision making. The man selected as the GIT is Fukujiro Sono, president of TDK Corporation. On the Fortune 500 list of companies outside the U.S., TDK ranks below Japan's largest, Mitsubishi, with more than 125 billion dollars in sales in 1981. It is even smaller than many of the Japanese companies more familiar to Americans, such as Fuji, nicknamed "Kodak-san," the photographic powerhouse, or the well-known automotive giants. But TDK is the world's largest producer of audio tapes and is also the manufacturer of a wide variety of electronic components. Mr. Sono is of prime interest among Japanese chief executive officers because TDK leads every corporation on the Tokyo Stock Exchange in growth during the five years ending in December 1981. Among an impressive group of companies on the move, TDK is moving fastest. The talks with Mr. Sono at the modern corporate headquarters located in the old center of Tokyo, and a visit to the company's Chikumagawa plant, the main magnetic recording tape production facility, produced the FW that will enable you to apply the "Power of the Pacific" to your business and personal decision making.

FUKUJIRO SONO

Great Inspiring Teacher
Japan's industrial success, as a tribute to the human factor, is amplified when you consider that the islands are particularly lacking in natural resources. The Japanese are forced to import the bulk of the raw materials used in industrial production, including virtually all of their oil. Yet the old meaning of "Made in Japan" has been totally reversed in our minds. But Sono is not content with the Japanese superiority at the copycat level, doing an exceptional job in the production of Western-originated goods. He expresses admiration for the American "pioneer spirit" and is striving toward a new era of Japanese-originated products. Since the Japanese have reached their present stage of industrial leadership by working smarter, there is every reason to believe that they will be able to make the leap from being imitators to innovators.

Mr. Sono said, "As Japan is becoming more internationalized, we are beginning to receive a few Nobel prizes here and there. And this is going to increase. It is not that there is no originality here. It is that circumstances were not those that bring out originality. Japan is an island nation and one not very close to the mainland. And for about 300 years, it closed itself off completely to the outside world. There was no outside influence and therefore no challenge. Nothing was produced for keeping up with the Joneses. There were no Joneses."

Fukujiro Sono is a very slight man, as are the majority of the Japanese. This is at least partially the result of a diet that consists largely of fish, steamed vegetables, and rice. He has a quick smile and although in his seventies, seems to always move at a half-run. I was told that when he is let off by his chauffeur each morning he begins to unbutton his coat. He times things so that precisely as he exits the elevator at the executive suite, his coat is just dropping from his arm into the hands of his personal secretary. "Mr. Sono, your office sent me the translation of your book *Stages of Growth: Reflections on Life and Management* so that I could get some feel for your decision-making approach before I came to Japan. I was fascinated with your description of a quality called *kan*, which is the essence of a good decision maker. What does it mean to be a person with 'good *kan*'?"

When I asked this question about *kan*, we were sitting at a long table in one of the two plush conference rooms we used for our meetings. The minute it was translated for him, Mr. Sono jumped from his chair, rushed to the front of the room, and pushed aside a section of wall paneling to reveal a green chalkboard. When an aide could catch up to him with some chalk, he began filling the board with ideographs to illustrate his explanation.

Our talks were conducted with the assistance of two translators from the TDK public relations department. One was a native Japanese who spoke English, and the other was British and fluent in Japanese. Mr. Sono was described to me by one of his employees as a traditional Japanese, "the real thing." He speaks no English. He prides himself on his calligraphy and illustrated many of his responses by writing elaborate and beautiful characters on the chalkboard. The written Japanese language is a hybrid composed of two fifty-character alphabets, *hira gana* and *kata kana*, as well as *kanji*, the characters that number approximately two thousand in the vocabulary of the average high school graduate. In this cumbersome system of writing, characters from all three sources are selected on the basis of expediency and mixed into a single sentence.

"Dr. Fleming, I think that being informed and having a lot of data is important, but there is more to decision making. In Japanese there are three ideograms that are pronounced *kan*. One has the meaning of feeling and sensitivity (感). Another has the meaning of intuition as gained from experience (勘). The third (観) means perception, looking at things in such a way that one looks into their true nature. I believe that for a decision maker, it is especially important to cultivate this last *kan*, the *kan* of insight."

"How can a person go about it?"

"To achieve this perception of things one must work earnestly at one's goals and I think one must also read a great deal—books on history, philosophy, and religion. In this way one will come to find out how decisions are made, whether in the samurai society or in modern society. Without making the effort to develop the three *kans*, a fine-tuned intuition born of experience and perception to see reality and discern the essence of things, no new creation will emerge."

"You mention the samurai. Do the writings of Miyamoto Musashi, who was a swordsman and who advocated the aggressive, warrior approach, actually have a strong influence on modern Japanese decision making?"

"Yes, it is very much the case. I have written down the character for *michi* (道). It means road or way. The same character is used to write *tao* in the Taoist religion and for martial arts, whether judo or akito or whatever. It means 'a way of.' In business it is a way of enterprise, a whole concept or way of life."

The samurai Musashi killed sixty men with his sword. He became unbeatable. One might mistakenly conclude that the decision making behind the Japanese way of enterprise was extremely aggressive. On Japanese television, for example, the samurai apparently holds a position in Japanese hearts akin to our fondness for the cowboy. Throughout the day TV stations show one samurai show after another. Not understanding the language is no hindrance to enjoying them. As in the westerns, the action begins with the bad guys' committing some misdeed. Then the good guys spend a half hour running up streets and down alleys in old Japan with swords flashing. Perhaps Mr. Sono sensed my perception of the samurai, for he found comparison with the Japanese businessman in this manner amusing. "It is not so much a question of following the very principles of Miyamoto Musashi and *The Five Rings* as using the same thinking process to create this 'way of enterprise.' I'm not saying in business or in private life that you've got to go around cutting down all your opponents and after that you can consider being nice to people. Rather than advocating competitiveness for competitiveness' sake, the way of enterprise is 'a challenging spirit.' This is carried out using fair play and taking the other person's stand into consideration. One tries to avoid outright confrontation as much as possible."

This last comment reminded me of a conversation I'd had over lunch the day before with my British translator and an English-speaking TDK executive. The Londoner and I were having a good-natured and very mild discussion about the merits of the British versus American translation of *The Tales of Genji*. It is a thousand-year-old Japanese-written book considered to be one of the first novels in the history of literature. Every Japanese student studies it. I noticed that our Japanese companion had grown quiet, and I asked him his preference between the two translations. His response: "Would you like some dessert?" Thinking I had been misunderstood, I repeated my question. He responded this time with "I haven't read it." This was my first lesson in the lengths the Japanese will go to avoid confrontation.

Learning that the Japanese are careful to value a challenging spirit while avoiding direct confrontation, I was not surprised to find during my stay in Tokyo that although many American television programs enjoy great popularity, the then-number-one U.S. show, *Dallas*, was being canceled. TV Asahi reportedly bought fifty-four *Dallas* installments at $3 million each. But even with special broadcasts to publicize the serial and a promotional tour by one of the show's stars, Victoria Principal, the viewing rate remained at 5 percent or less, compared to an average 53 percent in the United States.

I asked Mr. Sono about this, explaining J. R. Ewing, his rugged Texas individualism and his cut-throat competitive tactics. He was not at all surprised at the show's lack of success. "Yes," he said, "that sort of thing is bound to fail in Japan."

"Mr. Sono, just exactly how can one maintain a challenging spirit and yet not be extremely aggressive?"

"One thought prevalent in Eastern thought is that you will never get something if you go chasing after it. I can think of two specific instances. If you are after money you won't get it. And if you are after a woman and you chase after her, you won't get her. The minute you stop chasing you will. I think that in America, 'money grubbing' is too strong. Life is so short that I do not think so much emphasis should be just on profits."

"What is the logic behind business decisions if not the profit motive, or 'money grubbing,' as you call it?"

"When a decision is made, the deciding factor is whether the decision is correct or not—fair or unfair. What is not given any consideration at all is whether that decision will be of any personal benefit to the person making it. The person making a decision does not think of himself first and the company second. He has a pure heart. That attitude of the rugged individualist that you mentioned will mean that people will not be with you. It's not that they won't work for you, but their hearts won't be in the right place as they work for you."

"I have been told that the competitive spirit behind Japanese business decision making is the result of a strong sense of cooperation, a team spirit, within the corporation shared by labor and management."

"In Japan we are unified. It is like the rice, it all sticks together. This is a different concept from in America, where everybody is an individual. You know as a whole, in Japanese companies, decision making doesn't go from the top down. In our system, known as *ringi*, whoever wants to get a decision through has to fill out certain forms. These forms are then circulated throughout the company to all the people who either would be concerned or have positions of responsibility. Each person approves the form and then passes it on. In that way it finally ends up on the president's desk. There are cases when I will just look at it and sign it, and there are cases when I will send it back twice, three times, or four times asking for changes to be made."

The Japanese practice of consensus decision making is often hailed as the backbone of Japanese business success. It can be observed quite graphically in the use of the open-office concept. Except for TDK's half-dozen managing directors, there are no private offices. The typical working area is an open expanse containing fifty or more desks. The head of the accounting department, for example, sits at a desk among many people at similar desks. The desks are informally arranged in the rows or clusters that best serve each group. Asking a question of the boss or a colleague may not even require leaving your seat.

In these work rooms, everyone's behavior is businesslike and steady, and these terms best describe the Japanese worker. The areas are noticeably quiet. With the complicated writing system, typewriters are a rarity. They are just becoming practical with the introduction of the word processor. This is one reason that most business correspondence is handwritten or oral. Another reason lies in the importance given to personal relationships. Oral agreements are the rule in the business world, and lawyers have little role. The Japanese are perplexed when an agreement with an American company is followed by reams of legal forms requiring their signatures.

Most employees wear the company uniform, further reinforcing the consensus feeling. Several of the TDK directors, international businessmen of the highest caliber, proudly wear the same gray pants and "Eisenhower" jacket bearing the TDK logo that the factory worker wears. The Western idea that management's job is to think and the role of labor is to work is nonexistent. In the famous Japanese quality circles, for example, all employees involved in any given area, both labor and management, meet frequently to share ideas and help make decisions concerning production. "Harry" Takei, production manager at Chikumagawa, where 40 million audio and video cassettes are produced monthly, told me that there are fifty-eight quality circles at his factory that meet voluntarily and on the workers' own time.

I said to Mr. Sono, "To the Western reader, this type of cooperation, where everyone pitches in to make decisions based on fair play, will seem barely believable."

"Well, I am wondering whether the big difference may not be the fact that in the West, your job is what makes your life pleasant, whereas in Japan we live for our jobs. It is a question of what one centers around. We do not consider the job as simply a means to enjoy life outside it. The basic work concept of most Japanese people is that you make an effort to make life for the people around you pleasant rather than requiring that everybody make an effort to make your life pleasant."

"To be perfectly candid, Mr. Sono, most Westerners would view ideas such as making life pleasant for the people you deal with to be of minor importance where business decisions are concerned. Such decisions are made primarily on the basis of numbers: the so-called bottom line. It is generally believed to be more objective and businesslike to base decisions on the balance sheet. The connotation of 'businesslike behavior' or 'a business decision' is of one without regard for personal considerations."

"It is not so much the balance sheet, it is people. Because, after all, it is people who do the work. As you have been told before, internally we rely on the *ringi* system for decision making. Outside the company, even if someone lets you down one time, you give him another chance. It is a question of human relations, human ties. On the business side of life your decisions concerning your supplier are very much like those in a marriage. If you've married your supplier then there is a lot of give and take, but you have a responsibility. And that is the way to make a marriage work in the end. The American system is very much like the American marriage. A very high divorce rate. In Japan that is considered to be selfish."

"To put this on a more personal level, would you buy a suit from your favorite store, even if it could be purchased less expensively some-where else, just because you had developed a personal relationship?"

Again he seemed amused, this time by my skepticism. "Yes I would use the same place. I am never unfaithful to my shops or my restaurants or to my tailor." He laughed. "But this does not mean that I am a slave to them. If I don't like what they have I tell them. They learn from my opinion and they will make an effort to provide something better or some-thing more suited to my needs.

"Consider the word *en*, which means ties or links." He writes the character on the board (縁). "For example, when you are making a decision about using one of two outside companies, perhaps one is cheaper than the other. But if, of the two, one company has already done business with you, and even if not the cheapest, they have done things nicely for you, then I would be apt to choose that company."

"Do you believe that this is a good business decision?"

"Yes, because if you try to take human relationships as the basis for your business decision making, since most business is conducted with other human beings, the result is usually good."

"There is a certain amount of faith here?"

"Yes, faith in one particular company that comes about because you've had human relations with them for a long time. This is not the sort of decision you would make if you were simply looking at figures on a piece of paper."

"Good decision making contains an element of risk. From TDK's suc-cess it is apparent that you do not always choose the tried and predict-able."

"Well, there is risk and there is risk. Even when we take what we call a risk, it is a very healthy risk. The possibility of its going wrong is something like 10 percent. It is not a wild risk. It is the same thing as when you take risks with your family. Even if you are going to take a risk, you try not to take a risk that is going to kill them.

"But it is more our style to plan. Basically we make three plans. We have just made our first ten-year plan. But these plans are by no means definite, they can be changed if the situation changes. Again it is a ques-tion of people. From what I have heard from the States or in Europe, if a company does not have good results, the possibility of the president or the vice president getting fired is quite high. When TDK had a joint venture with an American company that lasted about five years, in the space of these five years all of the top management changed in the American com-pany. And so we didn't know which way to turn or who to contact because there was absolutely no continuity. As far as I am concerned, long-term planning is more a question of getting the right people, educating these people, and tolerating a certain amount of poor decision making as long as the long-term result is good. So, for example, if you have a plan which will mean that you have even somewhat of a loss this year, but you are sure you are going to have a net gain next year, then that is acceptable."

"It is surprising that a decision making system so grounded in labor–management cooperation would develop in Japan. Fifty years ago Japan was the scene of the most violent labor–management relations of any country in the industrial world. This was a legacy of the times before the Meiji period. [The young Emperor Meiji reigned between 1868 and 1912. His reign, referred to as the period of the Meiji Restoration, signaled the end of feudal Japan. Prior to this, the workers were controlled through force by the samurais, the warriors hired by the shoguns, or military governors.] How did such a dramatic turn-around take place?"

"I believe that from the Meiji Restoration, Japanese management decided that the way to success was through working together rather than employing the cheapest labor force, giving them the least possible in any other form of compensation, and firing them if they didn't satisfy them. If you think about it, this is quite logical thinking. If the management and workers don't work together, the result isn't good. Conflict does not make money for anyone, and so people as a whole try to avoid it.

"I must say that as a whole, within Japanese society, conflict is not a desirable thing. If possible it should be, and is, avoided." At his mention of this my thoughts went back to my conversation about *The Tales of Genji*. But the effort to avoid conflict and the genuine readiness to be cooperative in an effort to make life pleasant was again demonstrated to me that evening as I inquired of the hostess at a restaurant off Showa Dori, the main street in the downtown Ginza district, as to the location of another restaurant that had been recommended to me as specializing in sukiyaki. With a smile she led me down a long side street filled with unreadable signs to the door of the restaurant I was looking for.

As pleasant as is the effect of this Japanese attitude on everyday living, its impact on decision making in the business area is again the most dramatic. "Mr. Sono, one impediment to decision making that people express to me is the fear of the consequences of an incorrect decision."

"People who have worked with both Japanese and foreign companies, Dr. Fleming, tell me that foreign companies are always looking for someone to blame for bad decisions and spend an awful lot of time doing it. In Japan, people don't spend effort trying to find exactly one person who can then be fired. Within TDK, if someone has made a mistake at whatever level, in one particular project, we try as much as possible, when another opportunity comes up, to give the challenge to that person."

This attitude is very real in Japan and has resulted in the practice of lifetime employment. It is very rare to change employers in the Japanese system. An employee fully expects, when joining a company after high school or college, to remain with that company for his or her entire working life.

Thinking about the workday of American executives, wheeling, dealing, and with no one to catch their coats before they fall to the floor, I asked, "Mr. Sono, what is a typical workday for you?"

"The main thing I do is go around to the various departments and divisions of the company. I sit down and talk to people and gather information about what is going on at all levels. This is the information on which I base my decisions, and therefore I cannot spend all day in my office with the door shut."

I recall finishing one particular meeting with Mr. Sono. During the minute or so I spent trading some comments with the translators he had already pulled up a chair in one of the work areas, had his sleeves rolled up, was smoking a cigarette as all Japanese seem to, and was participating animatedly in a discussion group. He spends a good deal of time floating from one such group to another, taking the pulse of his company. He is then able to plan in the Japanese way, rather than being rushed into crisis-oriented decisions.

"There are those, Mr. Sono, who look at the Japanese success in the marketplace as a cultural flaw. I have often heard references to the Japanese as 'a nation of workaholics.'"

"Why the Japanese work steadily, rather than too much, is probably due to the Japanese weather. As you know, the seasons are very clear-cut in Japan. And in the old days, when everything was based on agriculture, there were strictly set duties. There was a time when you had to plant the rice crop by the seedling, to get in the rice, to prepare for winter, etcetera. And so each thing had to be done very steadily, in its time. There was no time to sit back. And as a result, the nation became industrious, rather than the derogatory term *workaholic*. There is a regular pace of work"—he begins to tap the table top softly, creating a metronomic effect—"which is very basic Japanese."

"Let's make another cross-cultural comparison. The successful American businessman is often pictured as an antacid-chewing demon, shouting into two telephones at once, making snap decisions machine-gun–style, and keeling over early with a massive coronary. The picture of the decision maker that you paint is vastly different. I wonder if the Japanese executives suffer the same occupational hazards from the pressures of decision making as do their American counterparts in terms of physical toll?"

"No. Because of the system of sending the *ringi* forms around, for example, which come back with the opinions of everyone, it is quite easy to determine whether a decision is a good one or not. There is not that ultimate stress where you alone must make a decision and if you are wrong, it is the end."

"And when you do make those big decisions, how does it feel?"

"Once the pressures have been removed from my brain, my general feeling is, 'Well, let's go out and have a drink.' "

"We have been focusing on the world of business in our discussion of decision making. Do you see any differences in making decisions in one's personal life?"

"It is quite natural that when things are going smoothly in a company, matters in one's private life will also go well. The most important thing while making a decision which has to do with business, or which has to do with your private life, is to go outside yourself. Rather than to consider matters subjectively, it is most effective to become as objective as possible and to make your decisions without selfishness.

"I've read Dogen's [an early Japanese zen priest] *Shobogenzo* many times. His term *teikan*, or 'clear vision,' means seeing through to the essence of things as they really are. *Teikan* is developed by doing something over and over again, whatever it may be. My British employee, Virginia, has become somewhat of an aficionado of the *kabuki*, the traditional Japanese theatre. The first time she went it was extremely boring. The second time even worse. The third time she fell asleep. But then, by the fourth or fifth time the haze begins to clear. *Teikan* is within you. It is not something you can buy."

As a reader of this book looking for FW in the area of decision making, you are concerned with *tao*, or "the way" of decision making. Depending on your personal values you will, at times, make choices that differ from those of others. This is as it should be. Our decisions always reflect our experiences. Nowhere is this more clear than when using examples of decision making from Asia. A TDK employee told me that management had recently been concerned with poor production at one of the factories. A thorough investigation was undertaken, and the decision-making process, the hallmark of the Japanese success story, was followed through.

It was concluded that the ranks of the employees at the plant were not sufficiently represented by individuals with Type B blood. The decision: New blood, literally, was needed. Employees were transferred to restore the balance of blood types. If the same decision-making process were followed at Westinghouse, an American company that has made strong efforts to become "Japanized," it is improbable, because of the Western value system, that there would be a similar result. But the Japanese take their blood types seriously.

Such contradictions between the ancient and the new occur in Japan because, although still the only fully industrialized country in Asia, its transition has come with incredible speed. Odd juxtapositions are everywhere. Women, and the occasional man, elegantly dressed in kimonos mingle unnoticed on bustling Tokyo streets. Clerical workers commonly do computations with computer-generated data using the ancient abacus. The rickshaw is rarely seen nowadays, but I did glimpse two on my last night in Tokyo as I walked through a wet snow to an ultra-modern Ginza-area hotel for late coffee. The antique vehicles had canvas doors closed tight against the weather. The men pulling them hugged the curb, fighting the steady stream of Toyotas and Nissans as they trotted down the city street— in jogging shoes. The Seibu department store, said to be the largest in the world, is brimming with couture items, designer jeans, art, antiques, sporting goods, and an endless selection of international restaurants. But it is only a few steps down the aisle from the Brooks Brothers suits to the oriental pharmacy where reindeer antlers and other sources of medicinal potions are displayed and prepared.

DECISION MAKING

Fundamental Wisdom
The United States Chamber of Commerce believes "overwhelmingly" that you work harder and better at your job if you are involved in the decisions that affect you. Psychologists will tell you that when you are effectively making decisions in your personal life you gain a feeling of control that grants immunity to most of common mental-health problems. The key units of FW that follow are derived from a man who, with a small number of his industrial colleagues, has created Japan, Inc. The special magic these men wield is the power of the human decision-making process at its best. Above the TDK organizational chart are these words from the managing directors:

The management is as a compass, pointing the way for the company. Most important, however, are human resources and a flexible management and organization which allow individual creativity to prosper.

It is decision making that points the way. You will find here the FW required to be an effective decision maker in your total world.

Background for Decision. "When it comes to decision making in business or private life, being well informed is a necessity. There are many times when a piece of information unconnected with what one is doing at the moment proves useful." Mr. Sono believes strongly in education and he has organized reading circles in TDK to encourage his employees to make learning a lifetime pursuit. Yet his view of what makes a well-educated decision maker is not the traditional one. "While I was working at Kanebo [a large Japanese conglomerate], I took a good long look at all the mistakes they were making. In my opinion, one of the major mistakes is that they were taking only graduates of one particular private university called Keio. Only if you were out of Keio could you become anybody within Kanebo. But we do not hire people because they are graduates of a particular university. We disregard that. I believe strongly in educating company employees after they have joined the company, rather than depending on the sort of school they have been to." Again Mr. Sono writes some characters on the board, this time from *The Analects* of Confucius.

Confucious said, "Those who are born with knowledge are the highest. Next come those who attain knowledge through study. Next again come those who turn to study after having been vexed by difficulties. The common people, insofar as they make no effort to study even after having been vexed by difficulties, are the lowest."

"Most people belong to the middle two categories. They are the people who become educated." This book is especially directed toward those in the third category. It provides the means to educate yourself. The more conscious you are of your alternatives, and the more willing you become to make choices, the more freedom you will possess.

Green Tea. Given the preeminence of the human factor in the decision-making process, it is clearly self-destructive to conduct human affairs in an atmosphere of distrust and confrontation. J. R. Ewing is fortunate that there is no oil to be drilled in Tokyo. To function in the Japanese system he would have to adopt a new attitude of supportive cooperation with employees, respect for and loyalty to suppliers, and consideration for his competitors. Decisions would be based on their overall fairness and their long-term implications. J. R. would become impatient with the Japanese practice of consuming endless cups of green tea during meetings in the executive suite. One employee told me that cup washing is done on a rotating basis, and when her turn comes, she washes cups a good part of the day and often far past quitting time. The tea serves to humanize the business world and helps create an atmosphere in which people can work hard at listening to and sharing with others. It is a concept that bears adoption in private life too. In every context, the humanizing of transactions through an added touch of civility enhances communication, promotes the inclination to consider the position of others, and encourages fair play. Sharing green tea or its equivalent in your own life will help discourage the formation of adversary relationships, which are counterproductive in business and in friendship.

Ringi. Consensus decision making has the dual advantage of adding the experiences and decision-making power of others to your efforts and taking the weight of making lone decisions off your shoulders. One of the tasks taken most seriously by Japanese chief executives is personnel selection at the top levels. Once good choices about key people are made, a large portion of the decision-making responsibility can be shared. This is a tool, not a weakness, and it is especially appropriate when others too will be affected by the choices made. Mr. Sono is aware that it is not only management that has the capacity for good judgment. He is, therefore, in a position to learn from many GITs. The message of this book too is that wisdom is present in the people around you and that you must simply take it. Everyone has FW to share. Applied correctly, this FW will often make decision making easier. Mr. Sono said, "I think we come back to the idea of human relations. If you have three years in front of you and you can go to school and study, or else within the three years you can meet three exceptional people, you will learn much more from these three people."

The President Sono Rose. The Japanese practice of hiring an employee for life is a reflection of the obvious decision to begin with good basic resources—whether people or materials. This philosophy has a major impact on the decisions that are made. Mr. Sono and I were discussing this when an aide brought in the latest issue of a Japanese business magazine. It ranked the companies by growth on the Tokyo Stock Exchange, where, I have already mentioned, TDK heads the list. Mr. Sono pointed to the bottom of the list, where the last position was occupied by Kanebo, Ltd. He began his business career with the Kanebo conglomerate in 1931 but in an unusual move switched to TDK six years later. He took no particular delight in the fact that Kanebo was last, but he was able to draw a lesson from it. "There is a very basic truth that in whatever you make, if your basic materials are not the best, then the finished material will not be the best. While I was working with Kanebo I was a salesman, and one of the things I went around the country trying to sell was embroidery thread. The biggest company manufacturing this was, and still is, in France. Kanebo was simply never able to get anywhere near that company. Our thread always lost its twist when stitched, wrinkling the fabric. They ended up by dropping this side of the business. I then did some research and found that the French company was having the cotton, which was the basis of the thread, specially processed and grown in Egypt and was sure of getting the very best quality materials to make the finished product. Kanebo was just buying from wherever it could buy. It is the same thing with a rose. If you don't have a good basic strain you won't get a good rose." Mr. Sono walked around the table and handed me a postcard. On the face of the card was a single, beautiful pale yellow rose. Printed along the bottom of the card was, "1977 President Sono." He said with pride, "It has been registered in the United States as a new variety." Mr. Sono's hobby as a rose fancier and his business philosophy consistently reflect the practice of basing decisions on the view of quality over the long term.

Nemawashi. In Japanese-style decision making, rash judgments are never made. The process of decision making is paced by the term *nemawashi.* *Nemawashi* refers to the binding of the roots of the rice plant, a step the Japanese farmer carefully follows when replanting the seedlings. The agrarian wisdom of hundreds of years has not been lost during Japan's emergence as an industrial power. *Nemawashi* in decision making describes the care taken in gathering data, seeking counsel, and objectively weighing various alternatives before making a decision. Mr. Sono said, "Good *nemawashi* often turns meetings into mere formalities. It entails obtaining the approval of all participants before the actual meeting through sounding out people, exchanging ideas and putting one's case forward." In this manner, using patience and the attention to detail, decision making is raised to an art. This is consistent with the Japanese practice of endowing the most mundane of conventions with flashes of art. The humblest purchase is always beautifully and carefully wrapped by shopkeepers. Routine food preparation does not exist. Even when I ordered what was listed as an "American club sandwich" on the hotel coffee shop menu, it bore the Japanese stamp. The added ingredient in the artful arrangement of the food by color and texture made even this sandwich special. If each step is followed with care, decision making can become enjoyable as well as effective: an exercise in art.

Mistakes. Very often, behind the tendency to procrastinate lies the preoccupation with mistakes. "In running TDK I have not made any major mistakes, but there have been occasions where a decision was timed badly. In *The Analects* of Confucius you will find these words: 'When you make a mistake, do not be afraid of mending your ways.' This means that when one realizes he has made a mistake, he should simply strive to correct it so as not to make the same mistake twice. There is no need to worry about the loss of face or prestige." In this book you will find this FW expressed by many of the GITs. The ability to learn from mistakes, rather than to become upset by them, is basic to many areas of coping. It is only in the example of the Japanese, however, that I located such a large group of people unanimous in their lack of concern with attaching negative conseqences to mistakes.

Shu, Ha, Ri. On the cover of Mr. Sono's book, a collection of topics given to employees, there are three characters, *shu, ha,* and *ri.* They represent Mr. Sono's view of progress in the growth of a human being. These three stages encapsulate the FW behind functioning as a master decision maker. *Shu* means training and discipline. "The first stage," Mr. Sono explained, "if you think of many of the traditional Japanese art forms, requires that you listen to or look at the teacher doing something and you imitate. You do not get philosophical. You are half-parrot and half-slave. This is how one masters the basics of anything. But realizing full potential goes beyond the scope of *shu* into the realm of *ha,* which means breaking away. *Ha* is where we find creativity. Once you have the basics in your head, this is the stage where the individual comes out. In *ha,* the teacher will be surpassed by the pupil. Finally there is *ri,* the realm of detachment. This is the stage where you become free from outside pressures. You do things in the purest form. Rather than surpassing your teacher, you surpass yourself." But Mr. Sono noted that the final stage of *ri* is a fleeting one. Life is a continuous growth process. During our lives we find ourselves continuously making our way up the ladder of *shu, ha,* and *ri.*

The hallmark of a maximally effective decision maker is *ri.* You will recall the realm of *ri* in your own decision making when you think of the times and the situations in which you have functioned best. These are the golden moments when the musician and his instrument become one. You can reach for virtuosity in decision making when you stop viewing decision making as something you must do to rid yourself of an unwelcome burden. As you develop your skill at decision making, your choices will much less frequently feel like chores and your performance will more closely approach art.

Procrastination. Have you developed the practice of avoiding decisions, perhaps even the simplest ones? If so, the serious intention to immediately begin to make choices as they present themselves will be enormously therapeutic. Procrastination only postpones the inevitable, often at great cost to you. Delays frequently complicate situations. But even if the cost is only in the increased tension that is produced by avoiding decisions, why accept it? The need to make decisions does not upset our GIT. He exudes an eagerness to grapple with them. The mental image of this smiling septuagenarian hustling from one problem-solving group to another with obvious relish is a demonstration of the vitality that coping with decisions brings. Mr. Sono told me that making choices produces a feeling of freedom. In truth, exercising choices is the definition of freedom. The only way to be a decision maker, as that Western sage Yogi Berra might say, is to make decisions.

Robert. One frustrating behavior of the Japanese, when speaking English with foreigners, is to smile and nod and communicate their understanding, whether they are comprehending what is being said or not. On the train ride to Chikumagawa, located in Komoro near the Japanese alps, I was very eager to learn of the extent of robotization in the plant that we were traveling to visit. Several times I mentioned my interest in the robot to my guide, a TDK junior executive, and each time he expressed his understanding in a noncommittal way. Finally I asked him directly about the presence of robots at the plant. "But we don't have any Japanese named 'Robert,'" he said, suddenly expressing his consternation about who this Robert was that I was so interested in meeting in Komoro. In fact, Japanese industry is quite heavily roboticized. I viewed long production lines headed by robots that travel on overhead tracks to computer-identified locations in the warehouse to retrieve needed materials. In one such line, "pancakes," or large spools of tape, are measured and cut into the desired lengths; a cassette is built around them, and they are wrapped, boxed, and shipped. The only humans involved were a young girl who patrolled the line doing small tasks at one machine or another, and another girl at the end doing quality-control inspections. Although such operations continue almost effortlessly, twenty-four hours each day, the human worker is in no danger of being replaced. In the TDK company guide, the following words are given prominence.

TDK believes that people should perform the work best performed by people, and that machines should do the work best done by machines.

What humans do best, of course, is reason. They are able to make creative decisions, an impossible task for the most advanced computer-directed robot. TDK is particularly strong in the degree to which it reveres the human factor. The reason lies in the origin of the company itself. Whereas the majority of Japanese companies were formed around patents purchased from their Western innovators, TDK was formed in 1935 to produce ferrite, invented in 1933 by Dr. Yogoro Kato and Dr. Takeo Takei. Ferrite is a Japanese innovation that is the basic ingredient in the coating of most tapes, as well as in ferrite magnets, coil components, and numerous other industrial products. If you have not been functioning as a decision maker, you have been denying one of the premier qualities that separate man from the machine. Using the decision-making FW that Mr. Sono highlights as responsible for the TDK success story will enable you to write your own success story. This requires only that you develop the decision-making *tao*, or way.

8 / Abbie Hoffman

USING ANGER

Anger's my meat; I sup upon myself,
and so shall starve with feeding.

"Coriolanus"

FUNDAMENTAL PROBLEM

Anger is an emotion. It flows from the righteous rejection of a situation or a behavior. It is a strong emotion and it is associated with intense displeasure. The word evokes the scent of rage and the potential for violence. Anger is often viewed as uncivilized and even sinful. We commonly disguise its presence by using euphemisms such as *resentment*. For some, it is easier to admit to feeling "disturbed" or "put out" than angry. People go to great lengths to deny the existence of anger as evidenced in the following actual exchange I had with a client in my office.

Me: "Do you think your husband is being unreasonable in his demand that you be home every day at noon to fix his lunch?"
Patient: "I do. It's the last straw. His taking me for granted has made me so desperate that I may divorce him."
Me: "You feel a great deal of anger at his feigned helplessness and lack of consideration."
Patient: "I've given up trying to change him. He is insensitive to my feelings and treats me like hired help. I truly feel that divorce may be the

only solution. But I won't say I'm angry."

Me: "You are not angry? You simply resent him?"

Patient: "That's it. I resent this in him so much I could kill him!"

Anger, then, is not in itself a problem. It is a legitimate emotional reaction. A Fundamental Problem occurs only when anger is handled ineptly. But it is not easy to find out what the healthy use of anger is. Our vocabulary is filled with unflattering descriptions of those who express their anger: "grouch," "malcontent," "rude," and "unfeminine." Anger's most commonly heard synonym, *mad*, is also used to describe rabid dogs and the insane. But significantly, the English language is conspicuous in its lack of words to describe those who possess the Fundamental Wisdom to avoid both bottling up anger and the equally unhealthy opposite extreme of expressing this emotion in self-destructive outbursts.

There are those who proudly proclaim that they never get angry. One might as well brag about constipation. What you really mean, if you are experiencing this side of the FP, is not that you never *get* angry, but that you never *express* anger. This behavior is learned and if it describes you, you have been effectively trained, probably under the guise of "good manners," to feel guilty regarding the existence of anger within yourself. Freud was among the first to describe the psychological devastation caused by blocking the healthy expression of anger. He described a process in which unexpressed anger is turned inward to produce hostility, self-hate, and even suicidal behavior. The professional mental-health literature is saturated with all manner of physical manifestations ranging from rashes to heart failure that can be shown to be directly attributable to the effects of buried anger.

The expression of anger also carries its dangers. If expressed incorrectly, it is equal to nonexpression in its role as an FP. The hazard is in expressing anger in a manner that ultimately tears down your view of yourself. Very often this takes the form of an interaction that is demeaning to others. This may be done quite directly with words such as "I hate you" or "You are an idiot!" Or it may be done more passively, as in the case of the woman who exclaims to her dinner guests, "Harry's golf drives me crazy." And then, *sotto voce* through clenched teeth and a tight smile, "Well, that's married life, isn't it, dear?" For all her subtlety, she might just as well hit him with a fire axe.

The Great Inspiring Teacher for the chapter on anger is the activist Abbie Hoffman. He was one of the Chicago Seven, defendants in a trial that resulted from the confrontation between the club-wielding Chicago police and the demonstrators, housewives, delegates, newsmen, and anyone else in the way at the 1968 Democratic National Convention. Said Abbie, "I think if anything remains of that era now, the first legacy is that you can stand up and fight city hall. That you can protest. We didn't have that when we entered the sixties. The fifties was just 'You can't fight city hall. You can't *win*. *They* have it all.' You had no examples to turn to in the history of the United States."

ABBIE HOFFMAN

Great Inspiring Teacher
Measured strictly in distance, the Veritas drug rehabilitation center is only about six blocks west of Manhattan's fashionable Fifth Avenue. In human terms it is much farther. Abbie reaches Veritas on the A train from the Lincoln Center Correctional Center to spend his day working with addicts, his job on the work release program. This is the infamous Hell's Kitchen area, the same streets where my own grandparents married and my mother was born more than sixty years ago. It was a rough neighborhood even then.

The sign outside the door is all that distinguishes Veritas from the other tenements. It is a small wooden rectangle framing a metal plaque thanking some groups for assistance in a landscape project. But with the cement sidewalk running up to the front door and the fire-escape-covered brick walls, without a square inch of soil in sight, it is difficult to imagine what possible contribution a landscaping program could have made.

I was waiting for him before our first meeting when Abbie phoned ahead to tell me he was caught in traffic. He was returning from a weekend furlough from prison. Only weeknights are spent in the overcrowded minimum-security lock-up with its mandatory urine tests to screen for drugs. I waited on the single torn chair next to the wax fruit on the scratched old table that served as a reception desk and watched the flow of the twenty-eight residents. Nine of them were female, and several had toddlers who seemed to enjoy the loving attention they received from everyone. The house regulations were posted over my chair: fifty-three rules on four pages. "Wake up at 7 A.M.; clean bathrooms daily; etc." There was also posted an elaborately drawn administrative hierarchy, the chain of command. It was headed by the name of the executive director, followed by those of the deputy clinical director, program coordinator, director of community outreach, deputy administrative director, and on and on. Finally I came to Abbie, misspelled "Abby," who was billed simply as "counselor." Only one person was lower on the chart, a girl with the all-purpose title of "assistant."

My observations were interrupted when Abbie came hurrying through the doorway. He raced by, giving me a hit on the shoulder as a greeting, and started up the stairs of the old house, taking them two at a time, yelling, "Frank's here." He shouted out instructions to hold his calls, but this was hardly necessary because he promptly reached under the desk and uncoupled the phone wire.

Abbie Hoffman, co-founder of the "Don't trust anyone over thirty" yippies, is forty-six now and bearded. The proponent of such slogans as "Kill your parents" quickly confided to me that he is concerned about the quality of the education his daughter is getting at college. Abbie was arrested in 1973 for the sale of cocaine. He was convicted and sentenced to serve from one to three years in jail. Rather than go to prison he jumped bail in 1974 and lived life underground as a fugitive. He had plastic surgery, straightened his hair, and assumed numerous identities to avoid capture. But just before turning himself over to the authorities in 1980, he used the alias of Barry Freed and led a successful battle as a conservationist in the small upstate New York town of Fineview, to stop winter navigation on the St. Lawrence River.

I did not know Abbie Hoffman during the turmoil of the 1960s. Yet from what I remember about him then and what I see in him now, I doubt whether the twenty-year interval has changed the basic Abbie. He told me, "You're not going to read this in the papers. No one is going to describe me this way in the mass media. I mean here I sit, a convict, a person who is identified as some kind of a hippie clown. But I am an organizer. That's what I see myself as. I organize communities and bring power to them. I suppose that is what revolution is."

Abbie's words are often fiery. As you read them, take care that you do not misread Abbie Hoffman. Abbie is quick to see the absurdity in life. No matter how passionate he feels about an issue he is discussing, he will always see the funny side of it and will invariably begin laughing at the silliness of the real world. Abbie once wrote that he believed the reason he and yippie co-founder Jerry Rubin made such an effective and enduring partnership was that Rubin's forcefulness and political instincts were softened and made palatable by Hoffman's silliness and appeal to the spirit. "One of the worst mistakes any revolution can make," he said, "is to become boring."

I asked him about this in terms of his role as a GIT. "I am spotlighting you in my chapter on anger, and you are about the happiest guy I know."

Naturally, he laughed. "And I'm in jail." Now he laughed twice as hard. "Well, I have learned to use jail as a positive experience in the last few weeks. It took me a long time. But now it's where I go to get away from the phone. People can't reach me and it makes a good excuse. I say, 'Well, I can't do that. I'm in jail.' Nobody argues. It's terrific. Only being dead would work as well. I mean I can really get away. But yes, I'm happy."

"I want to show the reader that using anger constructively yet being happy are not contradictory. Turning anger on and off has the sound of not being genuine."

"But what's the alternative? Having it there all the time? I mean, shit," he said, laughing again, "your muscles are so tense, your teeth are drawn, your face is boiling. You just can't lie down and go to bed. What are you going to do?"

As you read Abbie's comments you can experience them accurately and fully by being aware of his attitude, a kind of delight in the outrageousness of it all. I will give you his final words now too; they came after the tape was turned off for the last time: "You know, there is one more thing I wanted to say about anger. You always need to have the attitude that you will be making up with these people at some time in the future." When attempting to express anger constructively, remembering those words will enable you to maintain your perspective.

Abbie and I began by talking about the 1960s. I said, "My view of the sixties activism is that it was youth's collective expression of anger toward what America was becoming. Is that how you see it?"

"Yes, but anger follows disappointment. It followed this great stage of disappointment where you're taught this great mythology of justice for all and freedom and equality. And slowly you start to challenge the powers that be and you try to actually change the system along those principles. And you get a rude awakening that the mythology is quite separate from the reality. So that kind of gap is at first disappointing, it's then frustrating, and then you start to get angry.

"In something like the Vietnam War where you'd had endless carnage, where the war was dragging on and on, and where you, at a pretty early stage of the game, saw that the country had gone the wrong way, you start to oppose it. You start to oppose it with legal methods and then you see that society uses all of its techniques to isolate dissent. You know, it's not popular to oppose your government at a time of war. It's never been a popular pursuit. I mean our image of the Vietnam War struggle is that it was extremely popular with loads of people and congressmen yelling. But in 1963 and 1964, I can assure you, this was not a popular pursuit at all. And then, as you get stronger, society gets more and more oppressive. So there is always a rude awakening that I suppose leads to anger. But for anger to be effective, to be a catalyst for change, it must be organized."

"So effective anger is controlled anger."

"You have to learn to control the anger. You turn anger on and off. I mean I can use it as a theatrical device where it is almost completely faked because I think it is the right thing to show. Not completely, because I'm not an actor. People think I'm an actor. Actors come in and they study me all the time, but it's not acting if you are challenging the system. If you say that you think in your head you see some kind of direction that would make things better, there is anger involved. There is arrogance. Just by definition, you think you know a better way. The whole world's wrong and you're right. My father was always admonishing me with clichés. He'd always say, 'The whole world's wrong and you're right.' But I believed him then and I believe it today."

"I notice that people get angry about issues after the fact. People are angry about the Indians, 100 years too late. The country is fairly united in its sentiment against Vietnam, twenty years late, and it is currently fashionable to be liberal on civil rights. Do you notice this delayed anger?"

"Yes. Again we're talking about mythology. This is the story of Chicago. Chicago has become an event. People say they were in Chicago. They don't mean the city anymore, they mean the experience. So I'll bet I've met 80,000 people who were in Chicago, in that sense, demonstrating. And I'm telling you there were six or seven thousand people there. I don't tell them, 'You weren't there. I was there and you weren't.' I say, 'Right. I saw you. Sure you were there.'

"But I agree with *Mother Jones* [magazine] that you pray for the dead and fight for the living. I'm fond of saying that if you ask my mother she would tell you that my politics haven't changed since I was four years old. Although I hope there's a growth pattern, there's some consistency in reacting toward injustice. My picture of myself when I was six, seven, eight years old in school, is of this skinny little kid who took on the bully in the schoolyard and more often than not got beat up. But he put up a good scrap. That was my role."

"Where did you get that idea? You have written that your father always told you to behave; the day before your Chicago trial you got a letter from him telling you to watch your manners."

"I don't know where I got that idea. I could be short-changing him in terms of those years. If you grow up a minority-group member—we were a Jewish family in an Irish enclave—you're chased down the street. You are under attack for being different. And I guess how you come to terms with that is the difference between myself and a lot of my classmates who came out of Brandeis University and are good, stable Republicans."

"You came to terms with it by holding your ground?"

"I think I did, yes. I think I want to hold my ground. I mean I'm proud that I took that route. I'm not the most modest person. I don't respect a certain kind of WASP modesty because I don't think it's true. I mean if people are intelligent they have some self-awareness of their moment on the human stage. I'm proud when I stand and fight for the river as a fugitive, and it would be very easy and very understandable to everyone but myself to go another route."

"You had been underground almost seven years and avoided detection. Yet you couldn't let this cause pass without taking a stand."

"It was probably my most critical decision. They came along and said the Army Corps of Engineers is coming and this is what they're going to do. The farmers are telling me this, the river rats. They said, 'Barry, you're a smart boy. Would you read this little report? We think that there's something going on that ain't right in this report.' And I go up and I read the thing and I said, 'Holy shit.' This means the fucking dock that I just built and I'm real proud of, you know. I mean manual labor! On a river! For a Jew! Not since Noah have we done that. That was a great fucking dock. All of a sudden it's going to be blown away because U.S. Steel out there in Duluth, Minnesota, or someplace wants to do more business? They're going to ruin the whole river and all these islands? All this incredible way of life? The rugged individualism of the American pioneers and everything? Well, fuck that."

"That sounds like a very unlikely choice for someone hiding out."

"Yeah. I'm going to stick out like a sore thumb. I mean I didn't really have a last name up until that point. I'd been there since 1976, two and a half years, and I was just Joanna's friend Barry. 'Beery.' They talk like that. We evolved right there on the spot: Mr. and Mrs. Barry Freed. I thought I was sealing my fate. I said, 'What the hell. I'll take a shot, play it as close as I can, and go as far as I can.' "

"Going underground to avoid going to jail appears to be the exact opposite of constructively channeling your anger. It seems out of character for you."

"Well, the options get dramatically reduced when you are a fugitive or a prisoner."

"Taking yourself out of the ballgame like that made you mentally sick, didn't it?"

"Yes. I did something I never thought possible. I cracked up."

"Because you were biting the bullet instead of dealing with life?"

"Yes. There were scenes. We were in Mexico and I was driving the car and we came across an accident. There was a kid lying in the road, obviously with a broken leg, who had been hit by a car. And the police were lifting him when they shouldn't have been moving him. I knew enough about first aid to play a role. But that was in the early stage in my fugitive career, and even the Mexican police were very dangerous and threatening to me. I drove by and I got two miles down the road and I pulled off. I was vibrating. My whole body was shaking and I couldn't drive the car. I was pounding the wheel. And I said to my girlfriend, 'Don't ever let me do that again.' And I've never walked away since.

"I am a person who believes you bring a certain amount of will to the situation. But at that particular moment it just seemed that I didn't have any choice in what I was doing in life. I mean I would get physically sick if I was faced with a scene that I knew was unjust and I did not act. Now, this doesn't mean that I might not see it and I might not say, 'Well, I'm working on this' or 'I'm working on that.' It's a general direction that you are going. And it's not a question of my way being the stronger way. It's a gambler's decision. It is an educated gambling decision. What's going to pay off at the end of the rainbow? What's going to pay off now? What's going to pay off tomorrow?"

"What do you mean it's not the strongest?"

"Well, people look at me and they say, 'You're inspirational.' 'You're a hero.' "

"They also say that you are one of the most dangerous men alive."

This last idea made Abbie hysterical with laughter, and it was another minute before he could get any words out. "Who says that? Dangerous to what? To what?"

"To the establishment."

"Well, if it's the establishment . . . I mean I think of myself as an American dissident. Like I said, you're not going to pick up a newspaper and see Abbie Hoffman called a community organizer. You're going to see something else. You're not going to see 'dissident' because we don't have dissidents. Only the Russians have them. I'm a dissident. If the established authority is operating in an unjust, immoral direction I *should* become dangerous. There should be a lot of people that are dangerous."

"For the readers who may tend to think, 'I'm no Abbie Hoffman,' your statement that constructively expressing anger does not require that you be exceptionally strong is extremely important."

"It is the idea that you don't have to sell out every time. Every time you make a decision that is against your moral grain, in the existential sense—I'm not talking about what the church or society teaches you, I'm saying what you believe in your heart—when you go against that, you die. You die a little at a time. You become a little more hollow and you're going to get an ulcer or a cancer or something like that. So it is not a question of courage or strength or bravery or any of these other things. This is the road to health. This is the psychological road to health that I'm trying to take.

"The Jews that I've admired have been the ones that have gone for broke. They haven't been the ones that have assimilated that quickly into the upper-middle-class society of whatever country they ended up in. Those assimilationists, the people that take the government at its word, the 'good Americans' in the false sense, have some inner anxiety. Some inner dread there that erupts in anger that is unproductive."

"Do you see the ability to express anger constructively as the key FW here?"

"Yes. I asked Allen Ginsberg about that recently because I heard his poem 'Howl.' He read it at its twenty-fifth anniversary. I first heard it in 1959 in North Beach, where he had written it. I was a graduate student in psychology at Berkeley getting socially conscious. And in getting socially conscious, one of my petty angers was why was I so well educated and didn't know? I wasn't taught the darker side of American society: the lynchings, the Sacco-Vanzettis, the Rosenbergs, the Depression even. All this was hidden from me. I got A's in history, but I studied some other person's history. So at that moment in San Francisco the beatniks were attractive and I heard him read the poem and I got the record and I still consider it the great poem of our time: the real epic. And he was reading it at its twenty-fifth anniversary and although the imagery was all accurate, 'I saw the best minds of my generation gone down the drain . . .,' and all the great images of 'Howl,' I felt that his rage was gone. So I asked him later. I said, 'Do you see any value to rage?' And he said, 'Yes, I do.' And he quoted me something from William Blake, that there is a value to rage."

"And as an activist taking on a cause, you focus your rage on bringing about change?"

"Yes. And when I enjoin myself to a struggle, as I told members of the Salvadorian Front the other day, I don't lose. In that sense I'm an American. I play the game as hard as I can, and I play it to win. And the battles that I've chosen to fight have been successful. I don't waste energy. I speak at the colleges and hear somebody say, 'The great famine is sweeping the world. We have to feed it.' Or 'What are you going to do about the poisoning of the planet?' They pick battles to fight that are impossible to win. That only leads one to great disillusionment. To a sense of being burned out because you can't do anything about hunger in the world or the coming nuclear bomb."

"How does a person who is sensitive to the injustices in the world keep from being burned out?"

"I set my goals on the edge of utopia. They're not dead center. I consider myself a pragmatist. If there is any 'ism' I have, it is pragmatism. Right now I am organizing liberals. Here I was organizing addicts. In the civil rights movements it was sharecroppers in the South and ghetto kids. Where I work on the river it's rural conservatives. It is people who sense they have no power in this society. There are so many different groups of people in different categories.

"I was quite shocked when I went to upstate New York and I'm living as another person along the St. Lawrence River. That is as far south as you can get, I'm fond of saying. You know, the last Republican they didn't vote for was probably Lincoln. These are the real Americans. These are 100 percent WASPS. They *are* the rugged individualism. The only one-room schoolhouse in the East is there. I mean this is what America is. And these people feel they are not part of what's going on out there; the sense of victimization. The Army Corps of Engineers is coming along and is going to destroy their river. Thirty-two communities and a whole way of life. And either they've got the attitude that there is nothing they can do about it or that it is never going to happen. Either it is inevitable or it's never going to happen. And a lot of people manage to have those same views simultaneously. But the whole attitude is one of separation with the body politic, with the decision making. I've seen it in the black ghettos. I've seen it in the young people who had to go off and fight in Vietnam. People said go and fight and you had to go and fight.

"But this is the secret of community organizing: when people who have no power all of a sudden get power. If there are large numbers of people, well, then, the government is out. Right now it is strange because it is liberals, in quotes. Because there is no opposition, really. There is no organized opposition to Reagan and his policy in El Salvador. So here I sit, a convict, forming a committee. And we've got the president of Notre Dame on the committee, the biggest rabbi in the country, the first bishop from New York, a congressman and a Nobel prizewinner. We've got support from the street right up to the Senate."

"When you are paroled in March of 1982 will you be putting your energies into El Salvador?"

"Yes. I've got two main causes: the river and El Salvador. In fact they did a docudrama about me on PBS about a month ago. And in the [New York] *Daily News*, which really doesn't like me from my last "movie" [Chicago], the headline of the review was, 'If you've got the cause, he's got the time.' They had sort of given it a little jingle like Miller Lite." Abbie sings a few bars, "If you've got the cause, he's got the time."

"Meaning that you are a professional troublemaker?"

"Well, that I needed a cause. That I was addicted to trouble-making in some way. But what struck me was that it wasn't a bad thing, you see You can read it positive. I try not to let the critics get me down so I try to put things in a positive way. I choose my causes very carefully. And my primary cause will be working to reverse U.S. policy toward Latin America, and Central America in particular. I'm ideally suited to that. I speak the language. I've been down there and seen the thing on a visceral level. And I have my experience from the Vietnam years. The role I play in this society is ideally suited right now to bringing together opposition to the Reagan–Haig policy."*

"Presently such an organization does not exist?"

"Right. And my best thing is to set up new organizations. And ones that last, by the way. You go back to my home-town ghetto, and none of this story is ever told in the daily newspapers of course, to the community organizing structures that I set up seventeen, eighteen years ago. Community centers and things like that. They're still there. The yippies are still there, the Liberty House and the Poor Peoples Cooperative. That whole structure that I worked on down in the South, to some extent, is still there. And Save the River, and CLARO, the two organizations that I support financially."

"Is CLARO the El Salvador group?"

*Alexander M. Haig was secretary of state at the time of this interview.

"Yes. Central Latin American Relief Organization. The word *claro* means 'I believe,' 'clearly,' 'yippie!' It is the Spanish translation for yippie!"

"From what you have said, I would imagine you would have difficulty accepting pacifism, the passive or non-violent route to expressing anger?"

"Well, if you ask me if I'm a pacifist, I say no, because I reject all 'isms.' But I have to look at the people fighting in El Salvador. They are certainly using what I would call revolutionary violence. They are using defensive violence. They do not have the notion that peace is the primary objective, but rather justice. I think that is really what separates reactionaries from revolutionaries in my mind. Reactionaries want peace at any cost. Revolutionaries want justice at any cost. Those tendencies conflict. It is no wonder the United States has sixteen or seventeen holidays for peace and nothing for justice. When you are on top you always want peace. When the lion eats the lamb there is peace. I am sure there is a lot of peace in Chile today."

"So you are a believer that even the violent expression of anger, under the appropriate circumstances, can be constructive, healthy, and justified?"

"Again, it's a judgment call. Does an armed struggle apply to the United States? Obviously you had people like Thomas Jefferson and Abraham Lincoln not ruling it out. Lincoln's words were that when the government becomes so removed from the people, the people must exert their revolutionary right to dismember and overthrow the government. That's Abraham Lincoln. It's not Ho Chi Minh or Che Guevara. This is how Thomas Jefferson talked. In other words, all the rights that we have, all our constitutional rights, are all correct. But if those are removed, what's someone like me supposed to do? Just say, 'Well, okay, that's nice,' and put on a suit and tie and go get a job as an insurance salesman and forget about all those ideas I grew up with about justice for all?"

"Violently expressing anger is justified when there is no other way to make necessary changes?"

"Yes. I think when your options get severely limited. If I were a Salvadorian, well, I don't have the same options that I have here. You take this person and stick him in El Salvador right now and you would see me with a gun in one hand and a grenade in the other. You'd see me marshaling troops and attacking bridges. The justification for violence is the lack of politics. When politics breaks down you have war. When the interaction between humans cannot be solved through communication, then there is a breakdown and there is violence. Obviously we always have the option of picking up a rock and hitting each other over the fucking head. I mean we've had that option for probably 150,000 years or a million years."

"Is this the reasoning that led to the 'trashing' in the streets?"

"Trashing in the streets was necessary at that particular moment in the sixties—I knew you were going to get to that—because I think the history of the opposition to the Vietnam War shows that our options were being closed down. The pivotal historical moment for me is 1968, the demonstrations in the streets of Chicago. Now I'd been an organizer about six or seven years then in various movements in the South, in my home town, and in New York City. And I had begun to really get an understanding of the distance between mythology and reality in American society. And how one went about organizing and moving things. I had the notion that it was stupid to even talk about a belief in free speech unless you actually did it. I mean all these people running around yelling what a terrific thing freedom is but when it comes to exerting it they get a little icky. You know it gets a little sticky. 'Oh that. But that's in the streets and everything. Ugh, how uncivilized.' It's against everything you're taught in the suburbs."

"It is not polite."

"Yeah, right. It's a study in manners, really. We're talking about how manners are used as a controlling mechanism for meaningful change in a society. So we come to Chicago. A critical moment. We have to make a demonstration against the war in Vietnam. You have to go to political conventions. This is where the power brokers all gather. This is where the decisions are made that are going to affect the country for years to come. I had been to the 1964 convention working for the Mississippi Freedom Democratic Party challenging racism and the fact that there was an all-white delegation from a state that had 48 percent black people. So I already understood that this was something we had to do.

"Okay, so you see we are enjoined with the body politic. There are forces that have to move. So we go to Chicago and the city will not give us a permit. These are our rights to assemble and protest. Why can't we be here? Why can't we stay in the park? This is ten miles away from the convention halls. Most Americans, if you ask them what happened, they'll say that there were fifty or a hundred thousand people there and that they were banging on the doors of the convention halls. We never got within eight miles and there were never more than six or seven thousand people.

"Now here we have this event, you see, and this is a rather rude awakening. My God, you just can't go get a permit and get a lot of people together. The option of mass demonstration at crucial points and places in the American political process was squashed by Mayor [Richard J.] Daley and what the official government report called 'a police riot.' You can't rely on the constitutional rights that you have of freedom of speech and assembly. Meanwhile Nixon was closing down other options right and left. You say, 'Oh, my apartment got burglarized. So what, it's two fucking junkies.' And then you wonder. How come my Rolodex is missing? What the fuck do junkies want with all my addresses? Why do they want lists of people who are sending money to our organization? Hey, you know, something weird is going on that hasn't been going on before. You have to organize in a clandestine way because the government is sending infiltrators and informants to disrupt. Underground organizations had to begin thinking in terms of more militant armed struggle because the ability to organize among the masses was being curtailed. So to me, that was justified."

"When does the expression of anger, violent or otherwise, become destructive?"

"Well, in that same phase I was somewhat critical of certain actions. The Days of Rage, a title which I actually came up with."

"Because that was violence directed against the average guy rather than the power structure?"

"Yes, it was self-defeating. I didn't much like their [the Weather Underground's] philosophy, white skin privilege, their rush to be martyrs, to sacrifice themselves for the Third World. A lot of that was self-hatred. But in terms of strategy they attacked symbols essentially: the Pentagon, Congress. On that level I thought that it was useful. But it quickly outgrew its usefulness. It degenerated into the cultism and factionalism that is very common on the Left. When people start running around correcting everyone else's vocabulary every two minutes, that's a bad sign."

"Are you saying, in the context of the self-hate you detected in the Weather Underground at that time, that expressing anger destructively is expressing it in a way that lowers your self-image?"

"Yes. Let's take for example Jack Henry Abbott, the [Norman] Mailer protégé. This is a situation I feel very close to. My legal name is also Abbott and I am a convict and a writer. Mailer wrote the introduction to my book as well as Abbott's. Abbott and I were supposed to have met right here in this office just a day and a half after the murder."

Abbott, a convicted murderer with a literary bent, caught the attention of Norman Mailer. Mailer spearheaded a successful drive for Abbott's release, hired him as a researcher, and arranged for the publication of Abbott's book *In the Belly of the Beast*. Six weeks after his parole, while drinking coffee in a restaurant, Abbott asked twenty-two-year-old restaurant employee Richard Adan for directions to the restroom. In what Abbott called a misunderstanding, he stabbed the unarmed Adan to death.

"Jack Henry Abbott is a perfect example of the destructive use of anger."

"We obviously chose to handle things extremely differently, although our situations were, at that particular moment, very close. I was the most controversial prisoner in the state. I had been given what looked like a sweetheart deal. I had a foot-high front-page headline saying 'ABBIE WALKS' and way up in the corner it says, 'The Pope Goes Home.' But I already had four months in jail and I was within eight months of release. So if you are within a year and it is a nonviolent crime and you don't have a history of felonies, you can apply to be in the work release program. So I applied like everybody else in that situation and I was accepted just like anybody else would be if they had the qualifications. But the newspapers screamed and they attacked the whole program. It was as if they didn't know it existed. Like it had been invented for me, I'm not kidding. They said, 'If he got on, we have to reexamine the whole program,' and reactionary legislators started to scream in Albany about abolishing it. It is a controversial program in and of itself—the idea that you're half in and half outside the prison.

"I had to have a job to get out. And the publicity was the biggest want ad anybody could have. I got about thirty-six offers. I could have made $100,000 a year, all that is allowed under the work release program, but I didn't want to work in a publishing company or an advertising agency. Money is really not a primary motive in my life. I wanted to take a job that reflected well on the work release program itself. I had the very awkward role of being forced to defend a hunk of the penal system in New York. So I did it with gusto. I took this job working with addicts. I'm getting $200 a week. I raised them lots of money, helped get them a new building, I do my job as a counselor and got them a lot of publicity. I wanted it to reflect well on the program, and it has. I have made a big contribution, and the parole board gave me a nice sendoff.

"And so you take responsibility for the situation you're in. Jack Henry Abbot is someone who gets on parole. He's getting a chance. He's a writer with skills and talents being recognized. And what does he do? He destroys that whole connection between himself and the others. Others who are going to follow him. Others whose cases are being examined right now, two of which I've been working on for a good many years, writers in prison that I'm trying to get out. He destroys that tie between himself and the community. It is something very easy to do for somebody who has been in prison for twenty-five years, because the whole point of prison is to destroy those bonds, unfortunately.

"So he kills someone. I was on a talk show and this guy was lambasting Mailer. He says, 'Well, look, you and I, we deal with our anger. We start yelling at each other and I don't agree with your politics. But we're not going to start pulling out knives and killing each other.' Well, again, clearly the answer is options. I mean how many options do you have when you're twenty-five years in an American prison: isolated, no friends, no family? You can't compare it to the guy on the radio. He's talking to three million people at a whack every day, you know. If he's angry at the bus driver, at the subway system, he's letting it go."

"To take another well-known example of anger erupting in violence, what would you say about Sirhan Sirhan [Robert Kennedy's assassin]?"

"Well, there is a middle ground between pacifism and Sirhan Sirhan. I'm not particularly convinced that was a political act. At some point psychoses play a role here."

"For the sake of discussion, let's assume that Sirhan Sirhan was just an angry guy who believed in what he did: who thought of his actions as a positive contribution."

"I can't separate the psychoses enough so that I can say, 'Well, yes, we can consider this some kind of meaningful act.' But I mean, it is possible. Certainly political assassination can play a disruptive and educational role. I suppose if I'd gotten close enough to Hitler that I could have done him in and changed the course of history, I certainly would have grabbed at the moment. But there aren't a hell of a lot of Hitlers in the sense that there is one human being who controls an entire system. You have to look at individuals, no matter what role they're playing, as a product of the system. So therefore, when you bump off someone, you get the second in charge. If you look at the entire panorama of history, the assassination of one person, although it's been disruptive and led to war and chaos, has not really led to a revolution. Because obviously the powers that be have someone that they can quickly zap into place. In fact, one of the techniques of staying in power is to have someone second in command who is much more brutal and repressive. So that people will always say, 'Well, if you get rid of him, you're going to get this other guy.' "

"They opt for the lesser of two evils."

"The evil of two lessers."

"Well put. When it comes to expressing anger constructively, what turns a person into a doer? Your occupational title is activist. How does the average guy overcome inertia and make the jump from sitting around complaining, to becoming an activist with a capital A?"

"We have to purge the European in us."

"Purge the intellectualizer in us?"

"Yes. You know, Dwight MacDonald, the political writer, once said to me, 'Whatever gave you people the idea that you had to act on what you believe in?' I mean, that is so unintellectual. But I think it was a compliment, actually. I think he had seen it all gone down in the parlor rooms [café society intellectuals philosophizing without acting on their convictions]. I think with me personally, it's my extremely American upbringing, in the sense that I was plugged into all the sports and games. The people on the field or on the court were having a better time than the spectators. So I just wanted to learn every kind of game and every kind of sport and play them all as best I could."

"Life is not a spectator sport?"

"Right. Of course there is a dual edge. When people ask me about the trial in Chicago—you know everyone is so fascinated with that and the techniques we used and the cultural clash that occurred in that courtroom—I say, 'Well, I had the best seat in the house.' I mean you get to watch too."

"You know, since I have been writing this book I have never been able to come up with a word for what we have been talking about. There is no word for the healthy expression of anger."

"Boy, that is interesting. What about 'outrage'?"

"Well, it still doesn't imply expression. You would have to say, 'I'm expressing outrage.' "

"Abbie."

"What?"

"Abbie. How's that? That would be neat, huh?"

"Coin a new word?"

"Yes. In twenty or thirty years that will be the word for the positive expression of anger. 'Oh, that's an abbie.' 'He's abbying.' Words are important, you know."

ABBYING

Fundamental Wisdom

The first time we sat down together, Abbie asked me about the other GITs in this book. He was very interested in each one I mentioned. Then he started discussing his own role in this book. "Is this book about overachievers or something?" he joked. "Is this interview going to be a profile or my own words?" He seemed pleased that it would be the latter, and I explained Fuller's concept of the GIT and the book's emphasis on healthy coping. "I'm a big advocate of doing it that way," he said. "I studied with Maslow. That's the way I'd like to do it because I want to see this come out good." The fact that psychology was Abbie's area of study in college, which explains his qualifications for the role as a drug counselor at Veritas, is rarely seen in print. Abbie studied with the noted psychologist Abraham Maslow and was befriended by him at Brandeis University. Maslow is most often identified with his "hierarchy of needs," a pyramid-shaped affair with food, shelter, and other survival needs forming the base and "self-actualization," Maslow's term for optimal coping, at the top. It was Maslow's view that each individual grows toward maximum development by fulfilling his or her needs at each step on the climb up the pyramid. It is an extremely positive view because it recognizes the human potential to grow by mastering healthy coping skills. The late Abraham Maslow's student Abbie Hoffman possesses the FW that will enable you to cope maximally in terms of dealing with your anger the healthy way.

Maverick. "Abbie, you have written that you were told the collective action springing from the anger of the young people in the sixties will be a symbol of freedom for a hundred years to come."

"Andre Glucksmann told me that, this *nouveau* philosopher in Paris, a possible successor to Jean-Paul Sartre. We were having a hard time finding a similar example in Western history where a people rose up against their government's war of imperialism and actually played a decisive role. Foreign wars are usually very popular sports. They're really gung ho, jingoistic, go get 'em, eat 'em up, it's good for the fatherland. So as far as democracy goes, this was a blow for freedom. It's very unusual for youth to almost regard itself as a class. Yet people want to resist. We are taught from our John Wayne movies, all the westerns, to be mavericks. *Maverick* is a good old American word. It comes from out of the West. It was Colonel Maverick, a Texan. In the border wars in the 1840s, I think, he refused to brand his cattle. The other ranchers were demanding branding. They wanted to control things. 'How are we going to know whose cows are whose cows?' So the maverick refers to an American tradition of rebellion against authority."

"Do you feel it is innate to fight for what is right?"

"I think everyone who is oppressed wants to resist. Whether they realize that consciously or unconsciously is the problem. People want to resist but they manifest it in different ways. There is an internal need the way Maslow talks about certain kinds of needs."

"You once said you believe children should be educated to disrespect authority or else democracy is a farce."

"Absolutely. I think that's fundamental. In one of the first demonstrations in my home town, in fact the first anti-war demonstration of the Vietnam era, maybe the first anti-war demonstration in Wooster's history, back in 1965, we lined up outside the courthouse. Two hundred of us. You look up on the courthouse and there is this slogan: 'Obedience to Law Is Liberty.' Well, I don't know what that means, because law is such a transient phenomenon. It's so dependent on who is on top and who's on the bottom. To accept the seven million laws that we have in the United States on all kinds of levels, *in toto*, as some kind of divine force, I think you've got yourself a real problem if you believe in democracy."

"You used to say you were working on breaking every one of them."

"Including the law of gravity. I think at middle age you pick and choose your laws."

"You can pay a big price for that. Even death. Most people don't want to go that far. That's why so many people in New Hampshire scratched the state's motto off their license tags: 'Live Free or Die.' "

"Well, I'm willing to go that far. But I fear more the living death. Going back to that discussion we were having about bravery, I fear being hollowed out."

"And that's the maverick in all of us."

"Yes. When I talk to a college audience sometimes, I walk out and I stand there and I say, 'Well, I'm smaller than I'm supposed to be, right?' They all laugh. Everybody gets the point. Because TV is magic. You just fly and somehow you end up in somebody's living room." Abbie laughs. "And you must be over six feet tall to do that. If you ask people around here to estimate my bank account there ain't nobody that's going to get it. No stocks. No bonds. No real estate. But they all look at me as some kind of eccentric millionaire. They see me in *People* [pronounced *peephole* by Abbie] magazine and the fame makes you a foot taller and a million dollars richer. Once I announced to an audience at a school that I was going to kill everybody over six feet. Boy, I'll tell you, that was real popular. I catered to the majority."

The potential for anger, the drive to right wrongs, the David (of Goliath fame) love for the rights of the little guy, are inside all of us. This can be considered an American tradition. Recognize the existence of anger within yourself and don't let its presence scare you. Rather, learn what to do with it.

Controlled Anger. It is vitally important that anger be used rather than buried. Abbie commented, "You have to have some self-awareness of mood swings. You have to have some acceptance of the fact that you are going to be angry. There is going to be friction in human interrelations. You have to expect that as a natural phenomenon, and then try to see where it is justified and where it isn't. You have to make some decisions about whether it fits the situation or it doesn't. There is legitimate anger."

"What is involved in bringing anger under control?"

"We're talking about how people develop a self-awareness about their own emotional states. Anger is a problem if you don't use it correctly. I don't like losing causes. I watched the news last night and I saw Dan Rather do four-and-a-half minutes on El Salvador that would not have been done at this stage in Vietnam. And I know that this was because of a meeting five days ago that a friend of mine arranged between the foreign minister of Nicaragua and Dan Rather. This place called El Salvador, up until a few months ago, would be thought of by most Americans as a brand name of coffee or something. So in a sense a certain battle was won there—bringing people who have information together with communicators. Because right now the press is the only effective opposition to the Reagan administration."

Using your anger in a controlled manner will often call for more than the use of your vocal chords. It calls for intelligence, resourcefulness, and creativity as well.

Taking Count. Righteous anger demands a response. The consequences of feeling anger within, yet remaining passive on the outside, always call to my mind that scene of Abbie Hoffman driving past the accident in Mexico. "When I cracked up, my analysis of it is that underground living is functional schizophrenia. You are acting out another role. You're acting out false identities. You start to build these false identities and you start to play them so well that you start to become these other people. If you don't pick the right identities there is going to be a separation between who you really are and who you are pretending to be. And you are going to crack. It is something that can happen to anybody; you don't have to be a fugitive."

In order to lead a life that is not what our GIT called "functional schizophrenia," your responses must be consistent with your philosophy. If a particular situation, in terms of your values, provokes anger, then an expression of that anger is the only healthy way to cope with that situation. This, more than anything else, explains our GIT and the FW in dealing with anger. "I am middle-aged now, forty-six, and my position is that people are basically good. They're supposed to help kids who have broken legs in the street and get rid of regimes that are chopping people's heads off in San Salvador. My father went out bitter because I don't think he came to terms with what life was about. I think he was still trapped and intrigued by the—I hate to use the term—petty bourgeois drives. It was not self-fulfilling and I don't think he understood. That little lack of awareness there didn't suit him toward the end of his life. Although near the end, with Watergate and everything, I think he was starting to come around."

Healthy Anger. In our American society, we appear to be so cognizant of the destructive side of anger that there is little awareness of the benefits that accrue to those who learn to express anger constructively. Abbie's involvement in the El Salvador situation demonstrates this FW impressively. "I just saw the movie *Missing*," said Abbie. "What *The China Syndrome* is to the anti-nuke movement, *Missing* is to what I'm working on now, namely opposing U.S. military policy in Central America, in El Salvador. It's about a kid who's in Chile when the coup occurs under Allende. He disappears and everyone suspects that he's been tortured and assassinated by the military, but they can't find out. The father comes down, a father like mine. An upper-middle-class business father who accepts the mythology of American history: the land of milk and honey, the way of life, all is good, obey the government, the government doesn't lie to you. I think that's the real difference between the generations and the rude awakening that Watergate was—that 'the government doesn't lie.' And of course I believe it lies all the time.

"The father goes down, Jack Lemmon, and eventually he's led into the morass of the American embassy and diplomacy. And he realizes that the U.S. was involved in the overthrow of Allende and was involved in the assassination of his son. At the end they find him dead, of course. And I mean I walk out and I feel this sense of rage. And I say to my running mate, Joanna, 'This will keep me going for three years. This feeling that I feel now will be a driving force to tie me in solidarity with the people in El Salvador for three years.' I know of nothing else that can do this. Not money, none of the other things going on in society; the distractions in a sense. Right now I feel complete solidarity. I understand exactly the difference between good and evil, the moral choices to be made. And I understand what I am supposed to be doing in life. So that sense of anger or rage that is directed in a certain way can be as powerful as love in the sense that it integrates the individual with the society. I mean I felt it right there.

"When I was in the South in Mississippi, a lot of people would criticize me and some of the others, saying that we used the civil rights movement to find out who we were. You know, as a psychoanalyst's couch. I don't see that as a particularly bad thing. I see that as a very healthy thing. I think it is a good idea. People will find themselves if they get into society and try to change it. I don't even think you find out what power is about until you challenge it."

Revolution. You would completely miss the essence of Abbie Hoffman to see him simply as an individual whose principal strength lies in becoming angry at society's ills. At your best, in expressing your anger, you will manage to some degree to change the conditions that produce it. "I've got to have two reasons to get involved. I've got to believe completely in the cause and I have to believe that the strategy in my head is one that is going to produce victory. And the question of whether anyone is fighting inside or outside the system has always struck me as a metaphysical question, not a political question. We're all in the system and you use what you think is going to be effective. If people want to run for Congress, all those methods are good. If you fight hard enough and are good enough at it, you learn how the whole fudge is put together. I think this battle in El Salvador can be won. I watch the news and I see they've got all the fourteen-year-old kids, they've got the eighty-year-old men fighting on their team, you know? They ain't paying them money. What's keeping them going? There's some spirit there. And that spirit is going to win."

Participation. Abbie said he knew even as a boy that it was more fun to be playing in the game than watching from the sidelines. This is perhaps the ultimate payoff when you begin constructive action on the basis of your anger rather than holding back with a rationalization such as "What's the use?" Abbie, as Barry Freed, could not stand on the sidelines in the river dispute, although acting meant almost certain discovery and imprisonment. Curiously, however, this did not happen. "It never caught up with me. In the end, it looked good for my case. Senator [Daniel Patrick] Moynihan said, in front of 900 people, that everybody in New York state owes Barry Freed a debt of gratitude. We had never met and here we are on this stage with all these cameras going. I'm convinced that the *federales* are going to come running up the aisle and drag me away. And I'm giving my Barry Freed speech. Very different from Abbie's, very organized, very tight. A bit of humor but all underplayed in terms of the general principles. Like a responsible middle-class citizen presenting his views. '. . . For if we lose the river, with it goes part of America and our heritage. We will not let it be. . . .' You're making your stand right there. The speech is in the *Congressional Record*. And when I get through there's a huge applause. I always have good endings. And all the Northern WASPs are rising. So Moynihan says right into the mike, 'Now I know where the sixties have gone.' He connected with the activism and the involvement, the participatory democracy. That was the philosophy that we invented in the sixties."

No Vale La Pena. Just as I did when I introduced Abbie to you, I want to remind you now that the FW in dealing well with anger does not require that you adopt the demeanor of an "angry person." Abbie said, "The issue is that all of us want to live in a state of psychological health. Every time you take a bite out of one of those bullets, or you eat that little piece of shit, or you make a decision to play the rat-race game when your heart is saying that you are supposed to be doing something else with your talent, with your mind, with your energy—you die. Of course we all do it. I mean I do. I render unto Caesar's Palace that which is Caesar's Palace's. That is the modern parable. But it is a question of how you feel inside. The direction that you are going in. This is what I'm trying to do in life. I'm trying to stay psychologically healthy. I'm trying to enjoy life. And I think that an integral part of that is trying to make society a better place to live in. I mean the more I think about that experience in Mexico and a couple of other experiences with the physical problems of internalizing all this rage, or of exploding continuously, *no vale la pena*. That's what they say in Spanish. 'It ain't worth the ticket of admission.' "

9/ Carl R. Rogers

OPENNESS

Let thy tongue be equal with thy heart.

"II Henry VI"

FUNDAMENTAL PROBLEM

At the brink of the twenty-first century, the Fundamental Problem most typical is distancing. Distancing is a self-imposed alienation that few cannot feel tainting their transactions with the people around them.

The singer-philosopher Bob Dylan, as a sixties-generation activist, sang of "the prisoner of his own devise." Those who live in consciously selected isolation, prisoners of their own making, have failed to perceive the very obvious. Residing behind psychological walls with the drawbridge securely raised does serve as protection from other people. Yet the walls also function to prevent us from reaching beyond their confines. A "me–them" mentality, within the bounds of reasonableness, is of course prudent. But if excessive, this lack of openness hardens into a defensive posture that creates the all-too-familiar feeling of watching life from the outside.

Distancing is a learned behavior, and some people are more skilled at it than others. The most inept distancers are perceived by the people around them as angry, odd, or unfriendly. The better performers resemble the mythical swordsman who, because of exceptional swiftness with his épée, was able to keep the raindrops from falling upon him. Skilled distancers are modern-day swordsmen who use behavior cultivated to mimic warmth, friendliness, and openness to defend against all but the most superficial human contact. These master fencers speak and smile and put their arms around us, but after a time we find that they do not really register. They are like people without shadows who make no footprints. They are here but not quite tangible. Tragic for them is that not being knowable, they are unlovable as well. To the casual acquaintance they are perhaps cause for a shoulder shrug. Sensing that there is no one behind the mask, people have little incentive to work hard at trying to reach such a person. They simply move on to relationships that appear potentially more rewarding. For those who must try hard, such as a spouse, the result is chronic frustration. They eventually come to describe such people as "logical" or "computer-like." As hostility mounts, they may use terms like "inhuman." For the distancers themselves, the normals among us who are experiencing this FP, the result is simply, and terribly, loneliness.

The motivation to live your life as a walled-in person is fear. The fear centers specifically on how others will judge you. A failure to risk openness results from the belief that the judgment of others may lead to a painful personal rejection. In the distancing process, vulnerability takes on such a risky aura that life becomes an activity you believe must be carefully controlled. Spontaneity is perceived as particularly hazardous. Living by the seat of your pants as you react naturally to events around you is not conducive to maintaining a carefully constructed façade.

If you fear being psychologically open, you lead a double life. In your head you carry on a process very similar to presiding over an editing room in Hollywood. Messages to the "outside," be they words or gestures, are put on your mental screen for an editorial decision. "What will they do if I say X?" is always the issue. Words are deleted and others substituted. Gestures are added or omitted. Each is calculated to present a performance that will get you the desired response from another. This is manipulation of the highest order.

CARL R. ROGERS

Great Inspiring Teacher
As a veteran of thirty years of TV viewing, I unthinkingly assumed that California would seem very familiar. But the winding drive up the La Jolla cliff-face offered a spectacular vista of the slowly rolling Pacific that was as surprising as it was beautiful.

Picked like each Great Inspiring Teacher for the combination of celebrity and bounteous Fundamental Wisdom, Carl Rogers, the only professional psychologist in the group, had been a familiar figure to me from the early days of graduate school. The special quality of openness in his writing, speaking, and therapy fosters this closeness. It represents the greatest antithesis to distancing of which I am aware.

His secretary at the Center for the Study of the Person, where he is a fellow in residence, advised me that he was homebound that day, nursing himself through a bout of sinusitis. He had been widowed for less than a year, and she mentioned that he was just becoming accustomed to life as a widower. We met in his large living room with a glass west wall. He sat on the couch looking comfortable in a well-worn cardigan and sandals over his socks. The room was tidy, full of neat piles of recent books. Some were from publishers for him to review, others the most up-to-date publications from the world of psychology. A third category was composed of books for the retiree. We do, as Rogers says, all share the basic fundamental human problems.

The psychologist who gets so exquisitely close, through his books, that readers constantly write from around the world to tell him so, is a man who devised a system of psychotherapy hinging on genuineness, positive acceptance, and empathy on the part of the therapist. "A sort of transparency on my part" is how he describes it.

"Carl, I was very surprised to learn that you, *the* man in the field of psychology most associated with the idea of personal openness, were an early distancer."

"I think so. Let me talk about it a little bit, and see if you think I have the idea. I think that in my adolescence and younger life I definitely was distanced from people, to use your phrase. I would never have thought of confiding in my parents anything that was really important. I had very few friends, but I expect that if you'd asked me at that time I would have said, 'No, I'm not too distant from people.' But as I look back at it, yes, I was.

"That was a strange phenomenon. We moved to a farm when I was thirteen. The farm was my father's hobby. We had plenty of money and it was a well-to-do-man's hobby. But I became interested in the night-flying moths. And that was my first scientific project, I suppose. I just got very excited about it and read everything. Lefebvre—the French writer—and all the writers in this country. And I raised caterpillars and kept them in their cocoons. But it was a totally solitary project. To the people in the neighborhood, whom I didn't have much contact with at all, I was that boy who

CARL R. ROGERS   **147**

was interested in bugs. So they would call up and say, 'There are some great big bugs over here. Would your boy be interested in them?' Sometimes I was. Sometimes I wasn't. Anyway, that was the kind of life I lived then."

Rogers wrote candidly in *Becoming Partners: Marriage and Its Alternatives*, his book on relationships, of later distancing in his own marriage and the pain of working through it. "I began the frightening process of talking—*really* talking—with Helen about our sexual relationship. It was frightening because every question and every answer made one or the other of us so vulnerable—to attack, to criticism, to ridicule, to rejection."

"What have you found to be the catalyst that creates that special magic that links two people together into a close relationship?"

Up to this point Rogers had been hesitating and carefully thinking through his answers before responding. To this one his answer was rapid and sure. "Openness and sharing. If I can risk being pretty transparent with a person, then I will almost inevitably get closer to that person. When a relationship has deteriorated, I find that it is really helpful to say something like 'Well, I just feel we're not as close as we used to be. We don't work together as well as we used to.' Or, 'We don't seem to be as open with each other. I don't quite know why it is. Here's my perception of it. What's your perception of it?' That doesn't always or necessarily work. There are people with whom in talking it out like that, you come to the conclusion that you have gone apart, and the distance is real, and probably you won't be close. I can think of some relationships in my life which I really wished I could recapture and I haven't been able to. On the other hand, the other and more likely possibility is this will tend to close the gap."

"What about new relationships? We've all heard people say, 'I've never known a stranger.' These people have a quality about them that makes everyone seem like an old friend after just a few minutes. How do we reduce the distance as quickly and as comfortably as possible? Are openness and sharing still the FW?"

"Yes, definitely. There are times when I have quickly formed a relationship with someone, and a relationship which has lasted a long time. And it has always started first by, it seems to me, a kind of a chemical attraction or something. But then by being very open and very sharing."

"This is what interests the reader of this book. How do they go about doing this?"

"I think of one evening with an opera singer. I saw her for only one evening, and I'm not a music buff. It was by chance that I was seated next to her and she was an attractive person. I felt a liking for her and she asked me if I loved opera. I said, 'No, as a matter of fact, I really am not much of an opera lover. The musical aspect of myself is really not very much developed.' Oh, my God! You know that wipes me out in her eyes. She said, 'That's my life, and I'm just fascinated by it. It's really what I live for.' I said, 'Well, wait a minute. I understand that, because I'm just as involved in another field of endeavor that just fascinates me and is my life. So I know exactly what you're talking about. Only it's a different field.' Well, from that moment on, God, we became old friends by sharing the same kind of enthusiasm—different interests, together. In fact, into the evening she called to the man she'd come with, and she said, 'I want you to meet this man, because we have so much in common.' "

"So over the years the solitary butterfly collector has metamorphosed into a quite different person?"

"To jump clear to the other end, and speak of myself now, I would say that I live on two levels. I easily distance myself from people—social climbers, people who want to get to know me, people who worship me, people who want to be my disciples. And on the other hand, with people whom I trust or feel close to, I disclose myself almost completely. I just feel I like to share myself. That's what I do in the workshops that I conduct when I really get involved. I don't always get involved. Sometimes I'm just a facilitator in those workshops, but when I get really involved, I disclose myself. I really become very, very close, not only to one or two people, but to a lot of people. In my personal relationships, I'm kind of all or nothing. I mean some people I know and am just acquainted with, but for those I really know I'm just *all there*. They know everything about me, and my feelings, and my despairs, and my joys. The works—my excitements, my disappointments."

"I can ask you, as the only psychologist in this book, a unique question, Carl. Can you talk about your experiences in the therapeutic setting in helping people learn to become open in personal relationships?"

"Well, this may not be a direct answer, but it'll get to it, I think. I am certainly one of those people who are just terrified to walk into a room full of people they don't know at all. But I'm better at it than I used to be. I've learned to pick out people who look interesting and try to really make contact with them. But still, that is a situation I avoid if at all possible. On the other hand, the thing that fascinates me is we'll get 90, 100, 150 people together in a seven- to ten-day workshop. They are strangers to each other. They don't know each other. And yet, usually within two days at the most, it becomes clear that the thing everyone is most hungry for is real contact with other people. And we've learned some things. I don't think we've learned everything, but we've certainly learned something about how to create a climate where people can feel it's safe to be in touch with other people. It can be in angry touch with them, or in loving touch with them, or whatever. That hunger is so deep that it sometimes just amazes me. For example, I think of a workshop in Mexico, about 100 people, and the accommodations were lousy. And some of them, to save money, stayed in a dormitory, a basement dormitory that had a so-called bathroom facility where the water ran all over the place and ran into the bedroom. The living conditions were horrible. Nobody ever complained about that. Nobody ever complained. They were having contact with people of a sort that was not customary in their ordinary lives, and they loved it. That's just one example. I could duplicate it with many others."

"And do you believe that this new ability to break down distance barriers that the workshop participants learned became a skill that could be brought home to their real worlds?"

"Yes, definitely. Not everyone does, I don't think, but many, many people do. Some learn more, and some learn less. The frequent after-effect is that they form closer relationships with members of their own family. Come to think of it, just this last week I had a letter from a very intelligent university professor who was in a four-day workshop. This was when I was in New York state. And she wrote that the experience had opened up communication between her and her son that had been closed for years.

"This has been brought home to me time and again having done workshops in Rome, Paris, and England and various parts of this country. I've done them in Brazil, Mexico, and Venezuela, and people are so much like people it's incredible. In a workshop I did just a little while ago in Poland the professionals initially separated themselves quite a lot from the nonprofessionals by using their skills in hurtful ways. Somebody would speak up and would immediately be diagnosed or analyzed, you know. And this would just shut the person up for a time. But the group was very interesting for two reasons. One was that after a couple of days of that it became very painful. The group began to realize what it was doing to itself and they didn't like it. So they largely stopped that throwing barbs at each other. By the end of the week it really became a close community. Secondly, what I didn't know at the time of the workshop but learned by letter afterward was that those professional people were very hostile to each other in everyday life. They never spoke and had no association with one another. The letter said they had remained in close communication with each other and the workshop was being talked about as an historic event."

"Okay. For the readers of this book who hurt from their inability to touch others and allow themselves to be touched, where do they start?"

"By continually taking risks. That's why I think it's a never-ending process. You get through one situation very well, but that doesn't mean that everything is all settled. There are risks in every relationship. Risks in every professional attempt. I think for me, risk taking is one of the central themes of my life, and I don't quite know why or how that got underway."

"What is the fear that causes people to want to bottle themselves up?"

"Rejection or hurting the relationship or something like that is the price that might be paid."

"How real do you think the risk is?"

"Well, mine is not a Pollyanna view because I don't think men are all lovely and beautiful, but I do think that given the right psychological climate, people really are trustworthy. When they feel safe and feel trusted then they become very trustworthy."

"So you believe it's worth the risk?"

"Yes, I do."

"Now that you have developed a track record, a lifetime of professional and personal risk taking, does it get easier?"

"Yes, I guess a little easier. Yes, it does make it easier, though always the next hidden thing seems like it might be the thing that would bring about rejection. I mean it isn't as though, 'Oh, well, it's always worked, so it's going to work again.' It isn't quite that simple. It's, 'Since I do seem to have a pretty good track record . . .' I was thinking this noon while I was eating lunch of something that I really want to reveal to someone who is close to me. And it's a risk. And I know that my heart will beat faster and I'll have some qualms about doing it. But I'm going to do it.

"I think becoming more fully functioning is always a process and is never achieved by anyone. It is something one works toward, often makes progress toward, and sometimes slips back some. But I don't think it is a state which is achieved, period. The analogy that comes to my mind is the horrible attitude that some people used to have, I don't think they have it any more, that if they were psychoanalyzed, then they were analyzed. They were there. They understood everything. I don't believe that and I don't believe that anyone becomes a fully functioning person, period.

There may be moments, certainly, when he or she is functioning very fully and really is open to the world, and functioning in the way they would like. But it's a process with ups and downs. I think I've made a good deal of progress in that, but I wouldn't say I'm perfect."

"So you're saying, Carl, that in your experience, getting over the FP of distancing is not something that anyone accomplishes permanently, forever."

"I don't think anyone accomplishes *anything* permanently, forever. I think the same qualities I had as a boy crop up again. You keep learning the same lessons over and over again in new contexts. I guess I'd put it that way. I keep learning the same lessons over and over again, anyhow.

"You may not reach 100 percent, but you get to a point of normal, healthy coping. And you may be knocked off that base by something very traumatic that happens in your life. So even that, I don't think, is a fixed thing. It's like getting there is half the fun or all the fun. It's a process of moving toward being more than you are. That is what life is all about. And that's the really exciting part of it. And if you ever got there, whatever in hell that means, it would be like the golden paved streets of heaven or something like that. It would be boring as anything."

"Then what is the goal? Most people seem to think the goal is happiness."

"I almost never use the word *happiness*. I don't regard happiness as a goal. Happiness is a by-product of doing something exciting and risky and adventurous. And God, you find out it feels pretty good. *That's* happiness. But I think people who set out to try and achieve happiness, that's the saddest journey I know."

At the end of our time together the sun had set and in place of the cliff panorama was a wall of pinpoint lights. Where the ocean had been it was very black. Dr. Rogers discussed his plans to establish a training institute in client-centered therapy, his brand of therapy, for businesspeople, physicians, teachers, and all others interested in applying the ideas of openness and personal honesty to their own endeavors. He spoke of some "bright ideas" he was getting for research in client-centered therapy from recent developments in chemistry and physics. He had been traveling worldwide since the death of his wife and had apparently reached a point where he can comfortably face living at home again. Looking back to his trip to Poland, he said, "The interest there is very real, and a lot of people have read my books. Two of my books are being translated into Polish now. It seems to me they are very subversive. It seems to me that if they knew what they were doing, they wouldn't let those books be translated."

OPENNESS

Fundamental Wisdom

As a psychologist, Carl Rogers has spent a professional lifetime specializing in the murky area of personal relationships. That a man who describes himself as rather emotionally isolated as a child would be drawn to such an interest is not surprising. By nature, people seem driven to involve themselves in the areas that they find most personally challenging. Rogers has met this challenge through personal risk taking. Out of his experiences emerge these barebones items of FW necessary for you to make better contact with the people around you.

Trust. You will find the confidence to keep from flinching and holding back as others come close when you realize that the result is not likely to be painful. Human beings prefer—even crave—closeness over distance when the conditions are right. You can create these conditions for the people around you by demonstrating to them that they can trust you not to reject them. You communicate this message by dropping any jabbing, probing, or stinging behavior that forces others to keep their distance. Show them that it is safe to approach you. In return, you can be confident that once this message is broadcast you will not be jabbed in return.

Risk. Should I show them everything? The cost of admitting you to a world of openness and sharing is abandoning your lonely safety. This step toward emotional liberation can make you feel apprehensive at first. But you must place yourself in a more personally vulnerable position. It is a literal and figurative impossibility to see—much less touch—a person in a suit of armor. A trade-off is required. You must compromise a certain amount of safety and protection in exchange for becoming reachable. Do you want to be touchable? Expect to feel some occasional vulnerability.

Openness and Sharing. If you are feeling less than comfortably close, the key concept to reverse the sensation is "openness and sharing." This approach to relationships will make it possible to show yourself as you are. Others will be able to view the whole you rather than just the fragments of your feelings and ideas that you consider the most interesting or most advantageous to reveal, those that have allowed you to feign human touching without risking rejection. Such posing has created a barrier that makes the task of human contact akin to trying to get on intimate terms with someone who is on the other side of a high brick wall. Psychological walls put both you and the other person at a disadvantage by forcing each of you to work with limited information. Unless you've got a crime in your past, know the location of buried treasure, or work for the CIA, your first step in getting closer to people is showing them as much of your thoughts and feelings as you are able.

Genuineness. Spontaneously and accurately reflect to others your up-to-date thoughts and feelings "live," as in "live theatre," as your interaction progresses. Plotting and planning what you will say to people minutes or days ahead will cause you to come across as a psychological leftover— boring and stale to everyone, including yourself. Be fresh. Awake or asleep, your thoughts and emotions operate continuously. As one would turn up the volume control on a TV set, simply narrate what is going on within you. This will make distance immediately disappear.

Touching. Risking openness and honesty results in behavior that Rogers referred to as "transparency." If you emit transparency it will be immediately recognizable to everyone around you. Start by turning your statements into "I think" and "I feel" messages. Psychologically transparent people make the effort to bring their internal state out for us to share. This style of functioning establishes the aura of touchability, the psychological posture that makes giving and receiving physical and emotional contact possible. Test yourself to determine if you are functioning in a manner sufficiently transparent to allow touching. Put your hand on a friend's arm. Is this gesture accepted? Then allow that person to touch you. If you are radiating a sense of openness, people will quickly respond. The physical barrier, though, is only a half-step. Sexual experiencing without emotional contact, for example, is commonplace. Do you feel you are relating heart-to-heart rather than head-to-head? This is the ultimate. This is how to live life at its most exhilarating. It is described by those who do it as living "close to the fire."

Drift. Personal closeness in relationships must be maintained. Whether from sudden rifts or slow, barely perceptible cooling, personal bonds are subject to decay. Dr. Rogers describes the application of openness and honesty as the first step in rehabilitating rusting relationships.

Stripping. In forming new relationships, the name of the game is speed. How quickly can you strip off your layers of defense while at the same time creating an atmosphere that signals safety to the other person to do the same? The usual, and usually unsuccessful, approach in attempting a new relationship is to begin by probing for commonalities of background and interests. This is uncomfortable, smelling as it does of superficiality and distance. Frequently, in the end, it fails. Personal closeness can be immediately and successfully accomplished if you remember that the common denominator between any two people is their shared humanness. No matter how dissimilar your lives, like the opera singer and the psychologist, you can join with anyone in the certainty that you share striking similarities of thought and emotion in life's big issues, and probably similar feelings about the challenge of that particular encounter as well.

Style. As with all FW, the ability to be a distance reducer can be learned by anyone who cares to make the effort. This skill may be applied appropriately in virtually all relationships. Although psychological openness can be deliberately utilized selectively by raising and lowering defenses at will, you will discover that the new-found ability to get close to others feels good. It will probably become your preferred style of relating once you experience the taste of success. With reasonableness always the final test, there is no need to restrict your distance reducing to the close or loving relationships. Business, social, and casual relationships can all be enhanced through closeness, and they will all become more rewarding for you.

The Process. And what is the goal? Not the golden paved streets of heaven, says Carl Rogers. The goal is simply to try. If you have gone that far you will have succeeded. It isn't that you cannot do it better. You can always do it better. But the excitement is always in the trying. Swimmers don't swim because they yearn to see the other side of the pool. They enjoy the process. The process of risking and failing and succeeding will create your happiness. But once reaching the other side of the pool, when you have caught your breath and the momentary success is savored, jump in and swim across again.

10/ F. Lee Bailey

FREEDOM FROM APPROVAL

This above all: to thine own self be true,
And it must follow, as the night the day,
Thou canst not then be false to any man.

"Hamlet"

FUNDAMENTAL PROBLEM

You probably cannot state with any conviction that you do not enjoy the approval of others. A pat on the back for a job well done or as an expression of appreciation always feels good. Most parents have learned that praise for good behavior means far more to a child than any gift they can buy.

But although you quite naturally *prefer* another's approval, the issue can easily become a Fundamental Problem if your preference becomes a *need*. At issue, once again, is personal freedom. If your selection of one course of behavior over another is based primarily upon your consideration of each behavior's relative potential to gather approval, you are a psychologically dependent person.

Approval seekers are described by the people who know them as "fawning," "submissive," "wishy-washy," or "deferential." They really are parasites. The people who try to relate to them are taken advantage of. Because they are unable to function in a mature and healthy way, the people with this FP are unable to give to others in relationships. They can only take, and the people close to them eventually come to see them as draining and demanding. After all, to carry another on your back may initially require little effort. As time passes, however, the burden becomes intolerable.

"Going out with Derek is just too serious. He's all right as far as it goes, but he tries too hard." Or, "I wish Samantha could just sit down and enjoy herself. She runs around and can't do enough for you. I don't know, I just can't relax around her." People are uncomfortable around the Dereks and Samanthas because they are both approval seekers. They actually refuse to be the equals of the people around them. The result is that in spite of their good intentions, they make other people work. They unwittingly bleed their friends, family, and acquaintances of every last measure of approval. Their behavior is forced in whatever direction seems likely to squeeze out more.

As an approval seeker you find yourself grading other people, especially in the areas you view as your weakest. Relationships count the most with those you rate higher than yourself. Milquetoast approval seekers want approval from tough guys and often idolize sports figures. Middle-aged seekers of approval covet acceptance from the young. A poor student with this FP may seek approval from honor students but is just as likely to be attracted to those who most disdain school, the leading scoffers. This last behavior has caused mothers through the years to question why their children seek out "the worst element."

But the more you cherish approval from the people you have judged as your betters, the more elusive it will become. The explanation for this is simple enough. Picture the man who needs approval, above all else, from beautiful women. Perhaps he views himself as unattractive because of premature balding and a history of teenage awkwardness. Largely lacking in free choice, he chases after the approval of the most beautiful women he encounters. His approval need is so consuming that once he identifies a woman as an "A" or a "10," he will behave in whatever way he views as necessary to merit an approving word, glance, or smile. Here lies the trap. Ironically, his preoccupation with earning approval results in behavior that is not natural. He will seem odd, phony, and strange to the objects of his attention. He is *much less* likely to receive the much-sought approval than he otherwise might. But let a woman he judges to be unappealing enter his life. He rates her a "zero." Seeing no reason to seek her approval he acts naturally and at ease. The result is predictable. Under these circumstances he will receive the approval that he was unsuccessful in obtaining when he chased it. "Why," he asks, "do all the ugly ones love me?" As soon as you become free from the need for approval you will actually begin to receive a great deal more of it.

F. LEE BAILEY

Great Inspiring Teacher
His legs are wide apart. The strong, compact body balances on the balls of the feet. He lets his arms hang straight at his sides. Polished, high-heeled boots proclaim him unique and a little dangerous. He calls himself a renegade. He's a hired gun with a big reputation, and the town has turned out to see F. Lee Bailey work.

The prosecution witnesses facing him today across ten carpeted feet in the "pit" of the fourth-floor Dade County [Miami] courtroom appeared braced for the worst. Each left the stand surprised and relieved at their gentle handling. Bailey had warned me that there were only two witnesses in this murder trial that he intended to challenge. In his opening statement to the jury he had described the homocide detective as "not too bright" and the state's polygraph expert as "a liar." It was with these two that the shootout would take place.

For two days I observed everyone from opposing counsel to the local press affectionately address him as "Lee." The exception, according to Bailey, are the people in his office who, upon hearing Johnny Carson inquire one night "if he could call me F," have adopted this form of address. Observing his lightning changes from F. Lee Bailey, the best-known defense attorney in the United States, to F. Lee Bailey, show-business personality, one must occasionally remind oneself that both Baileys are very much for real.

He recalls leading a fairly sheltered youth in New England. "I knew I was sent to prep school because I was a problem kid in the public school. My mother was getting interested in marrying this fellow who was a cripple that I didn't get along with. Right now he is probably at least one of the two closest friends I've got on the face of the earth. I was at the very awkward age of fourteen, which is about as bad as it gets; high adolescence. At prep school I was a good deal younger than everybody else there. I had jumped ahead, and many of them were there because they had failed. Then at a fairly young age I went to Harvard. I intended to be a writer, but it was kind of a turn-off. I didn't belong in their community. I didn't live there and I was too young to be there. I mean I was reading poets like William Butler Yeats and I didn't know what the 'place of excrement' meant. I wasn't worldly.

"But once I got into naval flight training, all that changed very rapidly. One is very quickly thrust into a very high-risk situation and a very high-survival situation. Most of them do survive, although the accident rate is a bit horrendous. You hear maxims like, 'Stay ahead of the airplane; it's beautiful. Get behind it; it will kill you. Stay even with it and you'll be behind it.' So you get strong and you get, in a sense, conservative at the same time. You do that by having the shit scared out of you on a few isolated and juicy occasions. But I was among the elite of the world. They took only the very best. And if that were so or not so, they had everybody convinced that it was so."

Through a series of fortuitous events Lee was thrust into the position of chief legal officer for his Marine unit at Cherry Point, North Carolina. Before his discharge he would handle well over 100 cases and gain invaluable trial experience—all this before ever enrolling in law school. Graduating first in his law school class at Boston University, he argued the Sam Sheppard appeal before the United States Supreme Court at age thirty and won it. Grabbing the attention of the nation, he followed with a series of sensational cases including the Great Plymouth Mail Robbery; Albert DeSalvo, "the Boston Strangler"; Dr. Carl Coppolino; Captain Ernest Medina; and more recently the defense of Patty Hearst. His loss of the Hearst case carried with it heavy criticism by the press. But Bailey is no stranger to spirited and emotional attacks from within his profession and in the press, which have mounted in tandem with the spread of his fame. The "Johnny Ringo Syndrome," he calls it: the fascination with seeing the top gun hit the dust.

"I know that early in your career you were warned about showing too much vigor and rising too fast."

"I was warned constantly about appearing to go too far too fast. There was hostility that showed up very early. My colleagues should have rejoiced a little, I think in retrospect, over the breath of fresh air—a guy with some balls and stamina. And I have enormous stamina. I tried my first case by staying up all night every night for a week and reading 1700 pages of trial records so that I could finish a trial I never started. I came in two weeks after it was moving. But instead of saying that any newcomer who is showing a burst of energy but doesn't have the experience to balance it out is a pain in the ass but 'Oh, what raw material,' the reaction was one of intense jealousy on the one hand and a great resentment for trying to change things on the other. Massachusetts was a very stodgy community. California probably would have dealt differently with it. I ridiculed the hoary traditions of Massachusetts law which were nonsensical, but so encrusted that the greatest evil of all was afoot. That is, we ought to do things this way because we always have.

"But I don't think there is any protection against being hunted. I think the nature of human beings is that many perceive themselves as acceding to a throne by killing the king. That is what I call the Johnny Ringo Syndrome. You see it in various walks of life. And not always in contentious kinds. It can be a doctor in a hospital who is the second chief anesthesiologist and perceives the old man as slipping. He wants to knock him off. And he can be a vicious son of a bitch in his efforts to do that; politically, manipulatively, and every other way. Those kinds of people are always out there. There is always 'targetitis' when you get to be number one or in the top group."

"The Turner Case seems to be a pretty good example of this." This was the 1973 trial of Florida supersalesman Glenn W. Turner who was charged in Federal Court with deceptive business practices in his Orlando-based cosmetics conglomerate. Defense attorney Bailey had earlier made speeches on Turner's behalf and was subsequently included as a co-conspirator in some of the charges against Turner. Bucking the "fool for a client" adage, he decided to defend himself in the case. He brought a huge staff to Jacksonville to give himself what he calls a better defense, in many ways, than he had ever given another client. Much to his surprise, his friends stayed with him. Yet, although the charges were eventually thrown out, Bailey spent a year in Jacksonville tied up with the trial and he suffered. His own unavailability killed his practice.

"That's the trouble with being not only the spearhead, but also the threshold attraction. People will not hire my firm if they know I can't touch their case. If I could have said, 'Frank is going to try it but I'm going to supervise it,' it wouldn't have happened. But I couldn't do that. I was down in Jacksonville sitting on my ass. I expected to be vilified, have all my credit shut off, have important friends walk away, and suffer the indignities usually visited on a citizen of prominence who gets indicted. None of these things happened, although it cost me an enormous amount. I got three of the most prominent prosecutors in the country to agree to testify for me as to honesty and integrity. But it is an occupational hazard. Clarence Darrow got tried twice and finally agreed to leave California if they wouldn't try him a third time. But although I vilified the government, as I thought it well deserved to be, I escaped more unscathed from that than any criminal defendant in history. The first thing you suffer as the beneficiary of the 'presumption of innocence' in the United States is the total loss of credit where credit is predicated solely on your ability to pay. And the most startling thing of all is that two months after I was indicted, and before the trial ever started, Manufacturers Hanover Bank loaned me $400,000 on my signature. They said we assume that this case down there is a joke. I said it *is* a joke, and they gave me the money."

"Defending yourself in itself is a break from the traditional belief as to how one should handle such a situation, isn't it?"

"A lot of lawyers said you can't defend yourself, you'll have a fool for a client. That's an old axiom, and we tend to believe axioms without analyzing them sometimes. But no rule ever had a right to exist if it didn't have an exception under special circumstances. When I polled the senior members of the Bar and explained the circumstances, they said, 'We agree 100 percent.' That approval was very helpful. I was doing what everyone else was going to chastise, and I wouldn't like to do without it. But I do think functioning without needing approval is the measure of one who succeeds and maintains, consistently, a position of leadership. We see people up and down, new flashes in the pan, all the time. The news media are great at creating them, then beating the hell out of them because they made them too big. Then when they knock them down they get a little bit sympathetic. Richard Nixon is a wonderful example of that.

"You have got to be able to go to bed at night if it comes right down to it and say, 'Except for the advice of a couple of close friends who happen to be like I am, the rest of these people are full of shit and I don't care what they say.' I believe that and that's the only reason I can sleep."

"So you are not above risking disapproval for the chance to be a winner?"

"Being a winner is relatively easy. It's a toot. It's a flight into fancy supported by gaseous admiration. It's the people who survive being criticized, being a loser of the moment, who are around year after year and continually appear as a leader in some fashion who are the real winners. I have learned to enjoy myself no matter what the public is saying about what I've done, because I'm always sure I'm right or very close to it. If I should lose that confidence I think I would become a completely different person. In moments of stress I think back to the Joe Pine days. He was sort of the Wolfman Jack of the talk show. A William F. Buckley but at a different level. He was a one-legged former Marine who used to kick the crap out of everybody who would stand for it. If you looked him in the eye and said, 'Don't talk to me that way, you asshole,' on the air, he'd bleep the word *asshole* and you were his friend. That's the way we became acquainted."

"I hear you saying that trusting your own judgment and standing on your own brings with it the feeling of personal strength."

"I think once you learn to rely totally on your own judgment, and a good airman does that generically and without reflection much more capably than almost any other kind of person, there is a certain serenity that you can disappear into where you don't really have to have anyone—although I don't know people who don't have to have *anyone*. Most have a close friend or two always sticking with them and who, nonetheless, will say, 'You know, I think you're awfully bright but this time I think you're wrong.' I don't think any of us can go too long without some kind of approval without being riddled with self-doubt."

"It is this self-doubt that causes people to grovel to win approval."

"I think that people who brown-nose, immediately upon discovery, are disrespected very much. In the corporate structure, for instance, the minute an executive picks that up from a subordinate, unless he's weak himself and likes that even though it may not be genuine, he resents it. I have to be extremely careful about that in dealing with a jury. If a jury comes in thinking for better or for worse that I'm a pretty smart lawyer and that I'm kowtowing to them—just regular citizens who have suddenly been vaulted into a position where I have to lick their boots—I think they resent it. They suspect me. They feel a terrible creeping insincerity.

"I think it's perfectly all right to be decent to them, but I expect to be instructive. I expect to tell them, 'Now look, except for you over here who knows a lot about this subject'—as I did today—'you listen to me because this is important and this is what I know about.'

"With the one juror yesterday, I don't know if you were there, she wanted to 'fess up and cop out and say 'I'm not fit to sit because I was the victim of an armed robbery and I'll always be prejudiced.' She's the lady on the end, a gal about twenty-eight. I said 'Well, you're going to find out when we excuse people, whether or not we buy that. Mr. Gerstein [the prominent Miami defense attorney working with Bailey] and I know more about picking jurors than you do. If we should leave you on because we know what we're doing, and we do, will you do your very best not to be biased?' And she said, 'Oh, absolutely.' Now I was very direct with her and I wasn't patronizing at all. I wasn't even polite. And she's on."

The last line of his bestseller *The Defense Never Rests* is a warning to future defense attorneys. Bailey tells them about living without approval.

"The would-be lawyer should know about the loneliness of his chosen profession, and about the satisfactions of being a renegade. . . ." I asked him, "Lee, what are the satisfactions?"

"Vindication. Vindication when you've taken a minority or unpopular or irregular or nonconformist point of view. It's the approval of a substantial minority whom you respect or of a majority whether you respect them or not. Majority approval is always vindication. It's a kind of winning, but not the winning that I wrote about in *Secrets*, the Vince Lombardi winning where you have to be declared the victor. Having to wind up the trial with the highest score, *i.e.*, the verdict, isn't winning at all, although the press and the public constantly seek to make that the criterion.

"I've spent damn little time in my life with rubber knees," he declares. "And I'm thinking all the way back to the time when I gave my first public speech, which was a recitation in French of a poem by Victor Hugo. And I think I could probably still pull most of it out of the memory and have a fairly good accent."

"What would you say to the average man or woman who will be reading this chapter because they fear controversy and become upset if they aren't told they are right?"

"There is nobody with any magic, and I think that once you understand that fact you approach every situation, whether it's controversial or not, with confidence. Plus, the ability to lose. You've got to be able to lose, live with it, and be reasonably gracious about it. You don't have to pin a medal on your opponent, but sour grapes, unless you've got a real axe to grind and a good appeal running, although it may salve the wound a little bit, is really the tactic of a crybaby. No matter how right you thought you were, we live in an approximate world. With two guys, both of whom think they're right, only one can win. I'm a hard realist to this extent. I get terribly passionate about watching the [New England] Patriots play. I get as excited as any fan as the last minute grinds down and they're either going to pull it out or they're not. But then I can live with it a lot better than most people. I mean it takes them hours to get over the trauma. And man, I'm ready to turn on to something else."

"You mentioned the military as a key factor in gaining the confidence necessary to be free from the need for approval. Do you credit any earlier experiences as being important in this jelling of your strong sense of independence?"

"As a young fellow I was probably blessed in two ways. I was reared more by my mother than by my father, but she was very busy. She was a struggling and ultimately successful educator and businesswoman. So while I think I was given good guidance, I wasn't given hovering attention.

"I also had a grandfather who was typically German, a stubborn individual and the wrong person to say 'I can't do it' to. He taught me that. The minute somebody said, 'You can't do it,' all the erg joules [scientific units of measurement] of energy would suddenly become inflamed and I would say 'You *can* do it.' It's sort of like what Bobby Kennedy was saying when he said, 'Others ask why, and I ask why not.'

"I quickly became, at a fairly young age, persuaded that the average person was cursed with a great deal of lethargy. If inertia pointed him in a single direction, he'd tend to keep going that way until you went and changed his course. Also I learned that one ought to view revealed wisdom with caution, constantly check it, and not be at all afraid to take a contrary position if all the senses and the analysis one could bring to bear disagree with the axiom that was being pawned off as absolute."

F. Lee Bailey is a colorful person, at least partially because he exudes the aura that he knows what he is doing and that he is going to go ahead and do what he likes regardless of who approves and who does not. When, after the rather tedious process of jury selection, the prosecutor concluded his opening remarks and Bailey took the floor to address the jury for the first time on the merits of the case, this confidence was at its zenith. Unlike the other attorneys in the case, he speaks without notes at all times. An opening statement, he tells the jury, is a promissory note. The two opening statements, he warns, may sound like they are describing two different cases. He challenges each juror to decide who pays off as promised when all the evidence has been presented.

The fact that he is not concerned with garnering approval from anyone makes him a genuine individual. He is no imitation of anyone else but the personification of himself. I overheard one of the spectators among the huge throng that had lined up to be admitted to the public section of the small courtroom comment, "He looks exactly like F. Lee Bailey should look."

Whenever I picture Lee, I see him sitting up at the defense table before the eyes of everyone. He likes the spotlight. He calls it "the ability to be isolated; the ability to be the apex of the triangle." In the camaraderie at the table, the scholarly young man accused of putting six bullets into his girlfriend, several local Miami lawyers, and "Bad" Andy Tuney, Lee's investigator, shared a half-dozen rolls of multi-flavored Lifesavers. It's a little thing, one of many which contribute to the uniqueness of a man who clearly enjoys being F. Lee Bailey.

INDEPENDENCE

Fundamental Wisdom

F. Lee Bailey's manner of dealing with life successfully is instructive in many respects. He exhibits what Carl Rogers has called "trust in the organism." He has a strong grasp of the priorities that create a basic sense of direction. His confidence and single-mindedness give him the advantage. He believes he is in the best position to know what is right for him. This provides immunity from the FP of approval seeking. "A guy came to do a profile one day and he said, 'You know, I've read most of what has ever been written about you and I notice that everything falls on one side of the line or the other. Nothing is in the middle. It is either a hatchet job or a blow job, but they don't tend to be balanced.' And he was right. Your admirers say, 'This man is going to replace the Almighty,' and your detractors say, 'He probably should be running the store down below.' " The truth, of course, is in the middle ground. F. Lee Bailey is a "one leg at a time guy," but he is living life on his own terms.

Kowtowing. To prefer approval is reasonable. To behave for the express purpose of collecting approval rather than choosing an alternative based on its overall "rightness" is self-destructively manipulative. Before you make final decisions, run this test. Ask yourself: Am I certain that the determining factor in this choice is not the expectations of another? If the answer is yes, you're halfway there. Answer one more question before you proceed. If I receive no approval, is this choice still the right one for me? Yes? Go ahead. If the answer is no, the choice is a bad one.

Approval Seeking. Chasing after the approval of others will prevent you from coming across as your natural self. It will make others suspicious and may prevent the attainment of exactly what you seek. Bailey never underestimates how critical it is to avoid the appearance of pandering to a jury. He mentioned this several times to underscore its importance. The defense attorney whose reputation precedes him has an extra burden in establishing rapport with the jury. To attempt to be persuasive by means of courtliness would be calamitous. Such approval-seeking behavior would cause the jurors to view him as insincere and could cost him the case. In order to gain the trust and respect of the jurors, there is no other course for him but to be completely himself and to trust in his own skills. Lee said to me, "In a one-day trial I think I'd get killed or eulogized, I don't know which. But in a three-day trial we get to know each other." Self-directed individuals are willing and expect to sacrifice a great deal of approval as they lay it on the line. Although others may not continually pat them on the back for this, it is the most certain path to attaining the acceptance and respect that grovelers seek and never get.

Ignite. Just because something isn't done or hasn't been done is no reason not to consider it. The former approach, were we all to use it, would literally bring the progress of civilization to a halt. The mere existence of a hunch or a notion that a certain course of action "feels right" may be all the justification you need. If it helps, tack up portraits of the astronauts, Thomas Edison, Leonardo da Vinci, and others like them who routinely did what had never been done. For every one of these people, there were many who told them they were stupid or crazy.

Query. Challenge all maxims, axioms, and "proven facts." When people quote them to you or you catch yourself using them to put ropes around yourself, be on guard. For every "absence makes the heart grow fonder" there is an "out of sight, out of mind." Don't make twentieth-century choices on the basis of eighteenth-century wisdom. Trust only your own wisdom. Remember Bailey's decision to be his own client in the face of conventional wisdom. "I did defend myself, and I defended everybody in sight. And they all walked away except those who jumped off the ship."

Pride. The withholding of approval by others will only cease to be demoralizing to you when you come to believe that you know what you are doing. If F. Lee Bailey, wearing jeans, were to walk into a room of fifty tuxedoed and gowned couples, the first question to occur to him would be "Why do all these people have the wrong clothes on?" What would *you* do? Leave? Leave town? Make up sputtering excuses citing your own stupidity? Look in the mirror. You couldn't be all that inept or you wouldn't have survived as long as you have. Stand up straight. If you are not going to buckle under the disapproval of others, then *you*, at least, have to believe that you know what you're doing. If you don't believe it, why should anyone else?

"Targetitis." The Johnny Ringo Syndrome—if you step out of line, if you think for yourself, or if you go too far too fast people will try to shoot you down. The faster you go, the more snipers there will be. It probably happens to you in some form every day. You are praised when you conform,

and praise is withheld when you don't. One who does not behave for the express purpose of currying favor from others must expect to make some people uncomfortable. Those who have previously been described as being addicted to a perfect world, the distancers and the irresponsible, will feel threatened and view you as out of control. Their defensiveness and discomfort stem from the feeling that you are out of *their* control. Did everyone pat you on the back today? If the answer is "yes," you may be in a rut. Those with the greatest creativity, growth, and reach become uncomfortable with constant approval. They know they must be playing it safe and are stale. An architect, himself no approval seeker, told me of his twist on traditional business philosophy. "Just because the customer likes it doesn't mean it's bad." But, he says, too much approval and he knows he's foot dragging.

Winning. The real winners are not always today's winners. Winners, like every GIT in this book, are people with track records of success—not success every time out, but success over time. The question of consistency is the most telling. Considered by itself, one trial, one game, or a single loss in any arena is meaningless. I asked Bailey to give me a self-description. Here is his picture of one of the most successful trial lawyers in America. "You want to know what the book on me is? Here is the response that a well-seasoned professional who knows me well would give to a judge who said, 'Who have I got coming before me? I'm about to start a heavy trial with F. Lee Bailey.' Being reasonably modest but not terribly, I would say if put in that position, 'Judge, I've known this fellow for ten years. I've worked with him a couple of times. Here's what you should expect. A reasonable and professional attitude but only as it is consistent with a vigorous fight for the client's interests. You needn't worry about any deliberate subornation of perjury, manipulation of the court, and you needn't worry that once you rule something out he'll try and sneak it in the back door and dump it in the jury box. If he makes an objection you should listen carefully, because he doesn't like to object. And he won't unless he has what he thinks are grounds. And he knows the rules of evidence better than most people, and maybe you. Expect good help from the pit. [The pit is traditionally the area in front of the bench, inside the bar where the attorneys work.] You don't have to worry as to whether or not the party is getting good representation. On the other hand, if you think he's missed something, call him right up to the bench because he might say, 'Goddamn Judge, that's a hell of a question. I should bring that out.' And if you get rough, and mean, and equestrian you can expect the guy to make a record out of which to embarrass the shit out of you if he can—in the appellate court, not before the press. As far as the press is concerned you can expect him to say, 'The man is the trial judge in this case and I respect him or I wouldn't be here.' I am much more straightforward and unmanipulative than the person who has read the PR would believe."

That is as good a profile of a winner as you are likely to find. Winning, as F. Lee Bailey said, is not winning every case. How would you adapt this to a description of yourself, as a person in your shoes who knows what he or she wants and is willing to sacrifice the approval of others to get it?

I Don't Care! As Lee put it, the only way you can sleep at night is to disconnect yourself from the idea that you're supposed to please everybody. Abraham Lincoln knew that. Try this out. Roll it on your tongue as you turn out the lights or any other time the world is pushing you hard. "I think I'm right and for anyone who doesn't agree, I don't care! I really don't!" This, says Bailey, creates a certain serenity. Maybe everyone is at odds and running scared, but at least some people know what they are doing. You do.

Vindication. Everyone wants to win, at least occasionally, and the odds say that you will. Take your own direction regardless of who or how many agree with you. The certain periodic vindication that will come is sweet. Why? Because you did what you thought was right, and you were found to be correct. Following the advice of others brings no vindication. *They* told you so. The satisfaction comes with betting on yourself. "I have a kind of running affectionate hate for *Time*," says Lee. "We admire their rhetoric far more than we do their dependability and fact. I once sued them for more than they're worth. I told Henry Anatole Grunwald [*Time*'s publisher] I did it because I wanted to take over their magazine. I thought they were irresponsible. They told the world that Captain Ernest Medina shot a four-year-old boy in the face with a submachine gun. They admitted that the report had come from a drug addict and they shouldn't have published it. *Time* was quick to say, 'Okay we jumped the gun. We never checked it out'; just what I said. And the judge dismissed that count against Medina."

Consequences. If you are willing to take on life without seeking the approval of others and if you are even willing to tolerate disapproval when necessary, there is no small measure of comfort in the knowledge that the results are rarely devastating. You should ask, "What is the worst effect that this disapproval can have on my life?" Except for the loss of what Bailey calls "gaseous admiration," the consequences are usually insignificant.

Magic. No one has magic, at least no more than you do. F. Lee Bailey looks great as he is, crashing down the hall of the Dade County Courthouse only slightly slower than a charging bull. Pilot's glasses hanging from vest pocket, barking orders to the left and the right, he is, in a word, an individual. Get yourself some pilot's glasses, a $500 suit, and some Italian high-heeled boots. Bring all this and six assorted packs of Lifesavers to your next meeting with any two or more people. Fly your own plane into town if you can and inject the word *bullshit* into every other sentence. It works for Lee. What will it do for you? Probably nothing. Be the best *you* that you can and don't wait for the applause.

11/ Xaviera Hollander

CONTROLLING GUILT

Let guiltless souls be freed from guilty woe:
"The Rape of Lucrece"

FUNDAMENTAL PROBLEM

Think back to your childhood. If you can remember the experience of being told by a parent who seemed all-knowing and all-powerful that you did something bad, you can easily recreate the feeling of guilt. It is a nauseating brew of shame, disgrace, and often fear.

As an adult you experience this same feeling when you judge yourself in violation of the standards with which you identify. These may include the law of the land or the Ten Commandments. They can be personal codes derived from strong role models in your past, special codes of acceptable behavior for specific occupational groups, or standards you have self-imposed. If you begin to view your behavior as a breach of these codes, or if others can depict your behavior as such a breach, guilt is the result.

Guilt is an emotion that we all feel occasionally. But when guilt plagues you frequently or lingers over long periods of time, it becomes a Fundamental Problem and must be controlled. If allowed to continue, guilt blunts personal effectiveness. It is a barrier to happiness and causes depression—ranging from periods of feeling "blue" to black moods that can keep us from enjoying life or, at the most extreme, cause us to feel that ending our life is preferable to continuing to live with emotional pain.

The origin of guilt may be an act, such as a remark, made in the heat of an argument, designed to hurt someone you love. Or it may result from failing to act, such as forgetting an important anniversary. Guilt feelings can even result from having or enjoying something, as in the case of a person who drives a new car through an area of poverty or that of a "two beer" husband who watches television with feet propped up while his wife vacuums around him.

Guilt can also arise over matters with which we are not directly involved. The test of reasonableness determines whether these feelings are appropriate. The guilt in middle-class Northern whites that precipitated their journey to the deep South in the 1950s to participate in freedom rides would be seen by most as highly appropriate. Unhappiness at a Sunday picnic because of guilt associated with starvation in India would be inappropriate for the average American family.

Guilt can also develop without any apparent logical cause. Consider sexual guilt within a marriage with no basis other than parental prohibitions that cannot be turned off. Or picture the maddening, irrational guilt that occurs over housekeeping that, while acceptable, "is not the way mother would have done it."

Guilt that can't be shaken is always suspect. It may be a crutch that allows you to comfortably continue the unacceptable behavior that produced it. "I beat my wife regularly." This statement, unamended, would be difficult for even the best of rationalizers to live with. But add "and I hate myself so much afterwards that I've even considered suicide" and you are off the hook. Experiencing the guilt allows people to continue behavior they could not justify otherwise and causes them to indefinitely procrastinate on making serious changes.

Finally, guilt can take the form of self-abuse when it is used as a motivator. Not trusting themselves to accomplish all they would like without prodding, many devise outrageously excessive goals for this purpose. The hope is that the guilt caused by the unrealistic expectations will at least push them on to modest accomplishment. The actual result is a chronic feeling of failure and inescapable guilt.

Anger is usually an undercurrent in guilt, but sometimes it is deeply submerged. Most commonly, this guilt-producing anger is self-directed. It develops when you fail to act when you should, when you put yourself in impossible situations, and when you ask too much of yourself without ever a pat on the back. Guilt is an emotionally torturous FP, but you can learn the methods to control it.

XAVIERA HOLLANDER

Great Inspiring Teacher
The Great Inspiring Teachers featured in this book were drawn from a highly refined group of carefully researched men and women of international prominence. In preparation for this chapter I had listed as potential GITs various Watergate figures, including Richard Nixon. But of all the individuals in the world rich in Fundamental Wisdon to serve as a model to illustrate healthy coping in the area of guilt, Xaviera Hollander, the "Happy Hooker," was first on my list. She seemed fascinating. Her response to my query, a gracious invitation to be a guest in her Amsterdam home, led to four days of formal and spontaneous interviewing that provides the background, insights, and anecdotes for this chapter.

Xaviera Hollander was a lonely Dutch girl who fled Holland to avoid the traditional marriage at nineteen. She became a diplomatic secretary in far-away New York, and there she fruitlessly searched for her *beau idéal* among the gray-flanneled men in the after work, Madison Avenue watering holes. The short hours in the bed of her shared Manhattan apartment always ended with "Don't call me, I'll call you" in the rush for the last train back to the wives and kids in the suburbs. Resented by the ever-watching prostitutes for "giving it away," and encouraged by a visiting English stockbroker to demand what she was worth, she quickly rose from moonlighter to high priced prostitute to the biggest madam in the Big Apple. At a still young twenty-seven, her 1972 collaboration with author Robin Moore resulted in the all-time biggest-selling original paperback in publishing history. This simultaneously made her a household name and ended her career in prostitution. She was first expelled from the United States and then, in turn, from Canada and England. Finally Xaviera Hollander was forced to return to Holland.

Xaviera is a funny, quick, earthy, lusty girl who is so uncommonly beautiful that it is tempting to stare at her as if she were somehow not real. This independent-thinking daughter of a physician father and genteel mother has coped successfully with the all-American supreme producer of guilt, sex, in a way that has enabled her to keep her freshness and her ability to laugh at herself.

After several days together seeing the tourist sights, and several evenings at dinner parties, jazz clubs, and discos that the tourists never see, we planned a formal interview for the morning before I was to return to the States. It was the day before Easter. Little chance to catch up on the sleep lost in the trans-Atlantic time change and the challenge of keeping up with the intrepid Xaviera had caused me to sleep late. When I rose, I immediately went looking for her to remind her of the scheduled interview. She was ready. "Lets go upstairs," she called over her shoulder as she started up the tricky, sharply winding "Dutch stairs."

"You want to do the interview in your bedroom?" I called up, not sure I had heard correctly.

"Of course." I caught up to her and found her propped up in the middle of the king-size bed having a devilish laugh. "This is where your readers will think I do all my work."

Xaviera is a bit of a raconteur, as she says of herself. As I sat in the chair by her bed with a small table containing my tape recorder and her bowl of half-eaten corn flakes between us, the two ninety-minute cassettes were quickly filled with an entertaining and thoughtful discourse of guilt as she has experienced it and viewed it operating within the people around her.

"I am not guilt free," she began. "But I am in control of my guilt. In fact, I would not want to be guilt free. Sometimes the feeling is nice, or at least trying to solve it is nice."

"I am sure every reader will expect us to begin this discussion of guilt by looking at its relationship to the general area of sex."

"Basically I view sex as a subject that should be enjoyed. And this carries through in my writing. As one mother put it, 'I'd rather have my daughter learn about sex from your books than the back seat of a car and come home knocked up,' pregnant, you know?

"My father was rather Bohemian. I'm very much like him. He was a very free-spirited man with an eastern magic to him. He was a psychiatrist, of all things, and later became an internist. There was never any swearing in our house. There was never any coarseness. There was a lot of loving. I know up until the moment my father had a stroke that my parents' sexuality was very free. They made love up until his sickbed three times a week, which is a lot after thirty years of marriage, I think. He was also rather frivolous and had a few girlfriends, but would never stay away nights. He hurt my mother a lot because she was extremely jealous and possessive, but as a good Jewish father he never considered leaving his family for anybody else.

"I was growing up as the only child. My mother was strict. She came from a very strict German-French upbringing. I was told indeed by my mother to marry as a virgin and never accept anything else but cookies, candies, or flowers, especially never to accept money or bigger gifts than that from men. If she'd only known then. God, if she'd only known! You know the Canal (red light) District I took you to yesterday? We had a lot of international friends coming in and they would want to see Amsterdam and the Canal District. My father, who was quite a womanizer, didn't mind. I don't know if he paid whores but he sure didn't mind driving our car along the canals, and sometimes I would go along. I remember always when we passed those whores my mother would look at them in disdain, although my father had a jolly good time pointing them out. She said, 'Those girls should be secretaries or typists. I don't know why they do this.' So it was always being put down, prostitution, as a filthy job. I had never in my life dreamt I'd ever become a hooker.''

"Xaviera, tell me about the encounter with the English businessman that marked your starting point in prostitution.''

"It was Christmas time and I felt very lonely. So I went to Miami for a week. I had seen this man, about fortyish, in the Miami airport. Then I saw him again in New York and again waiting for the taxi. Eventually he put his suitcase up to mine, and to make a long story short we spent the week together. He was a married businessman, an Englishman from Paris, and he was rich. He treated me to the best restaurants and the best shows. We went to everything there was. I was treated like a lady, which I hadn't been for half a year.

"His last night he gave me a $100 bill. I said, 'For Christ's sake,' and wanted to rip it up. The night before we had seen *Promises, Promises* by Burt Bacharach, about a secretary who is in love with her boss. Instead of spending Christmas with her he gives her a $100 note and says, 'Honey, buy yourself something. I've got to stay home with my family.' She says, 'Promises, promises.' You know, like, 'Look what you're doing. I'm not a whore.' I felt exactly the same way.

"But I'd told him before that I would send my parents some money sometimes because they've been good to me all their lives. So he said, 'Your father is crippled. Put this money in an envelope and tell your mother to buy a nice silk pajama for her or something.' So I did and I had no more guilt. The next day he took me shopping and bought me $800 worth of clothes, and I had no guilt because it was like a gift. I was treated like a lady. I had told him about my life and he said, 'You are too charming.' I was very natural with no makeup. 'You are far too charming to just give it away to all those rascals.' So he gave me the number of a madam. 'Madam? What's a madam?' You know, 'whorehouses'? All I'd seen were hookers on the street, and it was really something that you didn't read about in those days. That's why *The Happy Hooker* sold so well.

"I went to see the madam and that's how it started, how I began working. He gave me the number of the madam and I got rid of the guilt. I said, 'Well, the hell with it,' to those guys. I kept my job with the consulate and sometimes I'd still go to the bar because I liked it. Then when they wanted to go to sleep with me I said, 'It's going to cost you fifty.' In those days fifty dollars was the normal price. Only slowly, a half year later, I got into the $100 bracket and up. But the funny thing is I was treated better as a whore than when I wasn't a whore. Because when I wasn't a whore it was just, 'Oh, she's an easy fuck. The flying Dutchman. You can screw her anytime for an orange juice.' But when I became a businesswoman it became real. 'Okay. She's got her job and we want those services and that's it.'"

"You are saying that your guilt was lifted by venting your anger at the Madison Avenue advertising executives by making them pay the price. Do you believe then that guilt can be dumped at will?"

"Let me tell you about a letter written to me through my column in *Penthouse*. They send me only the ones I'm allowed to answer. They have a very uptight legal department. But there was one I got that was related to guilt. It was a terrific letter that they did publish. It had to do with incest and it was the last incest letter they put in there. So anyway this woman wrote me a letter. She said, 'I'm sixty-five. I'm dying of terminal cancer. I have a few more months to live and I have something I must tell you because it's always been on my mind all my life; this guilt, this tremendous guilt. I've been having a sexual affair with my father ever since I'm fourteen to eighteen and my mother had died. Then I got married when I was twenty-one and my father moved away. We never had sex anymore, but I have never been able to get an orgasm with anybody else except with my father because of that horrible guilt.' And she said, 'I just want to tell the audience that there is nothing worse than living with guilt all your life because it fucks you up forever sometimes.' But she said, 'I don't regret having done this with my father, but I regret the taboo society puts upon incest, especially under those circumstances when there is no mother, where we really didn't hurt anybody.' This is what guilt does. Guilt should be eliminated when there is nobody that gets hurt emotionally, you know?

But she wrote her guilt off in that letter, I think. She said, 'I read and reread and reread the letter and I rewrote it five times and I finally got it out of my system.'"

"What did you mean when you said the feeling of guilt is a good feeling sometimes?"

"Like Emily.* She was guilty for no reason, but explaining her guilt was like taking it off her chest." A few nights before, Xaviera had had a small dinner party featuring Indonesian food—a cuisine quite common in Holland, as Indonesia is a former Dutch colony. In fact, Xaviera was born in the legendary Indonesian city of Bali. After dinner she encouraged me to turn on the tape recorder and she began to tell the group about my book. Mentioning guilt, she told the group about an incident from the preceding evening when she, her boyfriend, Fritz, and I had visited the *Kring*, or Inner Circle, the private artists' club of which she is a member. We sat around a large wooden table and were joined by many of her friends, including Emily, the petite, blond New Zealander wife of a prominent Dutch painter. Emily turned out to be such a study in inappropriate guilt that Xaviera told the story of Emily to the dinner guests.

"Emily was guilty because she gave me a jar of fish on the way to Paris. Like a real Jewish mother she made me a bag with fish. And then she realized, 'Oh God, Vera doesn't like fish.' She gave me figs and almonds and she realized, 'My God, she's on Weight Watchers. I shouldn't give that to her.' So Fritz, my boyfriend, Frank, and I were in the *Kring* last night and Fritz said to her, 'What a lovely scarf you have. What a lovely shawl.' So she says, 'Have it.' And then she feels guilty about having given it because I might not have liked it. So then Fritz has this beautiful ivory pipe [cigarette holder] and she says, 'Oh, I like your pipe,' and she was holding it. Now, Fritz is not the type to immediately give everything away. He has not quite that nature that she has. So Emily says, 'Oh, I love your pipe. Can I try it?' So I whispered to Fritz, 'Give it to her, for Christ's sake, because I don't know what to give her. Please, at least she has something she likes.' So he says, 'Have it. I have another dozen at home.' I whispered, 'For Christ's sake, how can you say this to her?' Like, 'Oh, where this comes from there are many others.' But later we decided that he did the right thing. Because if he'd said, 'Oh, God, this is my last pipe,' which it was maybe, she'd be guilty again." Xaviera laughed with the group and shook her head at the absurdity of it all.

But Emily had seen it too. She had told the story about the picnic

---

*All of the names used in this chapter, except Xaviera Hollander's, are fictitious.

basket on herself. "So expressing her guilt to us that night was a great relief. I could experience it like an orgasmic feeling. If I would have a heavy guilt I would talk it off and to take that guilt off my shoulders could be as satisfactory as an orgasm."

"Obviously, then, you are no believer that a person should live with guilt for the rest of his life?"

"No. That I don't believe. I mean to have temporary guilt feelings is like hating. It's like jealousy. It's like loneliness. They are all feelings and emotions, but you shouldn't get a hang-up from them. Otherwise, you make guilt a part of your life. If you're asking me if I ever had any regrets or felt guilty about anything, I felt guilty about having ruined that one and only family relationship that I've got with a step-sister. Because I've got no family other than my mother."

In *The Happy Hooker* Xaviera revealed an affair that she had with her brother-in-law while staying at the house of her step-sister and her family in South Africa. "When I wrote that book I was a hooker running a bloody whorehouse. I never thought that this book could go beyond American borders, much less become a worldwide bestseller that would be printed in eighteen languages. It was smuggled into South Africa through Swaziland. I knew it could never be sold in South Africa because of restrictive censorship laws. Little did I know some people would send it in. But I disrupted an emotional relationship, of course, which those two people had. I was disrupting trust and confidence and fidelity. They're still together, but she doesn't talk or write to me. I'm dead for her."

"All right. That is real guilt over a serious matter. Coping with something like that must be more than a matter of 'getting it off your chest.'"

"But you've got to have the right attitude. Look, I should have had so much fucking guilt with my type of life, and I don't. Even though, for instance, at one time my mother had tremendous guilt about me. After *The Happy Hooker* came out in Dutch she was very hurt and I had to promise to her not to ever publish any other books in Dutch. People would look at her like, 'Oh, your daughter this. Your daughter that.' Even though I was known worldwide I was nothing but a whore. I gave her a beautiful mink coat and she wore it in the street. On that street everybody knows everybody. So I gave her this beautiful mink coat right after the *Happy Hooker* scandal broke out. So she walks with the coat in the street in the winter and a neighbor, a woman, comes up to her and says, 'Oh, what a lovely coat you've got.' My mother says, 'Yes'—proud—'it's a gift from my daughter.' 'Oh,' she said, 'your daughter must have gone flat on her ass quite a few times to pay for that.' So my mother immediately gave the coat to the cleaning lady. She couldn't stand living with the guilt over wearing it."

"I know *you* wouldn't mind walking down the street in a fur coat, though?"

"No, I don't feel guilty about how I earned it, and I don't feel guilty about how many animals were shot for it either. You might as well walk down the street in sneakers if you don't want to wear animal skins."

"Well, what is that right attitude you referred to that prevents you from feeling guilty?"

"Well, *qui s'excuse, s'accuse.* He who excuses himself, accuses himself. But I don't feel guilty about my achievement. I've worked for it. I have never been a vicious boss who has beaten up girls physically or mentally. I haven't ripped people off or taken profits where I shouldn't. As a madam I never felt guilty.

"The women's liberation movement in America, at one point, accused me of being a female pimp, of abusing women. And I had a big press conference with them and I talked about it. They said, 'Are you a feminist? Are you in the women's liberation movement?' I said, 'I am not a feminist and I am not a women's libber. I am a liberated woman. I'm not for this whole militant attitude of ban the bra and 'Fuck you, Charlie. You wash your socks.' But I am very independent and a career woman. I don't consider what I have done should make me feel guilty toward women. I have never abused them. I have never forced anybody into being a prostitute. I never said, 'You must fuck that guy or else I'll kick your ass out.' They were greedy enough. That's the problem with hookers. They're often so greedy they'll take anything—some man that I wouldn't have taken, for instance."

"But what about sexual guilt? Is it ever appropriate?"

"The reason *The Happy Hooker* became so well known is not so much because it's about whorehouses but because it's about a healthy attitude toward sex. About the fun side of it. Of course there's the criminality, and blackmail, and organized crime, and the Knapp Commission [an investigation into police corruption]. But as far as sex is concerned you won't find much guilt in there. People should be guilty about sexual things only if one of the two partners does not seem to enjoy what the other does. So if you want to tie up your wife and beat the hell out of her and she digs it, fine. But if you whip her or spank her or you beat her up and *you* get a thrill out of it but she really doesn't, then I think one of the two should feel guilty. And then you must simply just stop it."

"It appears quite evident that the way you look at guilt has allowed you to emerge emotionally untouched from life as a Happy Hooker."

"The problem of having been a Happy Hooker is that you never shake the image of being a whore. Of being a sex object. Of sex. You can't say, 'I'm in love now and I don't care about fucking twenty other men. I don't want to share my man. I'm an old-fashioned romantic.' Because nobody believes it. You are caught in living up to the bloody expectations of the public. A perfect example. You know my parties. There are no orgies. Well, one day I met this lovely couple and that night I was organizing one of my soirees, we call it, house concerts. We have some musicians sometimes and they play what they like, jazz, classical, whatever. So I met this couple and I really liked the woman. They were from London. And they had heard about me. She had read the *Penthouse* or something. And I said, 'Hey, how long are you in town for?' And they said, 'We're here for the holiday weekend. We don't know anything about Amsterdam.' They had a little map like you had. 'Where should we go?' So I said, 'Hey, by the way, if you want to, why don't you have dinner and come afterwards to my house? I'm having a little soiree.'

"So ten o'clock passes, comes eleven o'clock and they are playing the violin and the piano and the doorbell rings. And here is this little tiny English bird and her boyfriend. She says, 'I'm sorry but we're a bit late. But I was a bit afraid that there was going to be an orgy.' They hadn't stepped inside yet, but she had seen a lot of dressed people and she said, 'But everybody is still dressed in there!' So she comes inside and here is the violinist playing and the pianist and everyone standing around with their clothes on. But people do expect it from you. And then they are disappointed if they don't have an orgy. They are afraid to come and then their curiosity drives them to my house and then they say, 'Oh, this is all there is? A bit of music?' To the public I'll always be the Happy Hooker. But, I suppose I'm being a sado-masochist, so I need to suffer a little bit myself."

"It sounds as if you, like the rest of us, play mind games at times with guilt. Looking back on your days as a madam, can you recall people manipulating guilt for their own purposes?"

"The perfect example of guilt with prostitutes is the following. A good-looking Jewish man comes into my house. I have a preference for Jewish men and I like to get my orgasms in too sometimes. So I wanted to kiss the man, right? He paid his hundred dollars and I thought, 'Oh, this one, He's going to do it to me. I'm going to get my satisfaction.' So I wanted him to kiss me. He said, 'No, I don't kiss prostitutes.' All right. So I wanted to blow him and then fuck him. Well, he wasn't into oral sex. 'I don't suck pussy. No prostitutes.' So finally I blew him but I didn't want him to come in my mouth so I wanted to climb on top of him and fuck him. At least get something going, right? He said, 'Oh, I'm not going to put it in you. You must be crazy.'

"I said, 'Why are you paying a hundred dollars if you don't want anything?' 'Just give me a blow job.' I said, 'Why a blow job?' He said, 'If I don't kiss, if I don't suck you, if I don't fuck you, I haven't really put it in you. Then I'm not going to feel guilty.'

"People are so stupid about guilt and their little games. I use the direct approach. No-holds-barred. I come on like gangbusters, you know?"

"You don't sit around feeling guilty that you should be doing one thing or another?"

"When I should see somebody, I call that person. When I should do something, I organize it. I'm the leader, a little Führer. I do it today if I can do it, rather than tomorrow.

"A sample of a little guilt was last week when I went to Paris. I needed a change. I needed a break and I knew Fritz would be there and I wanted him to enjoy a few days instead of always just staying with me in Amsterdam. But I also knew I couldn't afford it time-wise. I wanted to finish the book I'm working on."

"But you went. How did you cope with the guilt?"

"I'm going to start working in the next day or two. As soon as you leave. I don't have set hours and I will get caught up by working late, until five in the morning or so. My last book, *The Magic Mushrooms*, I did all on tape in Thailand. I was fasting and I locked myself up in my room and knocked the whole book out in four days. I had the whole book perfectly written and later typed out.

"Just like the small guilt you confessed to me the other day over not doing your share of the housework. If you are guilty about not having done certain work, not having cleaned house, there are two ways out. You can apologize or do it. I don't like apologies. Your other choice is to do it. Say, 'I'm sorry I didn't do it now, but next week you can take off and I'll clean the whole house.' You know, 'I'll do double chores.'"

When we finished the interview we left her bedroom and went for a drive. The first stop was a shopping mall nearby, the equal of any in the United States. She was in a joking mood, and as we passed a display of athletic equipment in a department store she began to mimic the earlier interview. She knew I had missed my morning run. "Don't you feel guilty about not jogging today, Frank?" She held an imaginary microphone to my face as we wound through the crowded aisles. "Not even a little? Huh? Huh?"

Then we headed out in search of a windmill. They are hard to find. I was told that only 150 remain in Holland, and I felt cheated at the prospect of missing the photo opportunity. As we drove along the green fields by the canal, with the sunroof opened to the fresh air, Xaviera, then thirty-seven, told me, "I have no regrets. I think about the past only in situations such as when you are asking me about it. The past seems so far away and so long ago. When I look at the whores and I look at myself I think, 'Have you really done all this? Have you run a whorehouse?' I have never reread my books, but I do intend to read them again when I'm about fifty. I'll read them one by one. It's like a diary, actually, for me. It's the only way to really keep track of the things I've done; the main events of my life. It's a good little ego trip to see where you've come a long way from or where you've sunk. I think I've come up instead of gone down."

We found what we were looking for and she stood patiently by as I took enough shots to satisfy myself. Then we began walking toward her car through the lush grass. The large, dark green windmill with huge white blades was surrounded by tulips of almost every color imaginable. The silence, in not an unpleasant way, reminded me of a cemetery. Xaviera apparently experienced the identical sensation. "Live life to its fullest! When I die I think I'll have as my epitaph, 'Here lies Xaviera. She lived a full life.' I can die today and say that."

CONTROLLING GUILT

Fundamental Wisdom
If your past has been plagued with guilt, consider this. Your future is a clean slate, but you are free to write on it for a short time only. You can go to Selma as some of the more socially conscious did in the 1950s and '60s or you can forget about it. Regardless of the choice, you are free to avoid poisoning your future with chronic guilt. Start living your life as Xaviera Hollander does. Remember, our GITs are presented for the purpose of providing you with specific coping tools. The use of these tools as they are practically applied is demonstrated in the context of the actual life of each GIT. Living your life as Xaviera does means utilizing the Fundamental Wisdom that follows in your life as she does in hers—in control and without apology.

Real Guilt. There is no denying that there will be many instances when you judge the guilt you are feeling to be rational and appropriate. This is the case when you have unquestionably violated your personal code. The issue becomes the control of your guilt. Xaviera pointed out that such guilt is a message to act. If you do, guilt disappears spontaneously. There is no need to make it an ever-present part of your life. She said, "I'm not a 'mañana bore.' I'm not like my girlfriends who say, 'Oh, honey, let's have dinner one night,' or 'We should meet and have lunch.' I hate that. I do it today." If there is something that you should really be doing, don't continue to put it on top of your list morning after morning. Do it. If you really ought to change your way of handling things, don't keep talking about the need to start behaving differently. Do it. Act quickly to remedy the situation that is perpetuating your feelings of guilt.

Dues Paying. If it seems that you are unable to shake the chronic, sickening feelings of guilt no matter how hard you try, you might be embracing your guilt. If you are playing this game, you have accepted guilt as the price of doing business as usual. Remember, dumping real guilt requires change. Are there some guilt-producing behaviors that you have been unwilling to change? "A small example of such guilt," says Hollander, "is the man who is cheating on his wife and he brings home roses afterwards." He does what he likes, feels his guilt, pays his penance in the cost of a dozen roses, and feels that he is even. He would have found it unthinkable to spend the afternoon with his lover and later arrive home with a smile on his face, a whistle on his lips, and no roses in his fist. What a terrible thing to do to his wife! Until he is ready to end the affair, the guilt is necessary to set things right with him. As with the man encountered previously who arranged with himself to avoid guilt by avoiding certain specific acts with the prostitutes he hires, the mental twists and turns using guilt in this manner can be intricate psychological works of art. "Like the Catholics," said Xaviera. "They don't have it so difficult, because they can always confess. So they just have to live with their guilt for a few days until they express it. And then they go do it all over again."

Personal Codes. Instead of expending intellectual effort working around the rules you have set for yourself, perhaps the rules themselves require examination with a critical eye. Do you sustain guilt week after week like the working mother who suffers over not spending more time with her children? She soothes her guilt by spoiling the children when she is with them and bringing home too many gifts when she's been away. A change in code could rid her of guilt immediately and permanently. To some this smacks of convenience and compromise, but your life is your own. You have the right to set the rules and mark off the boundaries. Such a change in the basic belief system for this woman might involve the acceptance that even though her own mother always met her at the door when she returned from school, family economics have changed. Although she might choose to do the same if she had a real choice, she is a necessary part of a two-breadwinner family. Her resolve to make the existing time with her children "quality time" may be all she can do. Xaviera's code is limited to stopping short of infringing on the rights of others. If you wish to place different limitations on yourself, be careful to avoid any rule that is unnecessary, that is not in line with your genuine beliefs, or that makes no sense to you. Otherwise you will create self-imposed demands that you will routinely ignore and that will, in turn, continue to create unnecessary guilt.

Imposed Guilt. Don't breathe easy yet. Even if you have now resolved to unburden your shoulders of guilt, others will try to load it right back on you again. Xaviera described the "guilt inflicted by the priests" that she witnessed during her stay in Uruguay. "There women really still marry as virgins at twenty-five and thirty years old. They are predominantly Catholic and even masturbation is out of their world. I met this young lawyer. She was about twenty-six. She said, 'I wouldn't dare to masturbate. I'd just feel so guilty I couldn't do it. I don't even know what it feels like to have an orgasm.' She had never had a man, nothing." The young lawyer's wishes regarding virginity and masturbation are not at issue. The issue is personal liberation. She apparently never considered her own thoughts or desires, she allowed herself to permit others to direct her behavior, using guilt as a bludgeon. "Act this way and avoid guilt," she has been told; "otherwise be ashamed." Accepting "shoulds" from others invites constant guilt. There are always those who will try to impose their values on you, whether they are in the form of overt figures of authority or in the classic tradition of the overprotective mother. Do not put this power into the hands of another. It is for you to set your own limits. Do so with prudence and restraint.

Carrot and Stick. Guilt quite properly can serve as a motivator, as motivation to bring your behavior more in line with your belief as to how it ought to be. But guilt is a powerful force that can be abused. It can be self-destructive if you begin to use it by asking of yourself more than you can reasonably expect. This sets up a chronic guilt/failure/guilt process that accelerates in severity and becomes difficult to disengage from. A patient of mine, a writer by occupation, came to the office one afternoon for his session and began with the statement. "I've been 'should-ing' all over myself today." "Should-ing" on yourself by imposing great mountains of unrealistic expectations in the misguided belief that the resulting guilt will be the best way to get a good effort from yourself always backfires. This ploy creates feelings of frustration and depression that can leave you emotionally defeated. As a result you will accomplish less than if you had begun the day with reasonable goals.

Anger. At times the righteous expression of anger is required to break free of guilt feelings that clutch you. For instance, there is no real behavior change you can make to defeat programming from your past. And another person's behavior that is causing you to feel guilty is also a situation in which any change on your part is irrelevant. Consider the woman who finds her way to therapy complaining of guilt feelings arising from a relationship with a husband she describes as "perfect." He answers every question with, "Whatever you would like, dear." Anything she asks for is hers. The resulting frustration causes her to push to the limit by taking advantage. She habitually sticks her never-complaining husband with the kids while she cavorts with friends. She insists on eating most meals at restaurants so she can avoid having to cook. She continues to push, her husband continues to oblige, and guilt mounts until she bursts into the office filled with self-loathing. She is startled by the suggestion that she express her anger at her husband. "How could I be angry at him?" she says. "The problem is me. I am mean and selfish." But a small amount of psychological excavation unearths, beneath the guilt, feelings of disdain for her husband. "He is not facing things honestly. He isn't sharing responsibility. He is leaving everything up to me. He treats me like a child. He is no man to act the way he does." The expression of such unacknowledged anger erases guilt. So long as the anger continues to be expressed when it occurs, the guilt will not return.

Liberation. And finally, hanging onto guilt when you know better and are free to do otherwise is masochistic. Is pleasure that is handed to you on a silver platter guilt-producing? There is a masochistic streak in the American consciousness that is best rejected outright. Why can Listerine ["tastes strong but lasts long"] be sold on the merits of its bad taste? Or conversely, why need good sex mean you are "cheap and dirty"? Xaviera said, "Women are punished more by this masochistic guilt. This is why American women cannot get their orgasms. A man might feel guilty if he is cheating on his wife, but the women feel more guilty about sex in general. They might not even know what they are guilty about. Generally they are guilty about having their desires. And they don't dare to express them without being looked upon as being loose. 'Good girls don't like to fuck.' That is definitely part of their education. In Europe it's different. In Europe there is less guilt, depending on the country. The French. My God! I just came back from Paris. They must be the horniest bunch of people I've ever come across. All they think about is fuck, fuck, fuck. To them sex is *pas de problème*, no problem. They are, sexually at least, liberated." And they are liberated because they refuse to fall for the perplexing but frequently accepted idea that bad, in the form of pain, trouble, or guilt, is good for them. You will be liberated emotionally when you control your emotions. Rejecting masochistic mumbo-jumbo in your thinking is the final FW that will contribute toward total liberation from the tyranny of guilt.

12 / R. Buckminster Fuller

LIVING WITH FAILURE

Cowards die many times before their deaths;
The valiant never taste of death but once.

"Julius Caesar"

FUNDAMENTAL PROBLEM

The courageous toddler sits with a pile of blocks between his legs. He piles one on top of the other until the column teeters and falls. He claps his hands and screams with delight. Then he begins to stack the blocks again. The behavior of the adult experiencing a Fundamental Problem in coping with failure is strikingly different. Adult block-stackers, whether attempting to lower a golf score or climb the rungs of the corporate jungle gym, become increasingly distressed as they progress. The prospect of failure unnerves them.

Here is a surprise. Success may upset them just as much. In the eyes of these deficient copers, success only sets them up for a fall from greater heights. We each know a fat Aunt Martha. All her life she has expressed a longing to be thin, but she weighs as much now as she did thirty years ago. Failing at her diet only makes her mildly unhappy. Success is worse. During the few times in her marriage that she flirted with being thin, Uncle William became jealous and irritable. And she fears social situations even more than Uncle Willie's jealousy. Remaining plump allows her to avoid a social life because she can claim she is self-conscious about her appearance and none of her clothes fit.

The fear of failure as a FP interferes with successful coping in several ways. It may intimidate you to such a degree that you are actually afraid to act, as in the example of Aunt Martha. Should you be strong enough to overcome such intimidation, a second hazard awaits. Your performance may be so impaired by the anxiety generated over the prospect of failure that failure may actually be the result. Finally, there can be negative consequences to success. People hampered by this FP who are successful commonly find themselves unable to derive genuine enjoyment and satisfaction from their achievements. The lingering fear of failure continues to poison them with insidious self-doubt. They view their successes as temporary and feel like the bubble is about to burst.

The willingness to take risks and the ability to function without hands tied by performance pressure is necessary to progress in any area. It is self-evident that unless you begin to behave differently, little will be different in your life. If you are now plagued by the fear of failure and timidly continue to play life close to the vest, hoping futilely that things in the future will be different, you are almost certain to be disappointed.

R. BUCKMINISTER FULLER

Great Inspiring Teacher
The Great Inspiring Teacher for this chapter is a man who lives the Fundamental Wisdom necessary for coping with the fear of failure. More than this, he conquered the FP that plagued him into adulthood through a deliberate effort to understand the failure process.

R. Buckminister Fuller, as noted earlier in this book, coined the terms "Great Inspiring Teacher" and "Fundamental Wisdom." He is variously known as an architect, geometrician, poet, inventor, and philosopher. Bucky, as he is widely referred to, holds twenty-three U.S. patents and has written twenty books, selling more than one million copies in total. In 1981 he stepped down from his post as world fellow in residence at the University City Science Center in Philadelphia, where his work was supported by a consortium of four universities. Routinely labeled the Leonardo da Vinci of our times, he is most closely associated with geodesic dome structures. Examples of his work include the 275-foot-diameter USA exhibit at Montreal's Expo '67 and his radomes, dome-shaped radar housings which dot the Arctic DEW [distant early warning] line.

Bearing in mind his significant and tangible achievements wherever his attention has been focused, it is surprising to learn that Bucky considers himself quite an ordinary person. "I made myself a deliberate experiment to see what an average, healthy human being could do." He was to repeat this theme often during the time I spent with him. It was an important message for him to get across. After all, were we to view him as simply an extra-intelligent aberration, we could dismiss his record of incredible achievement as irrelevant to what we should expect from ourselves. "The most extraordinary thing about me is my ordinariness," he proclaims, challenging us to settle for no less in our own performance.

Flying from Tampa to Boston, the first leg of my trip to Deer Isle, Maine, where Dr. Fuller was spending August before commencing another academic year of teaching, lecture, and research, I was silently pleased to find an article on Dome Living featured on the cover of the airline magazine. There among the advertisements for luggage, wine racks, and chronometers was a story about life in a domed home. The piece closed with, "Somewhere, Buckminster Fuller must be smiling approvingly. . . ." Apparently the author assumed that Bucky was dead. Instead, I found him at home in a sprawling white house with the date 1780 on the chimney, fifty miles south of Bangor on one of the numerous islands edging out to sea from the coast of Maine.

Unraveling extension cords to ready the tape recorder for our first meeting, which was to take place in the dining room of the big family house, I was slightly startled as Bucky appeared without warning through the door from the kitchen. Eighty-four years of age, he was smiling warmly. Not the cleric-like figure in black suit of his pictures, he wore bright red corduroy pants and an un-tucked-in casual blue shirt. My first gushing words as to the pleasure of meeting him, voiced too loud because of my awareness of his hearing aids, went unheard. He motioned to the aids and asked that I speak at normal volume. This initial awkwardness served to break the ice. From that point I was able to relax and genuinely enjoy the two days of the interview.

"Bucky, you said that you are an example of what the average person can do, yet only a handful of people in each generation accomplish what you have. What do you mean?"

"There is nothing I've done that anybody couldn't do," he began. As he warmed to the subject he closed his eyes and focused out the window behind me on a spot about a foot above my head. "But somehow or other we have gotten into the total mistake where we say nobody should make mistakes. We punish people for making mistakes."

Failure, I was about to learn, is not a dirty word to Bucky. "Then do you feel that the ordinary human being would be able to accomplish a tremendous amount more if he were not afraid to make mistakes?"

"I call it the Mistake Mystique. As far as I am concerned everybody is born a genius. People think of them as a very, very infrequent occurrence in humanity but I say simply that the survivors are very few. Most get de-geniused very rapidly by the loving care of their parents. One of the proclivities of genius is to inquire in unique ways. But this is exactly what gets discouraged. We say, 'Darling, don't. You'll get in trouble if you do that.' 'Don't do this.' 'Don't touch that.' This don't-ing by parents sets up the failure complex of humanity. Some of them live through it and we say they are geniuses. I say they are those who retain all their childlike sensitivity."

Bucky often concerns himself with the residents of what he terms "wombland," the sixty-three million unborn children. He feels strongly about what they require in their environment from their earliest experiences. "I'd like to get them the environment where it makes it easy for the parents to let them do the logical thing and where they can get the information they need without getting don't-ed and without getting hurt. I don't mind them getting a little hurt because that's very important information.

"I saw that human beings have been born naked, absolutely helpless for months, hungry, thirsty—with beautiful equipment—but absolutely ignorant. With the drive of hunger and thirst and curiosity, they are deliberately designed to learn by trial and error. The propensity of a child is just this way. All children seem precocious. We find at first that muscle is very important but then find that we have a mind that is very much more important than muscle.

"Inasmuch as we were designed to learn by trial and error, we had to make an incredible number of mistakes before we had 150 words in the Oxford dictionary. Humanity had to make billions of mistakes to get where we are. Yet now we've got this business of the Mistake Mystique where nobody should make a mistake. The concept of *failure* was invented by man. Nature doesn't fail. Nature does just what nature does.

"When man had the wrong expectancy he called it 'failure.' But it wasn't failure at all. Nature did just what nature does. Man's predictions were bad, that's all. But now, I see that humanity is preventing itself from really learning. It's getting paralysis by saying that nobody should make mistakes. A genius knows how to make mistakes and learn from them. If I were developing an educational system, I would fail everybody who got all the right answers. Because I would say they were just parrots; they were just trying to get the right answers and not interested in learning. I would give the highest marks to all the people who could tell me about the most mistakes they had made and what they had learned from them."

By 1927 Bucky was in Chicago and out of work. His first child, Alexandra, had died close to her fourth birthday. Just thirty-two years old, Bucky's sense of his own failure had become unbearable. "You don't tend to break out of the system unless you fail in the system one way or another. The great chance is at the bottom. I came to it myself when I came close to committing suicide."

"I know you reached the point of throwing yourself into Lake Michigan. How did you turn things around for yourself?"

"I said I was going to do away with myself and for the first time, at least, get out of pain. I decided literally that I was going to throw myself away. But first I told myself I must do some thinking about this. What do I know about what I'm doing?"

It was then that Bucky took stock. He decided on a dramatic change in self-perception. Rather than continuing to view his life as a collection of failures, he would now see himself as a "bundle of experiences." These experiences, he saw, could be drawn upon to make progress in nature's way, which, he had realized, involved the process of trial and *error*. "I understand that you spent two years in almost total silence preparing to tackle the world again."

"One of the ways I have gotten into the most trouble is with words. We have all kinds of extraordinary spontaneous reflexes in terms of words. So I said, 'I'm going to have as much of a moratorium on words as I can.' I couldn't have a complete one, but my wife let me be pretty silent."

"Why did you do it?"

"Because I wanted to be sure that when I began to make these sounds again I would know what it was really going to do to another human being. I would never ask anybody to listen to me ever again. I would talk only to people who would ask me to talk to them."

"What did you do when you started talking again?"

"Well, I'm a very hard realist. I said at the outset that I'm going to have to do my own thinking and deal in experiential information. Luckily, I had very good scientific training. But also I'll have to be very, very sensitive and use all my intuition. There will be nobody to mark my paper. So I began a process of asking myself what is the next most important thing to be done. Trial and error is like sailing. You go from a starboard tack to a port tack. And you must keep on tacking until you get the right tack to find out what nature does let you do. So that is what I have been doing for fifty-two years and I have been really very, very successful."

So the essential FW is this: Tacking to and fro, Bucky—and all who risk and sometimes fail—moves ahead. As a counter-balance to each failure, each error in the trial-and-error process, exists the potential for stunning accomplishment. "Then you are saying, quite definitely, that you believe a certain amount of failure is very natural if progress is to take place."

"Nature makes many starts. She doesn't take any chance on just one start. The more important, or the worse the chance of survival, the more starts she makes. For instance, the tree's function is to impound the sun's radiation. It can't have its young in its own shadow because it [the seedling] wouldn't have any radiation to impound. So all the trees are launching thousands and thousands of little gliders with a seed in them, hoping some of them get out from underneath their shadow and will land in places where things are propitious. But the chances that any one of them should be successful are extremely poor."

Living comfortably with the probability that from time to time a monkey wrench will be thrown into the middle of your plans as you progress by means of trial and error is the heart of Bucky's FW. If coping with this fear plagues you in FP proportions, you might have been surprised that bright Maine Sunday morning, were you sitting across the corner of the polished wooden table, as Bucky followed up these last comments with the statement that "the problem is a gift."

"What do you mean?"

He eagerly rushes ahead to explain, speaking by his own estimate at 7,000 words per hour. "I said there was nobody to mark my papers, nobody to tell me what to do. So you have to intuit your way. You say 'What are the first things that have to be done?' and try to attend to that. Then maybe this needs attention for a while, then it yields. You are always going from the starboard to port tack. Then all of a sudden you come to a blockage. This is the one thing I can find that's common to all lives in all history. Common to all lives, it's problems, problems, problems. But I think a great many people think of problems as being bad luck, and they try to have a problemless life." He appears amused by this last idea. Such an unnatural goal as striving for a problemless life, he seems to feel, would be as futile and unproductive as wishing for an exemption from gravity.

"But they never really do. Solving problems doesn't get you to Utopia. If you're any good at solving problems, it gets you qualified for bigger problems to solve. This is really the way my life has built up since I made this commitment, and I now find myself dealing with very, very big problems, and getting some good answers. And gradually, society begins to realize that those are good answers."

Bucky Fuller is a "normal"; an ordinary human being. Like the toddlers he describes as possessing the essence of genius, he has not been afraid to risk piling his blocks up high. His willingness to experience failure, based upon his understanding that failure is normal—even an absolute necessity for learning—has brought him a life of uncommon achievement. "Does one get used to taking such risks?" I asked him at the end. "Through a lifetime of confrontations, does the prospect of failure become less threatening and more comfortable?"

"Well, you have so much to comfort yourself with," he replied, alluding to a history of success with trial and error. "But the point is, you are always up against finding yourself worrying and then realizing you are defeating everything by worry. You have to go through it time and time again. There is no training yourself to be sublime, because it requires live thinking at all times. It never becomes automatic. You just have to time and time again say, 'Who am I?'"

COURAGE

Fundamental Wisdom
Bucky appeared to enjoy sharing his retrospective with me. He had illustrated his points with relish, quoting from memory several poems of Kipling at one point and a poem of his own at another. His arms and trunk had waved furiously to illustrate his analogy of the seed-launching tree. In our discussion of genius he reminisced about his friendship with William Faulkner. Later he rushed out of the room and brought back a long telegram he had sent off the day before to one of the state's U.S. senators about Maine's Dicky-Lincoln Dam project. Speaking of what he likes to call the "big picture," how the universe works according to a plan of which failure is an integral part, he again cast back to the dark time, at age thirty-two and poised for suicide, when he rejected the concept of failure. "I would say that since that time, only the impossible has happened." For the reader of *Being Better Than You've Ever Been*, grabbing hold of these insights will clear the way to unlimited accomplishment in your own life.

Failure Complex. Beginning early in life with the "don't-ing" of our loving parents, the concept of failure takes on a head-hanging connotation. It is grouped with such unpleasant concepts as sin and disgrace. In knee-jerk

fashion we develop the belief that failure is som
avoided. Bucky says, "I was brought up as a chi
mind what you think. Listen. We're trying to teach y
these people saying that to me loved me very much,
thing they could to teach me not to pay attention to m
to try to get over my sensitivities." If you are a parent,
to your children's success in developing the ability to
Make their environment safe to explore, avoid don't-ing   ᴖncourage
curiosity. Adds Bucky, "It is the type of loving environment that when
you say, 'Look, Mom,' Mom takes the trouble to look." As an adult it is
certainly not too late for you. When your intuition urges you to try something different, give it a try. There's no need to play it safe all the time.
Taking a risk is good for the soul. It reminds you that you're alive. You are
likely to learn things you would never learn being faithfully orthodox.

Mistake Mystique. The grim effort to avoid failure or even its appearance
sets up the phenomenon of the Mistake Mystique. Society sets up penalties
for mistakes. An error becomes something requiring an apology, an excuse, or even a denial. Mistakes, if too frequent, threaten our standing in
society and our view of our self-worth. A common practice is to unrealistically vow to try never to make another. Considering the number of
decisions we are required to make daily, often based on incomplete data
and without full control of circumstances, it seems reasonable to allow for,
at the minimum, a 20 percent mistake factor. The resulting 80-percent
error-free performance will be great, far above the level of mere chance.
As you progress through the day making choices and predictable mistakes,
simply toss your errors into the 20-percent-error column and keep moving.

Predictions. Rather than representing a moral lapse, failure is simply a
concept invented by people to describe an event that did not turn out as
expected. What you thought was going to happen did not. Unless you are
omniscient, own a crystal ball, or never do anything that is not absolutely
predictable, then the unexpected, as Bucky says, can be expected. The
more we veer from the already known, the more this will happen. There is
no morality attached to it. Get comfortable with the unexpected. If you
want to be concerned about something, watch out for perfect days. If
everything is on schedule and going completely as expected, then there is
cause for concern. You may not be trying hard enough. I asked Bucky if
this approach made him an optimist. "I consider optimists and pessimists
unbalanced people. I'm just an incredibly hard mechanic. I am a sailor.

or. The fact that I am able to tell you, 'I think I can get your
ss the ocean,' when I show you that you had options you didn't
you had, makes you feel better. You say my optimism has brushed
on you. But whether you are going to make it or not, I haven't the
slightest idea."

Mother Nature. Surprises, inaccurate predictions, or—if you can live with
the word—"mistakes" are part of nature's process of moving forward.
Mistakes are essential to progress. To resent mistakes by taking them personally and allowing yourself to become distressed by them is absurd. Just
like the tree that launches hundreds more seedlings than can be expected to
root and grow, plan to progress in shotgun fashion. Bucky guesses, "I
think Mother Nature must have many other kinds of starts in many other
parts of the universe." Set out for your goal by using as many means to
get there as you can devise. The advance expectation and acceptance that
most of your seedlings will fall upon barren ground makes you comfortable
with mistakes and makes risk taking tolerable. Bucky has had his share of
business failures, unbuilt design projects, and even inventions like the two-
foot "tensegrity sphere" that hung above our heads from the dining room
chandelier. For the moment, at least, while it incorporates interesting and
innovative design principles, this roundish geometrical structure has no
practical utility.

Gifts. At first you may find Bucky's labeling of problems as "gifts" rather
startling. How well you cope with the problems that will certainly come to
you is one measure of a life well lived. Nature and society so value effective problem solvers that the better they function, the more problems are
heaped upon them. Successful problem solvers have learned to steadily
deal with life's "blockages" one at a time, on a priority basis. As mountain climbers are always advised, "Don't look down." An easy and steady
pace, working at what lies before you, will allow you to deal with life's
challenges comfortably without becoming overwhelmed by what lies
ahead.

Learning. Although learning from success is easy, our failures are equally
instructive. Learning is there for all who are courageous and avoid waste-
fully expending intellectual and emotional energy covering up the very existence of their mistakes. Take stock daily. Look for the lessons borne by
your bad predictions. Refusing to learn from the mistake segment of the
trial-and-error process is like going to school on alternate days—you are

bound to miss some very important lessons. It was just this insight that allowed Bucky to stop short of taking his life. He decided to stop agonizing over his failures and to learn from them instead. He says, "All this extraordinary experience was really turned to advantage. You really need to find out how you *don't* work and how the system *doesn't* work, or you will never be any good in that system."

Shangri-La. So great is the mistake mystique that many have made striving to live the problemless life their greatest purpose. Somewhere in the distant future they envision a time when they can sit in a comfortable chair with their feet propped up, secure in the knowledge that all their problems have finally been solved. It is then, they vow, that life will finally become enjoyable. Anyone who takes a few seconds to think clearly will realize that this widely held notion is a fairy tale. During the course of each day, you and everyone else will face the usual variety of problems to solve. This is not a phase. It's permanent. Don't try to get over it. The goal is to learn to get through it, daily, as effectively as possible with the least emotional cost. Effective problem solving requires constructive and creative decision making while maintaining a reasonably steady and comfortable emotional state. Viewing the life task in this manner, consciously and frequently, helps promote such healthy functioning.

Genius. The nature of genius and uncorrupted children, Bucky tells us, is to poke into things in ways that no one else does. The willingness to satisfy natural curiosity through the deliberate suspension of caution by risking error is the only way, except for serendipity, to significantly tap into our potential to grow. With the rewards so alluring, the single most overlooked fact in the process is that failure rarely involves calamity. In most cases, it merely represents an inconvenience. If the consequences remain unexamined, failure always looms large and ominous. Many of us appear conditioned to assume that each toss of the coin spells life or death. At the next opportunity to exercise your genius in the face of failure, weigh what is to be gained against the potential loss. Intellectual and emotional risks rarely justify avoiding failure at all costs.

Risking. When Bucky talks about "nobody to mark my paper," he is talking about veering off the track of conventional thinking and going it on his own. Staying on the lighted and well-worn path offers security. People will mark your paper and tell you how well you are doing at learning what has already been learned and performing what has already been performed. It's all been done before. There is no risk, thus no potential for failure. The cost for such security is the sacrifice of your own genius: as if Picasso had been content to paint by numbers. It is important for you to take risks. R. Buckminster Fuller said goodbye to me at his front door after leaving me with a very sobering thought. "There is such an acceleration in the world today that the next ten years is about the limit to whether we can make good or not. I tell every audience I speak to that what they do matters. Everyone counts because humanity is on trial." When even one of us is blocked from realizing his or her potential as a human being because of the inability to live with failure, it is a loss to all of us.

13/Muhammad Ali

SELF-REALIZATION

All the world's a stage,
And all the men and women merely players:
They have their exits and their entrances;
And one man in his time plays many parts,
. . .

"As You Like It"

FUNDAMENTAL PROBLEM

This final chapter contains both the ultimate Fundamental Problem and the ultimate Fundamental Wisdom of *Being Better Than You've Ever Been.* If you have reached this point you have clearly identified various FPs within yourself. You are convinced that upgrading your coping skills in specific FP areas will make you more comfortable. But the final FP for you is that these new insights remain primarily in the realm of thought. They are not yet reflected in your behavior. While you might yearn to be more assertive or to distance less, these behaviors are still not part of you. They are goals but little more.

Think back to the psychological chameleon in Chapter 10. He is always struggling to play the part he guesses will please the people he is with. This chapter provides you with the opportunity to implement the role designed to please yourself instead of others. Here are the how-tos to make any of the FWs in this book your own. No matter how irresponsible you recognize your behavior to be, responsibility is yours for the taking. Regardless of how poor your self-image has been in the past, this chapter on self-realization provides the techniques to absorb confidence and become emotionally secure.

To some people the idea of deliberately choosing a role sounds phony. But which is more real? Is it real to go through life blindly attempting to follow a script that has been written for you by others? Or is it more real to consciously make an informed choice by deciding how you want to function and then perfecting the intellectual, emotional, and behavioral skills you select? If you have decided that the "real" you is to be based upon the FW you choose, here is the way to get started.

MUHAMMAD ALI

Great Inspiring Teacher

Tap tap tap. Tap-a tap-a tap-a. High-top white boxing shoes deftly perform an ever-changing choreography. The rope whirls fast and slow, backward and forward again beneath the shoes and stings the hardwood floor. Ali's body glistens with sweat and his reflection looks back at him from the full-length mirror. The nimble stepping belies his 254 pounds. Three feet above floor level and behind him is a regulation boxing ring featuring powder blue canvas. Three sides of the ring are bracketed with tourists and locals occupying most of the four rows of metal folding chairs. This gym, a log cabin building, is the focal point of The Muhammad Ali Training Camp in Deer Lake, Pennsylvania.

At a signal from trainer Wali Muhammad, or "Blood," the rope is tossed aside and Ali passively stands by the training table, still not turning to meet the eyes in the crowd behind him, as his outstretched hands are bandaged and the gloves are tied in place. The total silence of the crowd, heavy with station-wagon-type families, is a little peculiar. They appear to be taking home movies with their eyes, perhaps planning to replay this event on bar stools and at barbecues for the rest of their lives. Then Ali steps up to the red Everlast heavy bag and captures it in his unswerving gaze. The awesome, methodical smack of leather against leather continues for two three-minute rounds and the unavoidable thought of being struck with just one such punch is actually frightening.

This time the audience applauds after Blood's barked signal of "time" as a winded Ali walks to the open side door. He appears to simultaneously breathe in the fresh summer air and the pastoral view far below his mountain compound. Abruptly he turns, throws off the boxing gloves, and begins an impromptu talk to a crowd that he seems to have just noticed. He begins by telling them he is training for another attempt to win the World Heavyweight Title for the fourth time. No one was taking this attempt, at age thirty-nine, seriously. This fact combined with the decision of the American Boxing Federation to revoke his license after his dismal showing against Larry Holmes in Las Vegas provided him with the type of impossible challenge on which he thrives.

The talk is vintage Ali and he delivers it at a shout. "The word is I'm old! The word is I'm all washed up! Too fat! The American Boxing Federation wants to take away my right to fight—to make a living. Well, they're judging me through their eyes. If I could only see what they see, then I wouldn't be me, would I? I'm unusual. I'm unpredictable. I'm a prophet. I'm a poet. I'm a magician. I'll show you some magic before you leave. I'm the greatest of all time."

Ali paced back and forth next to the ring and for forty-five minutes delivered his thoughts to the crowd on religion, race relations, politics, romance, Muhammad Ali, motivation, philosophy, and boxing. During that time his sparring partner arrived, put on gloves, warmed up, hung around for a time, took the gloves off, and walked away. At the end of the talk, true to his word and assisted by Mr. Majestik, the black Hollywood magician who was part of the entourage, Ali put on an entertaining magic show to the delight of the many children present. At the show's conclusion he gave a final bow to heavy applause and invited everybody back the next day with the promise of a show that "will be even better."

A sports reporter from a Reading television station caught him as he turned to leave, and the champ obligingly stepped up to a corner of the ring to be interviewed. As the insta-cam man and his battery-belted assistant closed in, Ali teased:

> *I like your looks.*
> *I like your style.*
> *But your camera's so cheap,*
> *Don't come back for awhile.*

The reporter was young and this was obviously a big moment in his career. Smiling he stepped up to the corner with his mike and was surprised at Ali's deceptive size. "You're bigger than I thought," he muttered. "Did you call me a nigger?" yelled Ali. He brandished a fist and bit his lower lip in mock ferociousness. This is a classic Ali gag. The young man blushed and stammered and composed himself as best he could before the blazing TV lights. Ali then went through his "they say I'm too old" material for the six o'clock news and the afternoon's exhibition was over.

Back in the dressing room, behind the wooden door with the one-way mirror, the mood was quieter. Ali took off his shoes, stretched out on the green vinyl couch, and asked that the lights be lowered. Abdel, a nine-year Moroccan member of the troupe, massaged Ali's feet while Wali Muhammad and Drew "Bundini" Brown, Ali's long-time guru and trainer and the originator of "Float like a butterfly, sting like a bee," silently went about the business of organizing equipment for the next day. Jimmy Ellis, a former boxer and another regular member of the staff, sat silently nearby. I had barely begun to ask Ali about some of his comments to the crowd when Murad Muhammad, an Atlantic City boxing promoter and former Ali bodyguard, burst in the back door with Elijah Tilley. Tilley is a young cruiserweight (between light heavyweight and heavyweight) division contender with a 10–0 record who was hoping to spar with Ali. He looked much like the young Cassius Clay of twenty years ago. After sizing him up—"You look like Superman"—and testing the speed of his jab—"Throw me something"—Ali agreed to spar the proposed five rounds.

In contrast to his performance in public, there was never any clowning in Ali's dressing room. As soon as he nodded approval to Tilley, his men solemnly moved into action like a well-rehearsed pit crew. Blood carefully laid out the gear and Bundini helped Ali apply Vaseline to his upper body and face. Ali remained deadly serious and continued to stare into the dressing-room mirror as his two corner men finished their preparations. Then they pushed open the door and re-entered the gym. Bundini began to banter with Murad and Tilley. "Don't go getting in that ring trying to make your reputation, now. We just want to break sweat. This is just to snap a few pictures so you can go home and tell your mama you were in the ring with Muhammad Ali." Tilley shouts to Ali, "I won't hurt you," and Ali speaks for the first time. He is more serious than ever. "Don't pull any punches. I won't be pulling any either." He adds to me, "The reason I want to work with him is he is young and he has quick reflexes. If I can duck and dodge him I'll feel good. If I can't get away, then I'll feel it's over."

Only a few trailing members of the crowd remained as the fighters were helped into heavy groin protectors and headgear. Without any fanfare the first round was underway. Ali shouted to Tilley commands that were unintelligible at first because of his mouthpiece. Jimmy Ellis yelled out the translations. "Throw me something!" "Show me something!" Five hard-fought rounds passed with both fighters punching aggressively. At the end

Ali was still demonstrating his backward gliding and circling as he shouted incessantly, "Are you tired, young man?" "Show an old man something." Blood shouted the final "time." Tilley quickly peeled off the headgear and spit out the mouthpiece. He had given a respectable accounting of himself. But Ali was not ready to quit. "Let's go five more," he shouted. The kid looked uncertain. Since I was the only writer in camp, Ali had long before begun considering me the official representative of the world press. He leaned over the ropes to me and said none too quietly, "I'm thirty-nine and he's twenty-four. Look, he's had enough." That was all the incentive Tilley needed. He jumped into the ring without head protector or mouthpiece, ready to go. An amused Ali spit out his own mouthpiece and went out to meet him. It became a toe-to-toe slugfest. Although the jovial Bundini seemed to be enjoying it, Wali Muhammad was clearly not pleased. He took off his stopwatch and turned for the door, shouting over his shoulder, "You can box all day if you want to." The two boxers fought savagely, without the benefit of referee or between-round breathers, for almost ten minutes more.

The barrage eventually stopped, and soon Ali was back lying on the green couch, almost as if nothing had transpired. The taunting Ali of a few minutes before was now pointing out his cabin from the dressing room window. We agreed to meet again at eleven to talk undisturbed after he returned to camp from an evening television appearance. Toward the end of his talk to the crowd he had commented, "Many of you are so surprised to hear me talk today and see me do this stuff because you didn't know who I was or what I was mentally-wise. I may have shocked you." The fact is that there are two sides to Muhammad Ali.

"Do Not Disturb" was scrawled on a piece of paper tacked to his rough-hewn cabin door when I arrived at eleven o'clock. Some voices could be heard through the door but I did not hear Ali's. Abdel showed me in to the large one-room cabin. Ali was lying on his high bed that had four dark posts as thick as telephone poles. An advisor was talking to him about a fund-raising campaign for WORLD.

"What is WORLD?" I asked. He answered me and I repeated it back. "World Organization for Rights, Liberty, and Dignity."

"Not *whites*," he exclaimed in fake horror. He was going into his "Did you call me nigger?" routine. "I said *rights*! This isn't about race. When I finish fighting this is what I'm going to do with my life. We'll be an international organization and the world headquarters will be right here at this camp." He ticked off an impressive list of celebrities who had already agreed to help him raise money. "We will go to places anywhere in the world where people are suffering. We've been looking into freeze-dried food that we can take to any country in the world for people who need it. You've got to have something to do in life, and this is how I'm going to spend my time."

"You know, Muhammad, I've seen you work the crowds and we've talked a little behind the scenes and I'm beginning to believe what many people suspect—that the public personality of Muhammad Ali is all show business."

In the sleepy, almost hushed voice that is also part of the private Ali, he answered carefully. "I heard someone say once that the man who has no imagination, he stands on the earth. He has no wings. He cannot fly. So before I fought [Sonny] Liston my imagination flew. I named him the Big Ugly Bear. Do you remember that? And after I established him as The Bear I got a bear trap. At the weigh-in I put the bear trap on the ground and put some honey on the ground leading right up to the bear trap. The reporters came up and said, 'What are you doing?' I said, 'Shh. Shh. The trap's for The Bear.'

"It sells tickets, right? Floyd Patterson. I labeled him The Rabbit. I took a head of lettuce and some carrots to the weigh-in. I said, 'These are for you, Rabbit. I'll meet you in the garden.' Madison Square Garden, right? Earnie Shavers. Bald head. What was he? The Acorn. It's imagination. When I fought Ernie Tyrell I named him The Squirrel. George Foreman was The Mummy because that's the way he fights. I asked the press, 'How's The Mummy going to catch me? I'm going to shuffle and move.' Publicity! Ken Norton. Beat him unmercifully. I named that fight in South Africa, 'The Rumble in the Jungle.' Joe Frazier was The Gorilla. Where did we fight The Gorilla, of all places? Manila. So I worked with that. I said, 'It will be a thriller and a chiller and a killer when I meet The Gorilla in Manila.'

"I have enough sense to know that the people who we want to come to fights don't know a left jab from a left hook. So I say something to attract people from all races. I say something like, 'I'm pretty. I'm the greatest.' Some say, 'The nigger talks too much. The nigger needs a whopping.' And they buy tickets. Then for the Black Panther I holler, 'I'm bad. I'll kill 'em.' He says, 'Tell them whiteys, Brother. Talk to them honkys.' He buys a ticket. Then I say, 'I'm pretty. I'm a pretty thing. There ain't nothing like me.' That gets all the fags," he mocks in his best gay voice. He waves a limp wrist, " 'You tell 'em, Muhammad.'

"And people love mystery. So knowing that, I give them just what they want." He affects a pseudo–spine-chilling voice. "He will fall in seven." Then he pantomimes handing out tickets as fast as his fingers can fly. "Ticket. Ticket. Ticket. Do you know that since I retired they haven't filled a house yet? And all the boxers are talking now. Sugar Ray Leonard took all my stuff. But it's keeping boxing going today. And all those years I was playing on the public. I looked like a fool. But there is a saying. 'A wise man can act like a fool, but a fool cannot act wise.' Is that heavy?"

"A good number of people who know boxing believe that you really are the greatest in the history of the sport. Did you begin with this feeling from the start? Is it something you always felt?"

"I got it after I beat Sonny Liston in 1964. Couldn't nobody beat Liston. He knocked out everybody. One fist was bigger than both of mine. He beat up policemen and took their guns. He was a b–a–d nigger. But the difference was my mentality. The mind controls the body. I said, 'I'm the greatest of all time.' I didn't believe it but I kept saying it. 'I'm pretty.' I knew that was true," he offers mischievously. " 'I am The King.' I talked like that until I believed it. And I talked so much I had to beat his butt or I couldn't go back to Harlem."

"There are people who say, 'I would like to be different. I would like to be confident or guilt-free or a new person but this is just not me. This is not the way I am.' "

Ali had been lying shirtless and shoeless on his side on top of his blanket. He propped an elbow under his head and leaned his head directly toward the mike. "These people have no imagination and they will stay where they are. They drink the wine of failure. The world is like a big wine cellar with all sorts of wine collected. Man has only to choose the wine he wishes. He who is drunk with the wine of success knows no failure. But he who has drunk the wine of failure may be given every chance to succeed, but he will not succeed. The man who says, 'I can't make it,' 'I give up,' 'I can't do it,' has drunk the wine of failure."

"How did you discover for yourself that the mind is the source of power, even in something considered so predominantly physical as boxing?"

"I met Elijah Muhammad, Malcolm X, and the Islamic religion in Miami. I was invited to hear a lecture and I went to the Muslim mosque. The truth is powerful. The first words that I heard were, 'Why are we called Negroes? The Chinese are named after China. Cubans are named after Cuba. Russians are named after Russia. Germans are named after Germany. All people are named after countries. What country is called Negro?' " Ali snaps his fingers. "That clicked something. The minister said, 'Why don't we have our own names? We all have white people's names. Slave names. Silly names like Washington, Jones, or Smith. Why do we have a white man we call Jesus? The last supper was nothing but white Europeans. The angels are white. We're brainwashed.' I heard this type of talk and I was freed. I accepted the Islamic religion in 1965. I'm the only man to change his name in the middle of his career. Some blacks are waking up. Lew Alcindor; he's Kareem Abdul-Jabbar. Bobby Moore of the Minnesota Vikings is Ahmad Rashad. It's kind of getting out. I started to see it in 1960. Islam is a world religion and since then I've been a world wonder. Not an American Negro wonder, but a world wonder.

"It's the truth that I heard. People can't do things because their mother or father said, 'You'll never be nothing.' But it is up to you. What really matters is what you think. Do you know what I did this morning? I ran nine and one-half miles. Never in my life have I run *seven* miles. I ran nine. And your readers who jog will know how far that is. Every time I started to fall I thought of Howard Cosell.

"Attitude! My first wife left me in 1965. She didn't want to be a Muslim. She liked short skirts and mini-skirts. She got up one day and said, 'Kiss my ass. Damn the Muslims.' " Ali theatrically opens his eyes wide and his voice is hushed. "I thought I was going to die. So my manager took me to a party. He paid five prostitutes a hundred dollars apiece to entertain me. But I didn't know that. They just looked like real nice girls." A well-timed comic pause. "And all of them looked better than my wife. I wondered what was happening. All these pretty girls. Anyway I went home with one and forgot my wife until the next morning. The next day I was heartbroken again. So he called the girl back and she stayed with me almost six weeks until I got over this sickness. I got immune to that sickness with this girl. She got me to see that I could live without my wife. It is your attitude that controls the situation. If your attitude is not under control the situation will conquer you.

"You know, they've got a saying in boxing: 'They never come back.' I proved them a lie three times. I came back three times. Did you ever hear that, 'They never come back?' Well, hopelessness is worse than death. It is better to die than to give up and lose hope. We can achieve anything we want if we only believe. What's generally lacking in people is they don't believe. Let's say ten men are in the hot, scorching desert and dying of thirst. And they find a cool lake of water a half-mile away. And they can go to the lake and get as much water as they want. Every man won't take the same amount as the other. One will take a glass. Another takes a pitcher. One takes a rubber bag and fills that. But the one that brings a tank will take a tankful. This is the same way I believe. Some people can see farther than others. Columbus discovered America. The Wright brothers made airplanes. There was Daniel Boone and Davy Crockett. Americans went to the moon. The man who stands higher can see farther than the one who stands lower. You can see only as far as your eyes can see. You can hear only as much as your ears can hear.

"Look at the questions you are asking me. This is not what you come to ask a boxer. I have the most recognized face in the world. Since I accepted Islam I am a world man. More people know this dude than any human on earth. The name Muhammad Ali has gotten more wise people looking for me to talk to like you are. This type of interview is looking to find out what I think like. What's behind the man? What makes me tick? These questions are not the ordinary sports questions, and this is good. It's an honor to be asked questions that you would ask a governor or a senator or a president. And I'm a boxer. Maybe I'm more than a boxer, but that's all I'm famous for is boxing."

"If you had to credit one thing, what would you say made such a spectacular level of self-realization possible for you?"

"Part of the Islamic teachings is that everything that God made has a purpose. I have a lecture I give in colleges called The Purpose of Life. The sun has a purpose. The moon has a purpose. Buzzards have a purpose. Pigs have a purpose. Sand. Grass. Rain. Sun. Clouds. Large or small, everything God made is made for a purpose. What's my point? Most surely His highest form of life, which are humans, has a purpose too. A wise man, the wise woman is he or she who knows their life's purpose. Ten people with the knowledge of their purpose are more powerful than a thousand people working from sunup to sundown without the knowledge of their purpose. My purpose is to inspire people. Black people first, because charity starts at home. But all people. And because I know my life's purpose, things happen to me all the time that don't happen to an ordinary athlete.

"A black man in L.A. wanted to jump off a building. You heard about it. He was going to jump from a building! Ten white psychiatrists couldn't talk to that bad Brother. He was bad. He looked like King Kong on the building. Cameras were everywhere. People were waiting. They call me. Last try. I go to the scene. I walked to the top of the building and said, 'What's the trouble?'

" 'We don't know if you can be any help. You might not want to try. It's a black guy. He's got a pistol in his hand.'

"He was yelling, 'I'll kill all of you white bastards.' All of them, the FBI, all scared.

"I said, 'Brother?'

"He said, 'Who that? Who that?'

" 'It's me, Ali. Come on down. It ain't worth the trouble. Let's go.'

" 'It ain't Ali. I don't believe you.'"

Ali begins to peek his head around an imaginary corner. "They said, 'Don't go around there. He might shoot you.'

"I said, 'I'll take a chance.' I said, 'Brother!' "

Ali now pretends to poke his head all the way around.

"He said, 'No shit!' I got him down and do you know someone hired him and now he's making $16 an hour?

"I could go on naming incidents. President Carter had some trouble with Russia invading Afghanistan. He didn't want America to go to the Olympics in Russia. He wanted five African countries, four of which were Muslim, to pull out. Who did President Carter call to convince the African countries not to go to Russia? Muhammad Ali. I was in New Delhi, India, at the time. He called and said, 'I am sending my plane to you in Bombay, India. Keep these countries out of the Olympics.' He sent a whole staff— security, cooks, and secretaries. I had the White House in my lap for five days. I was a big, big nigger that day, boy. Three countries went along and two didn't. He called me for that. I'm not just an ordinary man you see punching bags here in Deer Lake and chopping trees.

"It's your attitude that controls your life. I started talking in 1953. In 1953 I told my mother I was going to be the World Heavyweight Champion. We had just heard Marciano defeat somebody on the radio. They said, 'Ladies and gentlemen, still heavyweight champion, Rocky Marciano.' From that day on I liked the sound. *World Heavyweight Champion*. But I wasn't encouraged because my goals were so high and so big only I believed. Even my friends and brother, mother, father, and closest relatives didn't believe like me. So it wasn't very encouraging because I was in a world of my own.

"Imagination! I used to sit in Louisville Central High and write on a piece of paper: National Golden Gloves Champion. I would draw a jacket and write it on. I would draw it all the time and imagine myself walking around Louisville. I was big then. I was seventeen years old. The National Golden Gloves Champion? Champ of all America? Man, I won it! Then I used to draw a jacket after that of the World Olympic Gold Medal Winner. I would draw that and I went to the Olympics and I won it. Then I always would draw a sign written on the side of a bus I would buy: World Heavyweight Champion. I saw Floyd Patterson once in Indianapolis. That was in 1960. I was in training. On the bus I saw, 'World Heavyweight Champion,

Floyd Patterson,' and it looked so big. It doesn't look big now. But then I was imagining it: World Heavyweight Champion. All my life I wanted to do that. When I got the title I wrote on the bus, 'World Heavyweight Champion, Cassius Clay.'"

It was after midnight and we were both getting tired. We agreed on a time to meet the following day. I got together the tape recorder, papers, and cassettes and was rising to return to my room. I said, "Thanks, Champ. I'll see you in the morning."

Instantly the big fist was inches from my nose. "Did you call me tramp?"

SELF-REALIZATION

Fundamental Wisdom
In spite of his high media profile it took me almost two years to contact Muhammad Ali. My files contain "Return To Sender"–stamped letters for a dozen different addresses in Los Angeles and Chicago. Finally I located a reporter who had the private number for Ali's training camp. I called for three days from morning until night and usually reached a busy signal. The few times the phone was answered I was put on hold, only to be told that Ali was boxing in the gym, resting, or otherwise unavailable. After one such wait I was astonished to hear that unmistakable voice come on the line proclaiming, "This is still the World's Greatest." I explained my project and he immediately invited me to "come on up." He briefed me on airline connections, supplied driving instructions, and signed off with "just call if you get lost." I arrived at camp the next day and found Muhammad Ali to be the ideal Great Inspiring Teacher for the chapter on self-realization.

"You know in life there is a minor purpose and a major purpose. The minor purpose is a steppingstone leading to the major purpose. My minor purpose is to conquer the boxing world. My major purpose is to do all I can for my religion, God, and humanity. To inspire people. I've got a million-dollar home in Los Angeles. I've got a beautiful, twenty-five-year-old, tall, pretty wife. I've got two beautiful young daughters. I've got two pretty Rolls Royces, a pretty private neighborhood, money in the bank, fame, discos, and theatres. But here I am in bed in my camp. I'm losing weight, training at my own expense, paying my own crew, and I have no license yet. I have an old, beat-up rental car to drive around in and I'll be causing myself pain again tomorrow. I'm training for a fight that might not come off. This is the type of thing you see in a movie and we don't know the outcome."

Although Ali was granted a license to fight in Columbus, South Carolina, a few weeks after these talks, and then scheduled the Bahama fight with Trevor Berbick, he was speaking at a time when obtaining a boxing license anywhere in the country was very uncertain. "There are all kinds of rumors about me. 'Why's he fighting?' 'He needs the money.' 'He misses the public.' 'He misses boxing.' But my comeback is not to make money. It isn't to show off and be seen. It is because people need heroes. And I inspire them. You know what a white newspaper man just told me? He said, 'Champ, if you come back I'm going to lose fifty pounds. You don't have to win. Just get in the ring.' Fifty pounds. I inspired him.

"Do you know how great it would be? When the man says, 'Ladies and Gentlemen,' Ding Ding Ding, 'the decision. Four times Heavyweight Champion . . .' They start hollering before he even says my name when they hear him say, 'Four times.' '. . . Muhammad Ali.' Ding Ding. All the pain and missing the family and the house and cars. It will all pay off." We moved on to talk about other things, but later he came back to this. He repeated wistfully, "Four times Heavyweight Champion. Think about that." Muhammad Ali has achieved some incredible heights. He credits imagination and a belief in himself.

Happiness. Happiness comes through self-realization—being the best John Smith, Mary Jones, or (Your Name) you can be. "Some think they have bad luck because of lack of wealth. Some think bad luck comes from the lack of acquaintances. Some think they are doing bad from a lack of love from those who they love. There are many reasons they will give you for being unhappy, but do you think any one of these excuses is entirely correct? Do you think that if they possessed all of them it would suffice? No. They would still be dissatisfied. The yearning for true happiness is found only in the heart of man. Little Richard is now a minister. The Beatles turned out to be spiritual. Many whites and blacks today are born-again Christians. Because after getting money, after getting fame and property, they aren't what they thought they'd be. So I went to Hollywood. I got to California and my mansion with my Rolls Royces outside. I looked out one day and said, 'Is this all there is to it?' The same house I have was built in 1917. Five men owned it. They're dead. When I'm dead the house will still be there. We're going to die. Your mother, your father, relatives you once knew are dead now. You saw them in the casket. One day you're going to be dead like that. I've been to funerals of people I used to know. You can watch them in the casket. The people are like this." Ali puts his hands across his chest, closes his eyes, and lies still for a long, long time. "I knew him. I talked to him. I walked with him. Now he's cold and hard. Man, I straightened up. This is why I'm so spiritual. I had all the money, sex, fame, pretty women and still it didn't do nothing."

The chances are that you will not make $8 million paychecks nor attain the fame and material goods of a Muhammad Ali. The only opportunity you may have to learn this lesson and avoid spending your life chasing fool's gold is to take the word of this GIT. Realizing your full potential as a human being means uncovering the treasure that lies buried within yourself.

Brainwashing. Most of your limitations are self-imposed. Over the years you have drawn a circle around yourself. It exists in your mind and defines the point past which you believe you cannot go. Becoming all you want to be begins with erasing that artificial boundary. This is not an activity with which you can expect much help. Few people were able to share the enthusiasm of the black teenager from Louisville. We have to dream our own dreams. That you believe is enough. Start with a blank slate and a willingness to add all the coping skills necessary in this process of self-realization. The size of the job is not important. What is important is that for perhaps the first time you have a concrete picture of the person you would like to become. And this new image is not filtered through the prejudice you or others may have formed about what you are capable of achieving.

Imagination. This book offers the menu of all the coping skills you need to function as an effective human being. Review the FPs and select the ones that fit. Then pull together the FW that bears on each that you need. There has never been a time in your life when it was more important to be creative and organized than in selecting the skills that will move you into the range of effective coping. Use your imagination. "The man who has no imagination, he stands on the earth. He has no wings. He cannot fly." Lay out on the drawing board exactly the person you want to be and circle in red the FW that is yet to be part of you. You will fly.

Step One. Now look at your drawing board. This is the crunch point. It can be threatening. Doubts are raised. "How do I start?" "I don't make decisions because I don't have it in me." "I don't act like a perfectionist because I am not one." There is only one way to get started. You begin by doing. Infants must constantly lose their balance *before* they can gain their balance and begin to walk. Adults must get behind the wheel of a car without experience and step on the gas *before* they become competent drivers.

In a short span of time the baby will walk and the adult will drive without giving more than a minimum of conscious thought to these behaviors.

Act One. There is a way to begin playing the role of a guilt-free person, or self-confident person, the nondistancer, or whatever FW is on your drawing board. You can begin right now, even while these qualities feel foreign to you. The technique was discovered by Constantin Stanislavski, founder of the Moscow Art Theatre. It is The Method, the famous acting technique that is based on the discovery that internal changes develop *following* the mechanical incorporation of specific qualities into a person's behavior. You begin by answering the question "What would I *do* if I *were* . . . (a perfectionist, comfortable with failure, a rational thinker, etc.)?" Stanislavski terms this "building the part." Real personality changes will begin as soon as you alter your behavior to reflect the FW you have selected. If you want to become a person no longer plagued by conflicts, you begin by playing the part as such a person might—by weighing alternatives and risking decisions. Even physical changes help accelerate the internal changes. Start to walk, stand, and speak in the manner you believe an effective decision maker might. Only this will lead to a personality that is different from what yours is right now.

Purpose. Playing your new role in an effort to realize your potential will not seem easy. But it is not that difficult either. More than anything else it is just different. It requires the determination and effort to overcome inertia and stop functioning with the sameness that has characterized your behavior over your entire life. This takes a sense of purpose. You must fight the tendency to respond with the old, familiar reflexes. Change might even be costly to you at first. Ali often proclaims proudly, "I fought the Vietnam War." He doesn't mean what you might think. Ali refused to fight in the Vietnam War. "I knew killing all those innocent people was wrong and I said, 'I'm not going.'" The price? Ali was stripped of his championship title at twenty-four years of age, in his boxing prime. Three years later he was forced to fight to win it back. "I gave up the title and $13 million and all I had to do was go to the Army and entertain the soldiers." But this was not in Ali's personal plan for himself. His purpose did not include contributing to that war. Once you know your purpose, you cannot pull your punches either.

Attitude. It is surprising for those who don't know him to hear Ali refer to his conquest of the boxing world as just a steppingstone. He sees boxing as just one step along the way for the person he has become. And for his successes he credits not his fists but his attitude. Remember his analogy. Becoming the person you want to be requires drinking the wine of success. He attributes his comeback attempt to being inspired by the attitudes of others. "Most people who sincerely believe in themselves can accomplish whatever they want. And just as many people fail because of their attitude. I was sitting home in my mansion and saw five men climb a mountain with a Braille map. Along with one epileptic, two deaf people, and a Vietnam veteran with one leg. That inspired me. They climbed Mount Rainier where eleven people who could see were killed the week before. Another man ran a thousand miles across Canada on one leg. Hell, I met a woman in Bangladesh who was 135 years old and she danced like a kid! And who is going to tell me, 'It can't be done'?" If at this point you have picked out the coping skills you need, and you combine them with this attitude, you will be unstoppable.

The Real Thing. The last FW before you set out on your own course of self-realization was voiced by Bundini Brown. Back in the dressing room when the young fighter and his handlers were trying to sell Ali on sparring, several statements were made about Tilley's boxing skills' looking "just like Ali's." Bundini rebelled loudly, "Don't say that. Only Ray Charles"—the blind singer—"would say he looks like Ali. We are the original. There is no other Billy Eckstine or Sinatra. We're like Coke. We're the real thing. And your man has to be himself." I asked Ali about this later. "Well, it isn't bad to imitate or pattern your life after another. I did mine with Sugar Ray Robinson. I talked with him. I copied some of the stuff he had too. It got me so far. Then I got independent. And this Elijah. He imitates me on things. That can help him get started. But then he will have to make his own style." There is only one of each GIT. This book is not directed at instructing you to *become* any one of them. This chapter on self-realization is offered to show you how to take what you need from the best. Put the FW you collect together to be the best you that you can be.

FINAL WORDS

The physician setting your broken leg and the dentist filling your tooth can only aspire, at their absolute best, to return you to your previous state of functioning. The promise of this book is to make you better than you ever were. If you have read this book, you are now striving for a degree of Fundamental Wisdom that will enable you to function in a reasonably comfortable and effective manner in every area of coping.

Such goals are absolutely realistic. The psychologist Carl Rogers, a Great Inspiring Teacher, made this comment. "These days I must say I feel highly optimistic about individuals and groups but very concerned about the world as a whole. I don't know if we'll blow ourselves up, but I do feel our culture is deteriorating. I think we're coming to the end of the age of technology so my view of the social scene is not rosy. But my view of man and humankind and of persons is basically an optimistic one."

GIT Bucky Fuller expressed this same thought another way. "At the present time muscle and cunning are still running human affairs. Mind is not in control of human affairs; mind is gaining but is not in control. I see all humanity born in a group womb of permitted ignorance. It has taken an enormous amount of resource by trial and error to finally get to a point where we discover that mind is everything and muscle is nothing. We are on that threshold right now."

What both are saying is that we, as human beings, have evolved to the stage in our own development where we possess the necessary insight into human affairs to take positive control over our lives. If you as an individual are not pleased with your present functioning, this book tells you how to change it.

You should not be discouraged nor alarmed if you identify significant difficulty with many or all of the Fundamental Problems. A long list is rather common and is no cause for concern. Many people have approached me with a list of their FPs and expressed confidence. "Finally," one told me,' "I have in my hands a tangible accounting of the things that have been making me unhappy all my life. The fact that these problems can be named and listed means to me that other people have them too. And that they can be understood and dealt with. I feel relieved."

Despite the information presented here, the consultation rooms of mental-health professionals will remain full. Haltingly dependent and not believing in themselves, tens of thousands each year will continue to seek to be told by professionals what is here for the taking. Yet I can state that a large number of those I have treated in my practice could have accomplished all that they did without therapy if this book had been available to them.

The first requirement for change is the intention and willingness to do so. The fact that you have reached this point in *Being Better* suggests that you are motivated. The second necessary step is to identify and place in order your Fundamental Problems. You were instructed to do this in the last chapter. Finally the time comes to act. Buying this book is like buying a set of plans from an architect. Although a very necessary first step, it takes a lot of sweat to get from a set of plans to the completed building. If tangible changes are to be made, the time comes to spread the blueprint on the ground, roll up your sleeves, and get your hands dirty. You now have the tools to begin.

INDEX

Words:
   and emotions, 73
   importance of, 76, 138, 190
   learned use of, 74, 102, 146
   see also Language, Semantics
Worry:
   and acting in the present, 30, 44, 66,
      119
   controlling, 11, 18, 72, 79

Worry, *(cont.)*
   effect on success, 41, 192
   vs. simulation, 55, 70, 71
Worthlessness, 39, 40, 46, 48, 89
Wounded Knee, 90, 93, 94, 95, 102

Y

Yippies, 125, 132, 133